Jim Nantz has been named National Sportscaster of the Year four times and is the signature face and voice of CBS Sports. He has covered nearly every one of the network's sporting events since 1985.

Eli Spielman is an award–winning marketing consultant and writer. He has won seven Emmys during his twenty-five years with CBS Sports.

ALWAYS BY MY SIDE

THE HEALING GIFT OF
A FATHER'S LOVE

Jim Nantz

with Eli Spielman

GOTHAM BOOKS

GOTHAM BOOKS
Published by Penguin Group (USA) Inc.
375 Hudson Street, New York, New York 10014, U.S.A.

Penguin Group (Canada), 90 Eglinton Avenue East, Suite 700, Toronto, Ontario M4P 2Y3,
Canada (a division of Pearson Penguin Canada Inc.); Penguin Books Ltd, 80 Strand, London
WC2R 0RL, England; Penguin Ireland, 25 St Stephen's Green, Dublin 2, Ireland (a division
of Penguin Books Ltd); Penguin Group (Australia), 250 Camberwell Road, Camberwell,
Victoria 3124, Australia (a division of Pearson Australia Group Pty Ltd); Penguin Books
India Pvt Ltd, 11 Community Centre, Panchsheel Park, New Delhi–110 017, India; Penguin
Group (NZ), 67 Apollo Drive, Rosedale, North Shore 0632, New Zealand (a division
of Pearson New Zealand Ltd); Penguin Books (South Africa) (Pty) Ltd, 24 Sturdee
Avenue, Rosebank, Johannesburg 2196, South Africa

Penguin Books Ltd, Registered Offices: 80 Strand, London WC2R 0RL, England

Published by Gotham Books, a member of Penguin Group (USA) Inc.

Previously published as a Gotham Books hardcover edition.

First trade paperback printing, May 2009

1   3   5   7   9   10   8   6   4   2

Gotham Books and the skyscraper logo are trademarks of Penguin Group (USA) Inc.

Unless otherwise indicated, all photographs are courtesy of the author.

The Library of Congress has cataloged the hardcover edition of this book as follows:
Nantz, Jim.
Always by my side: a father's grace and a sports journey unlike any other / Jim Nantz with
Eli Spielman.—1st ed.
p. cm.
ISBN: 978-1-592-40361-5 (hardcover)   978-1-592-40408-7 (paperback)
1. Sportscasters—United States—Biography. 2. Fathers and sons—United States—Biography.
I. Spielman, Eli. II. Title.
GV742.42.N36N36 2008
070.4'49796092—dc22   2008006661
[B]

Printed in the United States of America
Set in Bembo   Designed by Elke Sigal

While the author has made every effort to provide accurate telephone numbers and
Internet addresses at the time of publication, neither the publisher nor the author
assumes any responsibility for errors, or for changes that occur after publication.
Further, the publisher does not have any control over and does not assume
any responsibility for author or third-party Web sites or their content.

To my family, especially Mom—a woman of deep faith,
fierce loyalty, and unconditional love.

To dads everywhere, who encourage their sons and daughters to dream
big dreams—and inspire their kids to pursue them.

And to all who cope with Alzheimer's patients—may you, too,
find grace through the legacies of your loved ones.

FOREWORD
By
PRESIDENT GEORGE H. W. BUSH

One of my chief complaints since leaving my previous day job is the fact that nobody concedes my short putts anymore. There was something truly magical about being president of the United States out on the golf course when, after you've rolled up a horrible putt six feet from the hole, people fell all over themselves saying, "That's good, sir! Put that one in your pocket!"

When I "commit" golf these days, however, everyone seems to have forgotten my going toe-to-toe with Gorbachev or Desert Storm, or when I stared down the nefarious broccoli lobby by publicly declaring my lifelong aversion to that insidious vegetable. No, since leaving the White House, everyone seems to develop lockjaw around me on the greens. As a result, those "gimme" putts are in short supply. But when my good friend Jim Nantz asked me to pen the foreword to this entertaining, enlightening, and often touching book, there was no question what my answer would be. In golfer's parlance, this was a hanging-on-the-lip, falling-in-the-hole gimme.

I say this *not* because of Jim's many accomplishments in his chosen profession, even though he is one of the great sports broadcasters of his generation. Jim's early rise to the top and his enduring success speak for themselves. Some things are just meant to be: Tiger Woods and a golf club; Yo-Yo Ma and the cello; James W. Nantz III and a microphone.

Jim knows what it means to be a true friend. He understands that loyalty is a two-way street. Jim is also an extraordinarily bright Point of Light who selflessly supports so many charitable causes. Most of all, as you will soon discover, Jim Nantz is a devoted father and son. Spend ten minutes around Jim and you will know that the deepest currents that shape who and what he is come from his own family.

While Jim has always been right on target in his family and professional life, even a perfect tee shot can find a fairway divot; when it does, men and women of integrity have no choice but to play the ball as it lies. Few of us will walk this earth and not be touched in some way by tragedy, but there's an old saying that adversity has a way of introducing you to yourself. That is the essence of the real story inside these pages. To me, the heartbeat, if you will, of this tale comes from the classy and courageous way Jim and his family have confronted the good—and the not so good—that life brings to every door.

A master storyteller, Jim shares some rich anecdotes about some of the leading sporting events over the last twenty-plus years, including a key horseshoes match that involved, at the time, the great governors of Florida and Texas. To this day, I find that I'm constantly defending Nantz and his character against a widely held Bush family charge that he altered the rules. Ten years have passed since that controversy, but I will confide that the forty-third president of the United States continues to be miffed over this matter. Nonetheless, we Bushes love Jimmy and we regard him almost as a surrogate member of our family.

So sit back and enjoy this remarkable personal journey that spans Super Bowl XLI, the Final Four, and the Masters. But those headline-grabbing heroics turn out to be a mere subplot within this endearing real-life story of the transmission of cherished values from a wonderful dad to a loving son.

CHAPTER ONE

May 26, 1995, had been shaping up as "just another day at the office"—albeit an office whose desk faces a television camera, a monitor bank, and a bay window that, on this one Friday afternoon, was set up to overlook the 18th green at the Colonial Country Club in Fort Worth, Texas. My parents, Doris and Jim, had come up from Houston to visit me, and as a bonus they got to cheer on one of my college roommates, Blaine McCallister, who was playing in the PGA Tour's grand old tournament, the Colonial. I was also blessed to be surrounded by my CBS "family"—in particular, Ken Venturi, our analyst, who sat to my right; the legendary producer/director Frank Chirkinian, who was, as we say in TV, "in my ear"; and Frank's protégé, associate director Lance Barrow, who sat just to Chirkinian's left in the production truck. There I was, thirty-six years old, and about to celebrate my tenth anniversary at CBS Sports, the very network where I had envisioned

myself working ever since I was in grade school. In my first
decade, I had already been privileged to broadcast virtually every sport the network had to offer. In short, I was fulfilling my
lifelong aspiration to narrate the great stories of American
sports.

What would I have done with my life had I not been fortunate enough to defy the odds and land behind CBS's anchor
desk? Well, perhaps I might have been content to *sell them* that
desk, joining my father in his office-furniture wholesale business. That was always the fallback plan, something I could do
to help make life easier for Dad in his later years. Now, though,
I was developing a far better father-son business model—one
that centered on the three things, besides his family, that Dad
loved most: traveling, meeting people, and sports. My schedule
was growing more and more hectic. Wherever I turned, the
demands on my time continued to increase. So I thought, why
not enlist my father as my full-time, on-the-road business
partner? He had plenty of management experience, and no
one had better people skills. We'd work as a team, traveling together regularly, just as we did when I was growing up.

"Everywhere you go, people absolutely love you. Besides,
there's no one whose advice I value more," I told him as I tried
to pitch this concept. "Dad, there will be plenty for you to do,
and besides, I need you!" I must have told him on a dozen
other occasions—and I really felt that way. No matter how I
worded my argument, he would invariably deflect it with a
noncommittal, "We'll see, Son."

My father's fierce independence didn't surprise me. He
never wanted anything handed to him—or even *perceived* to be
handed to him—from anyone, including me. For the time being, Dad was more than content to remain a "free agent."
Whenever our schedules allowed, he'd join me at a big football

game that I was calling—or the Final Four or the Masters. Then, when it was time for me to go on the air, he would stop watching the event—and simply stare at *me*. Somehow, he could do this for hours on end—sitting silently just off camera, listening on a spare headset as the producer orchestrated all the different elements that bring a telecast to life. Out of the corner of my eye, I could see him beaming with pride, that beatific smile etched onto the world's friendliest face, as if he could hardly believe that all of this was really happening to his only son.

. . .

"Oh, my God!" I muttered reflexively when my father entered the tower that day with about three minutes to air. I'd never seen Dad like this: His eyes were disoriented. His face looked confused. His speech was halting and barely coherent. We rushed to get him something to drink and some towels. Dad was a "young" sixty-six—vibrant, active, and strong. But on this sweltering afternoon, the heat and humidity—and his haste to make it back to the tower in time for the start of the broadcast—had left him seemingly overcome by exhaustion and dehydration. Instead of taking a few sips of water, as he might usually do, I watched him gulp down two full bottles.

"Listen, Dad, why don't you go over to our CBS hospitality suite in the clubhouse. Cool off, catch your breath, and then come back here," I told him. "We've got all weekend together, so you take your time—there's no rush." Normally, he would have waved off my suggestion, insisted that he was "just fine, Son," and propped himself into his regular front-row seat so he could fixate on my every move. Instead, he nodded slowly and turned for the door at the back of the tower and started down the steps.

. . .

And so for Ken Venturi and all the crew, this is Jim Nantz, saying so long from Fort Worth, Texas. We'll see you again tomorrow at three Eastern time on CBS.

The moment I finished signing off, Frank Chirkinian gently instructed, "Jimmy, don't get off headset yet." Frank's booming bark was now modulated to a solicitous whisper as he asked me, "Are you sitting down?" Instantly, it dawned upon me—and on Ken Venturi, who was at my side, also listening—that my father had not returned to the tower. I had assumed that once Dad had gone inside, he probably made some new friends—as he invariably does—and decided to stick around, tell some jokes, and watch the broadcast with them from the comfort of the air-conditioned clubhouse.

"First, let me assure you that your dad is *just fine*, Jimmy," Frank said. "But he was taken to a nearby hospital. Apparently, as he left your tower, he collapsed at the base of the stairs. Your mother insisted that I not tell you while you were on the air. I've been getting regular updates for the last ninety minutes, and we've got a car waiting to take you to see him. Now, Son—don't you worry. Everything is going to be all right."

At times such as this, Chirkinian instinctively referred to me as "Son," and he and Venturi were among several individuals who were important father-figures to me—and they remain so to this day. The one saving grace for my father was that the 18th hole at Colonial was directly across from a first-aid tent, and just a few hundred yards from where ambulances were parked on the other side of the clubhouse. The paramedics stabilized my father and rushed him to Harris Methodist Hospital, less than ten minutes away.

Kenny and Frank both offered to go with me, but I knew

that Mom was there, and I figured that in this situation too many people in a small hospital room might overwhelm my dad. Quickly, I packed my briefcase and bolted down the same sixteen steps that had fatefully altered the course of my father's life and mine.

When I reached his bedside, Dad's eyes brightened—he still had his gift for communicating by eye contact—and he tried to speak. But the left side of his face was droopy, and it caused him to slur his speech. I couldn't make out every word, but the gist of it was clear: He was apologizing for putting us through this, and he was sorry for having ruined all of the great plans we had made for this weekend. This was so typical of Dad—to be concerned about everyone in the room but himself.

My father had suffered a mini-stroke (technically called a transient ischemic attack, or TIA). But this episode was probably the latest in a series of setbacks that we had failed to recognize for what they were, dating back perhaps to the untold amount of head trauma he had incurred playing football in the era of leather helmets. In fact, there had been numerous other warning signals. For instance, my sister, Nancy, recalled a recent incident on a vacation, when Dad went to the hotel lobby for a quick cup of coffee and forgot what room he was staying in. We also remembered Dad's sudden difficulty in correctly pronouncing the name of our longtime next-door neighbor. We had laughed off these awkward moments to put my father at ease. But these and other cognitive data points were hiding in plain sight.

In the weeks following Fort Worth, my dad's condition improved. His speech returned and the partial paralysis of his left arm also disappeared. Still, something was amiss. We became more conscious of his inability to "connect the dots," and our suspicions and fears mounted. Finally, we took my father to be evaluated by a prominent neurologist, Dr. Stanley Appel. He confirmed the clinical diagnosis that several other physicians had previously made. It was the single word we all had come to dread most: *Alzheimer's.*

With foresight and sensitivity, Dr. Appel had arranged for a specially trained social worker to brief and console my mother in an adjoining room. Meantime, the renowned specialist, upon whom we had unfairly pinned so much hope, was not having an easy time convincing me that we were out of miracles. "There are a few medications that might slow this down in the short term," he told me, in deliberate tones and measured words that were perfectly appropriate to this life-changing moment. "There's nothing that can stop the inevitable." Just then, we heard my mother's anguished wailing; it penetrated through the walls and sent shivers up my spine. Dr. Appel reached over compassionately and took my hand in his. "Jim, she's going to need you to be strong now and take charge as the leader of the family," he said firmly. "The one thing I *can* tell you is that soon you're going to have to make some important—and frankly, very painful—decisions."

· · ·

My dad was the personification of hope, confidence, and success—and I like to think that he passed those winning attributes on to me. But this joyful, can-do attitude also came with a flip side: I was simply not programmed for failure.

"You hang in there, Dad," I kept thinking to myself. "We'll figure this out and fix it."

If I was aggressive enough ... creative enough ... persistent enough, I would find a drug, a treatment, a therapy; if not a cure, then at least something to buy us some more time. My old basketball mentality surfaced to suggest that all I had to do was come off the bench, hit a few three-pointers, and we'd be right back in the game. It didn't matter that the doctor had declared, "Game over!" I refused to concede defeat. I was in a classic state of denial.

Months passed before it finally sank in that there would be no last-second game-winning heroics—even though I would more than gladly have paid any price or made any sacrifice for them. These months took *years* off our lives. Everything was playing out exactly as the medical experts had called it—including the extreme toll that Alzheimer's takes on a patient's family.

From 1995 to 2000, my mother and sister bore the brunt of tending to Dad with a devotion that bordered on saintliness. I made it to Houston at least once a month, tying in my CBS travels with a stop in Texas either on my way to an event or on my way back home to Connecticut. Eventually, even the most stoic among us had to wonder, how long can one reasonably expect a petite woman to drag her 220-pound husband up and down the stairs? How can a daughter, busy raising an infant son, effectively handle the demands of her own family life while being on call at a moment's notice? We had full-time care, but it never seemed to be enough to satisfy every need. Would there ever be a second's rest, when everyone could stop worrying that Dad might turn on the stove and accidentally scald himself—or, for that matter, burn down the entire neighborhood?

Only someone who has had to deal first-hand with Alzheimer's can fully appreciate the grim litany of vile and demeaning tasks that become part of a caregiver's routine. Yet these physical chores may not even constitute the worst of what a family must endure. In the early stages of the disease, you tend to focus on covering up for embarrassing public gaffes so that you can preserve your loved one's good name and maintain his reputation. Later, when there are no more public moments, the ongoing struggle shifts to preserving his human dignity, even when he can no longer control his own basic bodily functions. Finally, as Dr. Appel had warned me from the start, one is forced to make brutal end-game decisions.

Mom's love for the man she cherished "in sickness and in health" remained inexhaustible, but after five grueling years, her physical and emotional resources were almost fully depleted. Nancy was also totally spent. Clearly, something had to change. Caring for Dad *at home* was no longer a viable option. Intellectually, the decision to place my father into a special-care facility made perfect sense; in fact, it should have been implemented much earlier. Emotionally, however, everything was suddenly surreal: One moment, I was all set to take Dad on a whirlwind tour of the sports world, and now I was kicking him out of his own house. What kind of loving son could even think of doing such a thing to his father? Ultimately, it was the loving son who realized that he was on the brink of losing his mother, as well.

Just as Dad never sought sympathy or pity, neither did I. So every Saturday and Sunday, I would soldier on, seemingly without a care in the world other than "Would so-and-so sink that putt?" Or, "Would XYZ advance to the Sweet 16?" CBS Sports wasn't paying me to share my problems with our viewers. For many of them, *we* were the ones who were providing an escape. Being on the road and so far removed from the day-to-day problems in Houston was frustrating. Knowing how much Mom and Nancy were suffering only added to my already overwhelming sense of guilt. I had long gotten past the denial stage—I knew that Alzheimer's was tantamount to a death sentence—but I was becoming increasingly despondent.

In June of 2000, I was in Carmel, California, where I hoped to snap out of my emotional funk by spending time in one of my favorite places. The sounds of the surf, the scent of the salt air, and the bracing coolness of the ocean waters stirred fond memories. Both of my parents loved the beach, and they had passed that appreciation on to me. To this day, when I need a tranquil setting in which to ponder life's difficult questions, I immediately head out to the town beach that's only a mile from my house and walk along the water's edge. This time, however, no serenity or healing was to be found. Instead, I found myself trudging aimlessly up and down the sand at Carmel. I was, in a word, "lost."

After a few days, though, I started making peace—albeit an uneasy one—with the plan to move my father into a private-care facility. *Had we "given up" on him?* That issue haunted me emotionally. Only when I concluded that, no, we had not given up on Dad, we were doing what had to be done, did my pervasive gloom begin to lift. I raced inside to call my mother, begging her and Nancy to take the next flight out for a much-needed break.

"What about your father?" Mom asked me. "Who's going to look after him?"

"I am!" I replied. "I'm on my way to Houston. You two come out to Pebble Beach. I've already rented this cottage, so stay for as long as you wish."

I returned to Texas that evening knowing that it would be the last time I would ever experience being in my old house with Dad. For five days, I watched him, I fed him, I bathed him, I dressed him, I entertained him, and I protected him. In short, I did everything for my father that one would expect a parent to do for a very young child—everything that Mom and Nancy had been doing on a daily basis for the past five years.

.   .   .

I have mentally replayed these scenes countless times. It's the eve of the Super Bowl—Saturday night, February 3, 2007—and they're churning again, like the loud waves of the angry ocean beyond my hotel balcony. With the rest of the family joining me here in Miami, I feel my father's absence acutely. But he remains bedridden in Houston, staring at the ceiling. He continues clinging to life, yet completely oblivious to it.

Such is the pernicious pathology of Alzheimer's. It ravages the human brain the way a computer virus attacks hard drives, disabling programs and erasing all stored memory. Earlier in the day, I had managed to get out for a run along the beach. Once again, the magic of the ocean conjured up memories, and I thought back to that time, only a dozen years earlier, when I really believed that I was going to have it all: my dream job, traveling from championship to championship with CBS Sports—with Dad, my hero and inspiration, by my side, to share my world and all the excitement, satisfaction, and fun that I've been privileged to enjoy.

This Super Bowl marked the beginning of a journey that took me from Miami to Atlanta for the Final Four—then on to Augusta for the Masters. This would have been the ultimate father-and-son road trip, and in a profound way, it was. Now it was time to celebrate a man who'd spent his first sixty-six years on this earth living life the way it should be lived. Over the course of this journey, I reflected on the legacy that my father had lovingly bequeathed to me as I continued to seek his grace through the goodness of others.

In my mind and in my heart, Dad remains *always* by my side.

CHAPTER TWO

My father was born on September 23, 1928—exactly four hundred days before the stock market crash that spawned the Great Depression. Black Tuesday had disastrous repercussions on the textile industry in the rural Southeast. Many mills were forced to shut down in an economic blow that would last more than a decade, until World War II created a major demand for textile manufacturing.

My grandfather—the original Jim Nantz—who, like most everybody else, lost his job at the local mill, was fortunate to find a new job as the town postmaster in Mt. Holly, North Carolina, the real-life embodiment of Mayberry, USA. It was a good career match for a man of great integrity who was also kind and friendly. He knew every citizen personally and interacted with their lives on a daily basis.

Dad was always so proud of his Mt. Holly upbringing. When I'm in Charlotte, I often make the half-hour drive out to the country to walk along Main Street and to imagine what it must have been like when my father worked the fountain as a teenage soda jerk at the drugstore—that is, when he wasn't making mischief with my uncles Kenny and Mark, and their cousin Henry Kale. The locals of that era invariably come over to tell me all about my grandfather and my dad—about how loved they were, and how much they are missed.

Like his father, my dad was tall and athletic. He graduated from Mt. Holly High School, in a class of twenty-eight, after eleventh grade. Football was his ticket to college—and at age sixteen, he enrolled at Guilford, a small Quaker school in Greensboro, North Carolina.

As a freshman, Dad earned a starting role as an end on both offense and defense. The season opener took place on September 28, 1945, at the University of Maryland. The valiant, but overmatched, Quakers were crushed, 60–6. Dad later took comfort in knowing that, although Guilford was the first school beaten by an untested rookie head coach, it would not be alone. The Maryland coach making his debut that day was Paul "Bear" Bryant. He would go on to record 322 more victories and six national championships. My father, who could put a humorous spin on almost any situation, liked to joke that he was responsible for helping to teach this Hall of Fame legend what it took to win at the college level.

After finishing his college studies at Belmont Abbey and his army duty at Fort Jackson, South Carolina, Dad had a pair of infatuations—one old and one new. The former was football, and he pursued this passion by trying to play for the semi-pro Charlotte Clippers, until a shoulder injury forced him to give up the game.

Dad's other infatuation was Miss Doris Jean Trull. Never short on confidence, my father called her for a date one week after meeting this sophisticated city girl at a big-band dance. "Hi there, I'm Jim Nantz," he said by way of introduction. "I'm the guy all the gals in Charlotte are talking about!" There was a stunned silence. He sure sounded conceited, thought the woman on the other end of the line, who would become his wife and my mother. On the other hand, she thought, he *was* so charming, amusing, well-dressed—and such a good dancer—that all the girls in Charlotte *were,* in fact, talking about him.

Whether he was selling himself or "soliciting freight," as he would do as a young salesman for McLean Trucking, Dad certainly had a knack for piquing the interest of potential customers. And he was the consummate closer. Within a few months, he got Doris Jean to say "Yes!"

.   .   .

My father was 100 percent loyal to his employer, Sea-Land (which Malcom McLean founded after selling his trucking company). Whenever they wanted him to help out in a managerial position somewhere else in the country, he felt it was his duty to accept the challenge. "The company made a decision!" he would announce every time he had to break the news to me and to my older sister, Nancy. (Yes, the alliterative Nancy Nantz was Dad's idea of an unforgettable name.)

When I was six, we left Charlotte for New Orleans. Three years later, the company asked Dad to transfer to the East Bay of California. We had lived in the Oakland suburb of Moraga for less than a year when we headed east to New Jersey, where Sea-Land had set up its headquarters and major port operation.

Every move was difficult for me. Just as I was making new friends, I'd have to start all over again—although to my dad's way of thinking, he was providing us with a chance to broaden our horizons. In retrospect, this itinerant lifestyle might have been a blessing in disguise by exposing me to a variety of regional sports cultures, with different teams and fans. What's more, perhaps because we moved around so often during my formative years, I never picked up the distinctive speech patterns characteristic of any single region. Many viewers have claimed that they detect a faintly Midwestern accent when they hear me, but that's actually the only region of the country where we never lived.

Where I really came of age was in Colts Neck, a small town near the Jersey shore that was making a gradual transition from a rural farming community that produced delicious Jersey tomatoes and sweet corn into more of a New York commuter suburb. The Garden State was also known for its home-grown football talent, and a few of my classmates tried to plant that seed in my mind. Since I was taller than my fifth-grade peers and thus weighed more, the coaches placed me in a league with seventh- and eighth-graders. My heart was willing, but my body was physically not mature enough—and I just got mauled.

I recall coming home from the first night's practice, totally exhausted, racked with pain, and reeling from a splitting headache that my mom's mother, LulaBelle Trull, cured with a glass of Alka-Seltzer. When Dad came home from work, eager to find out how I had fared in my first day on the gridiron, he was stunned when I told him I didn't really think that football was for me, and that I had no interest in going back out there to face more physical punishment the next day.

"Yes, you are, Son," he informed me in no uncertain terms. "You wanted to try this—and you are not going to be a quitter!" Dad had that old-fashioned football mind-set. He thought this experience would be a good way to toughen me up, and as usual, he was right. I gutted it out that season but did not play again until the summer prior to my senior year at nearby Marlboro High School. By then, I was the captain of the golf team and co-captain of the basketball team. But the football coach—who had been watching me in gym and intramurals—convinced me that if I dedicated a few months to training, lifting, and one-on-one coaching, I could possibly be the starting quarterback. Whether it was my need to accept the challenge of making the football team, or perhaps some deep-seated desire to show Dad that I could also play his sport, I decided to go out for the team.

Believe it or not, I was hanging tough and making progress in my crash course to learn how to run the offense. But, before you could even cue up the *Rocky* theme music, my underdog struggle was over. With less than two weeks remaining before the season opener, as I was working on a drill to help the defensive backs practice their closing-and-tackling techniques, I ran a short route, turned, and caught the football. Just as I planted my cleats to turn upfield, I got drilled on the side. To my teammate's credit, it was a clean hit. To my great disappointment, it was a classic football injury—a blown-out left knee. Go straight to the orthopedist's office. Do not pass "Go!" Do not suit up for any games.

As much as I enjoyed playing sports, I was absolutely obsessed with *following* them. Growing up in an era of information *under*load required resourcefulness. While kids today surf the Internet and join online fantasy leagues, our primary source of scores, news, and feature stories was the daily newspaper. By the time I was eleven years old, I realized that timely access to the newspapers was a necessity. But the local ones didn't make home deliveries because the houses in our area were spread far apart. So I figured out that the best way to get hold of *The Asbury Park Press* and the *Red Bank Daily Register* was to sell subscriptions to a few of our neighbors and deliver the papers myself.

In today's digital world, the speed of information transmission is a function of available bandwidth. How many seconds will it take to download? Or, can you stream in real time? As a teenager, I had my hands and feet instead of a modem—and on a good day, I could access the information I craved in about one hour. That's how long it took me to fold and deliver my papers, and walk the route with a sack slung over my shoulder and a transistor radio tuned in to talk-radio pioneer Bob Grant on WMCA-AM. Then, since my folks made it clear that only when my work was done could I get to my reward, I would devour the sports pages.

While Dad encouraged my enterprising method of getting the daily paper, he soon began to fret that I was too focused on the sports section. He was naturally curious about everything, and he was always looking to find ways to get me to expand my range of interests. One day, he challenged me to pick a stock and to invest my paper-route and lawn-mowing earnings in it. That way, he figured, I would at least check the financial section a few times a week.

By then, I had scraped up almost $500 in my savings, and I told Dad that I wanted to "put my money into Chrysler." He was a bit taken aback, knowing that the famous automaker was enduring financial problems. "It's okay, Dad," I told him reassuringly. "I like the fact that I can get a lot of shares for five hundred dollars." True to his word, Dad gave me free rein to succeed or fail. Dutifully, he drove me to the bank in nearby Holmdel, where I withdrew the funds from my passbook sav-

ings account, and then to his broker's office, where I bought
fifty shares.

I *still* own that investment, but only for sentimental reasons. I enjoy seeing my dad's name on the statements as the
custodian—I never wanted to change that—and I look forward to passing the account on to my own daughter, Caroline.

.   .   .

Our house in Colts Neck was a rambling ranch with a finished
attic loft area that served as Nancy's bedroom suite. Just in front
of her room, you could pull down a ladder and climb up into
the attic, where we had a large swivel-mounted indoor television antenna with six-foot arms and prongs. By rotating the
antenna to the far right corner of the attic, you could bring in
television signals from Philadelphia, to the southwest. The de-
fault, or "New York," position was directly facing the staircase.
Adding a degree of difficulty to this maneuver was an obstacle
course of Christmas decorations, unused furniture, heirlooms,
and old clothing. Catching an ornament on one of the prongs
could get you called out by Mom for making a mess. And if
you thought baseball was a "game of inches," antenna-moving
was all about finesse and touch. If you were the slightest bit off,
the reception would be too snowy to watch—and that meant
you had to race up two flights of stairs to fix it.

To me, at least, all this effort was worthwhile. This was the
only way I could see the *ACC Game of the Week* with Jim
Thacker and Billy Packer on the old C. D. Chesley Network.
None of the New York stations carried it. The real action, however, took place on NFL Sundays. After church, it was game
time—and I was in my own world. Under ideal conditions,
Mom would take Nancy into New York to see a show or to

shop. Sometimes, Dad would join them in Manhattan, or he'd decide to spend the day puttering in the garden. While Dad loved to play sports, he didn't have the patience to sit and watch games on TV. That patience, though, was one of my virtues. Simply being left alone in the den with a couple of peanut-butter-and-strawberry-jelly sandwiches was my idea of heaven.

With the Giants and the Jets "protected" in the New York market, the flexibility of bringing in signals from Philly meant that I could check out extra NFC games if the Eagles were on the road, or pick off NBC's AFC game. At the same time, I was listening to the Giants on the radio, so if their game suddenly tightened up, I could barrel up to the attic, reposition the antenna, and catch the end of it. Years later, as host of *The NFL Today* and the NCAA Tournament, I would be moving audiences from one game to another and constantly updating the highlights with the help of scores of producers, directors, remote coordinators, technicians, and operations people. But in my Colts Neck fantasy studio, I was a one-boy network—the technical crew, the producer, and of course, the anchor.

As much as I was into watching the exploits of the Roger Staubachs, the Bill Russells, and the Tom Weiskopfs, what totally consumed me in those "Wonder Years" were the marvelous voices that chronicled the heroic deeds of these champions. Once I locked in on a clear signal, I would drape the microphone cord of my tape recorder around the television's channel-selector dial so that the microphone hung just in front of the speaker. Every weekend, I would diligently record and label the broadcasts so that I could play them back, over and over, from Monday through Friday.

When I listened to a Dick Enberg or Pat Summerall or Jim McKay, I was mesmerized by their cadences and phrasings, and by the timbres of their unique voices. I dreamed of being able to emulate their keen eye for detail as well as their poetic command of the language. I loved listening to them spin out one memorable story after another, effortlessly segueing from relaxed humor one moment to high drama the next.

Above all, these eloquent heroes of my childhood had the gift of articulating Dad's unspoken vision, passion, and idealism about athletic competition. They shared a reverence for tradition and were not ashamed to celebrate all the quietly wonderful aspects of sports. Their broadcasting priorities were straightforward—to maintain the integrity of the event, and to focus on the *story,* not the teller.

· · ·

In my senior year of high school, my parents would move one last time—to Houston, where Dad began a second career in the wholesale office-furniture business. Nancy was already a student at Clemson, and since I only had a half year until graduation, I was allowed to stay in New Jersey to finish out the basketball and golf seasons so that I wouldn't let my teammates down.

When I finally arrived in Houston, my parents' new neighbor Dick Brown, whom Dad had told all about my interest in golf, was kind enough to invite me to play at The Woodlands as a welcome-to-the-neighborhood gesture. Afterward, he introduced me to the pro, Ron Weber, who told me he'd love to take a look at my game.

A few days later, I followed up on Weber's offer and met him at the practice range. It was one of those glorious days when the ball was just flying off the clubface—long, straight, and pure. About halfway through a bucket of balls, he finally said something: "Are you playing college golf this year?" I replied, "Oh, no, Mr. Weber. I'm going to the University of Texas to study engineering." That was where my guidance counselor back in New Jersey had directed me.

I pounded a few more golf balls, and Weber followed up, "I think you could play college golf." He suggested that we continue our chat in his office. He had been an All-America golfer at Houston and a PGA Tour player back in the 1960s. He handed me a Rolodex card and asked me to write down my contact information. Then, as he was inserting it in alphabetical order, I noticed him slip it in just ahead of the card that read NICKLAUS, JACK. That was *very* cool!

Weber then picked up the phone and called University of Houston golf coach Dave Williams. It was a quick conversation, and the only part of it that I heard was "Coach Dave . . . we have a kid who I've been watching here, and I think he can help us out."

Within days, I had an audition for Coach Williams. Back then, I was *fearless* on the golf course. Sometimes that would get me into trouble. But this time—in front of college golf's most famous coach—it paid off handsomely. I started out birdie-birdie right out of the box. Even though I was four-over the rest of the nine, Coach Williams still walked over, put his arm around me, and uttered words that even in my wildest imagination I had never dreamed that I would hear: *"Jimbo, how'd you like to be a Cougar?"* Houston had won thirteen national NCAA golf titles by then, and the program was considered the UCLA of golf. Now the legendary "Coach Dave" was inviting me to join his golf team, the defending national champions. I could hardly believe this was all happening to me.

On August 29, 1977, I was one of four walk-ons who showed up to meet my fellow freshmen on the golf team. There

were also three recruits who were on half-scholarships: Fred
Couples, Blaine McCallister, and John Horne. We had an instant connection. We were all crazy about sports. As the semester unfolded, just as I had suspected, a huge talent gap appeared
between the rest of my teammates and me. I began to realize
that Coach must have seen something in me that day out at
The Woodlands that was beyond golf talent. In retrospect, I
think Coach liked the old-fashioned "Yes, sir," "No, sir" polite-
ness that my parents had instilled in me. He already knew that
he had reeled in a bumper crop of freshman talent; what he
wanted was someone who appeared diligent and buttoned up
to add some gravitas to the team.

Coach Dave, who was a demigod on campus, always had
the big picture in mind. His famous advice to new head coaches
who came to Houston was "Tell everyone that you're going to
win the national championship." Like my dad, he believed in
aiming high and going for the ultimate goals in life. Both men
were supreme optimists, always building you up and making
you feel as though you could accomplish anything. For instance, Dad used to always tell me, "Son, one day you're going
to be the next Walter Cronkite . . . people trust you, Jimmy!"
And Coach would walk around telling everyone, "One day,
Jim Nantz is going to be president of the United States." After
you listened to them say it over and over, you almost began to
believe it.

· · ·

Fred, Blaine, John, and I shared a two-bedroom suite in Taub
Hall, and we were inseparable. On Saturdays, we'd get up at the
crack of dawn to caddy at the Houston Country Club or at
River Oaks. We tried to get our names on the list by 5:30 A.M.

Then we'd put on white coveralls and sling a bag over each shoulder. At the end of 18, on a good day, we'd get $30 for double-bagging it. That would give us some valuable expense money for pizza and a few lunches at McDonald's.

By and large, we were good kids pursuing big dreams. Every now and then, though, there were a few minor distractions. For instance, we couldn't resist hitting screaming one-irons down the narrow fairways better known as the corridors of Taub Hall. Or we'd transform the center of campus into our own make-believe golf course. Occasionally, a stray shot would be followed by the sound of shattered glass and a madcap chase by the campus cops trying to track us down and nail us with a $25 citation.

In the spring, when the PGA Tour rolled into town, we'd go watch the pros at the Houston Open, which was being played at The Woodlands, the very course where Ron Weber had recruited me to UH. One moment, in particular, jumps out in my memory: We were standing near 1973 U.S. Open and 1976 British Open winner Johnny Miller. His ball had landed on a cart path at the 18th hole, and he was waiting for a ruling. He could play it or take a free drop. The official took a long time to get to Miller, and we were exasperated. Finally Fred blurted out, *"Come on, just hit the ball!"*

Miller shot one of those withering if-looks-could-kill glances—not at Fred, but right at *me*. I was just standing there with my arms folded, trying to keep a straight face. To this day, Miller has no idea that he was heckled by Fred Couples, whose path he would later cross many times as a competitor and then as a broadcaster. Or that sixteen years later, the innocent bystander he appeared to blame would present him with the trophy and the check for his final PGA triumph, at Pebble Beach in 1994—on CBS, of course.

In 1979, we continued our annual rite of spring. Once again, ignoring the final exams that loomed only days away, we made our pilgrimage to see the pros at the Houston Open. Fred, John, and Blaine were dreaming of one day being inside the ropes, while I was more interested in learning the network setup. All of us had long known that I had a better shot at becoming a professional broadcaster than I did at becoming a professional golfer.

After watching golf all afternoon, we were walking up 17, and there was the NBC Sports compound looming just past the corner of a dogleg. "Hey, Jim," Blaine said. "Why don't you go ask for a job?" Why not, indeed, I thought—momentarily channeling Dad's and Coach Dave's anything-is-possible approach to life. I motioned to one of the security guards, and when he came over to us, I said, "Can you please get Mr. Ohlmeyer for me? I'd like to have a word with him." The guard then asked, "May I say who wants to speak with him?" "Sure," I said. "Tell him that Jim Nantz is here to see him."

The guys were blown away that I even knew enough to ask for Don Ohlmeyer by name. As the guard disappeared into one of the office trailers, I thought we'd all have a good story to tell everyone back at Taub Hall. Just then, as we were still enjoying the moment, I noticed that the guard had reemerged—and someone was walking beside him. Now, I knew Don Ohlmeyer's name because I had memorized all the network credits, but I had absolutely no idea what he actually looked like.

Like so many of his generation of producers who had worked in the glory years of *Wide World of Sports, Monday Night Football,* and the Olympics at ABC Sports, Ohlmeyer, now the executive producer of NBC Sports, seemed larger-than-life—a burly, thirty-four-year-old, chain-smoking Notre Dame alumnus. I could tell by the look on his face that he seemed genuinely startled to have been summoned from his work by four young kids.

I had the sinking feeling that I was trapped in the middle of some typically dumb college prank—which, in fact, was exactly the case. "Mr. Ohlmeyer," I said, realizing there was no turning back, "my name is Jim Nantz. I'm a communications major and I'm on the golf team over at the University of Houston, and these are my roommates. We all got to thinking that . . . maybe while I'm here, that I ought to use this opportunity . . . to . . . *er*, ask you for a job."

"Well," he said, as I envisioned myself having wrangled a rare audience with the Great and Powerful Oz himself, "what kind of job are you looking for?"

Before I could even compose my response, John said, "He wants to be one of your announcers!"

Ohlmeyer burst into a laugh, appreciating the audacity of a group of nineteen-year-olds, three of whom would one day become PGA Tour members. "I already have all the announcers I need," Ohlmeyer replied, "but I'll tell you what. I could use someone to drive my announcers from the parking lot up by the clubhouse over here to the compound and take them back at the end of the day. I won't be able to pay you for this, but would you still be interested in doing it?"

Would I? Of course I would. Not only was I thoroughly relieved that my buddies hadn't accidentally burned a bridge that I aspired to cross, but I thought that being able to spend some quality time in a golf cart with network broadcasters whose work I admired would be a great learning experience.

Each day, after I had safely dropped off my last VIP at the compound, I would go back to the production truck, where

Ohlmeyer motioned me to come in and observe. I was completely transfixed by the bank of monitors and wondered how in the world anyone could make sense of it all.

"Hey, what are you doing next week?" Ohlmeyer asked me when I went to thank him for giving me this opportunity. "I can use you up at the Byron Nelson. You can be a spotter. And for that I can even pay you—although you'll have to handle your own expenses." I told him that I had a week of finals coming up, but he could count on me to be there on Friday. What started out as a lark with low expectations, if any, was starting to take on a life all its own. Within days, I had gone from shuttling the commentators around to working alongside one of them during the broadcast.

This happy turn of events reinforced a number of valuable lessons that I had learned from watching my dad. He had always taught me that it never hurts to ask—because you never know when you might be in the right place at the right time. Second, do your homework! In addition to knowing the stats and personal bios of the golfers inside and out, I had taught myself as much as possible about how a broadcast works and about who the key players were at each network—and it paid off. I probably knew more about Don Ohlmeyer's background than anyone else outside his family—and this was well before we had the luxury of simply Googling someone.

With his easygoing manner and his knack for remembering details, Dad was a master at developing relationships. He took a personal interest in everyone he met and treated everyone with genuine respect and courtesy. As a result, I understood intuitively that even if Ohlmeyer couldn't provide anything for me to do, at the very least I had established a relationship.

Simply put, I was delighted to have the chance to see what it was really like at the network level. This had been my dream for so long—and now I was right there in the middle of it. That's why I didn't care that I was doing a relatively menial chore or that I wasn't getting paid. Heck, to gain this kind of experience and exposure, I would probably have gone right out and sold all of my precious Chrysler stock.

Dad also believed that you made your own breaks. I applied this proactivity principle as soon as I reached Dallas for the Byron Nelson. Four hours after handing in the blue books for my last final, I arrived at Preston Trail, a course I had seen many times on TV over the years. After walking the course and watching the golfers play out the second round, I began phoning the radio stations back in Houston that I had called a few weeks earlier on behalf of Coach Williams to offer them reports on our latest tournament results. This time, I was calling on my own initiative, to let them know that I was "covering" the Byron Nelson. Would they be interested in having me call in with reports on the action?

Sure enough, two stations took me up on the offer. One was KTRH, the city's only fifty-thousand-watt station. The other was KPRC, where my original contact was local legend Anita Martini, the first woman sports anchor in America, who, five years earlier, had been the first female reporter ever admitted into a Major League Baseball clubhouse. I had gotten to know Anita while covering the Rockets and the Astros for KUHF, our college-radio station.

My knowledge of the broadcasting industry was growing exponentially, but I had not yet learned that, in almost all cases, when stations assign you to report on a story, they want an "exclusive"—not the same story that you are sharing with one or more of their competitors. Nonetheless, each morning, I got up early to write a forty-five-second script and rehearse it out loud. I wanted to make them believe that they were dealing with a real professional.

As for my new "day job," I was situated in the tower on 15, right next to NBC commentator John Schroeder (who would finish in a tie for fourth at the U.S. Open two years later). My headset linked me to the scoring operation, and I would update the scores on a board in case Schroeder had to read them. I also had a color chart to help identify the players, so that I could report to one of the associate producers in the truck that, say, Lee Trevino, wearing a red shirt and black slacks, was making his way up the fairway toward us.

Once the last contending players finished up at our hole, Ohlmeyer asked Schroeder to climb out of the tower and become one of the "foot soldiers," as on-course reporters are called. I was right behind him. Somewhere, I thought, the boys from the dorm must be watching and maybe even catching glimpses of me out on the fairway in the middle of a playoff as Tom Watson was defending his title at the Byron Nelson. To top it all off, NBC was paying me $20 a day to do this! I couldn't imagine anything better—except if one of my guys had won the tournament, which is exactly what Fred would do eight years later.

Dave Barrett was the sports reporter at KTRH who took in my phone reports from Dallas. He himself had attended UH only a few years earlier, and I met him while covering events around the city for the student radio station. Barrett, who is now a radio correspondent for CBS News, told me that he admired the Sony TC110 tape recorder that I was carrying around, and he encouraged me to keep in touch and to visit him at KTRH in the fall. The station, he was sure, could find a few things for me to do.

Coach Williams was delighted to hear that I was making progress on the broadcasting front. On many occasions he had told me the story of Terry Jastrow, another Houston golfer he'd coached a decade earlier, who had worked the Houston Open for ABC Sports and, eventually, became that network's acclaimed golf producer back in the days when they had the rights to three of the four majors—except, of course, the Masters.

I told Coach that, despite my broadcasting successes, I still wanted to give myself one last chance to improve my game. Before my junior year at Houston, I went back to Battleground Country Club in New Jersey, where I had worked in the pro shop every summer since I was fifteen years old. My hope was that by working with the head professional, Tony Bruno, I would be able to find that elusive "magic in the dirt." Perhaps another couple of months under his tutelage, I thought, and I might be able to lift my game to another level—especially my short game.

Unfortunately, none of my efforts over the summer made a significant impact on lowering my scores. When I got back to Houston, I told Coach that I felt I was wasting time. While he wanted me to move ahead with my broadcasting career, he also wished that I would remain around the team in a leadership role.

Over the summer, I had periodically checked in with Dave Barrett at KTRH radio. Now that I was back for the fall semester, Dave suggested that I come over to the station so he could introduce me to the sports director, Jerry Trupiano. That meeting led to a part-time position as an unpaid intern. There was no class credit, either, but I sensed *opportunity* written all over this. Now I was on the inside, with a chance to learn the business first-hand from the bottom up.

Since I no longer had to practice golf every afternoon after classes and turn in a scorecard, I reported instead to the radio station. Often, they would assign me to a game that night—the Astros, the Rockets, wherever I could get postgame audio for the next morning's programs. After five months of free labor, Trupiano hired me as his new weekend guy.

I was juggling many jobs—the college-radio-station, KTRH, public-address announcing at Hofheinz Pavilion and as a backup at the Astrodome, my first play-by-play gig doing the high school game-of-the-week on Gulf Coast Cable, and hosting UH basketball coach Guy Lewis's show on KPRC-TV, the local NBC affiliate. That meant I was able to attend almost every sporting event of note in the Houston area and rub elbows with the top guns of the local sports-media world. So, when KHOU-TV, the CBS affiliate in town, was looking for a fill-in sports anchor, sports director Dan Patrick—now a Texas state senator and national political commentator—asked me to audition. But the ultimate hiring decision was up to news director Jerry Levin. (He later became a CNN reporter and was held hostage for eleven months in Beirut.)

Jerry called me into his office and told me that he knew within twelve seconds that he didn't need to watch any more of my audition tape. I had the job, he said—but he could only pay me $25 a show, and he couldn't guarantee how many weekends I would work. Then he asked me, "How old are you, anyway—about twenty-seven?" I said, "Yeah, about that." I was only twenty, but I didn't have the nerve to tell him that I was a student living in the dormitory over at the University of Houston.

Just one year after John Horne had blithely suggested to Don Ohlmeyer at the 1979 Houston Open that I should be one of his announcers, I made my on-air debut as a TV sports anchor on KHOU. Ironically, one of the highlight packages that I narrated that night included action from the 1980 Houston Open. (Thank you again, Mr. Ohlmeyer.)

This little crazy-quilt career that I was developing also included submitting sound bites to Win Elliot at CBS Radio's *Sports Central USA*. He paid $37.50 for each cut he used, and if I had a play-by-play cut *and* a winning player's sound bite, that was worth $75. But getting the play-by-play sound in this case meant calling the action. So I sat in the Astrodome and set up each pitch, hoping it would be the game-deciding moment. And if it was taken or fouled off, I had to set the scene all over. Today, it's standard procedure at the network to do a "re-set"— who we are, where we are, etc.—at the top and bottom of every hour for the benefit of viewers who are just tuning in. Win had me doing re-sets on every pitch.

A loving father of ten who always said he wanted his epitaph to read GREAT DAD, Irwin "Win" Elliot doted on his stringers, students, and interns as if they were his own children. He, more than anyone else, taught Dave Barrett and me the snappy use of tape. He perfected the style of "talking to" the sound bites, then responding to them, as if *he* were having a conversation with the interviewee.

"Don't ever be afraid to make a mistake on the air, Jim," he told me a number of times. Then, I learned that he would *intentionally* include mistakes in his copy every so often so that he could correct them on the air ("Oh, silly me! What am I saying here?") and enjoy a laugh at his own expense. He felt that random missteps helped him keep his audience, if only because listeners never knew what he might say next.

The notion of not worrying about the flubs that we all make every now and then was tremendously liberating—and no one else, in school or at any of the places where I worked, had ever taught me that. When I knew Win made those few errors *on purpose,* I never again worried about any mistakes that I would make by accident. I realized that the key to an effective delivery is to be conversational. Even the great Jim McKay of ABC Sports had an irregular delivery, full of starts and stops, just as he does when he speaks naturally in conversation—which is why it worked for him on the air.

.   .   .

One of the greatest days of my budding career took place within weeks of my graduating from college. Paul Marchand, who was one of my golf team pals and is still a major influence in my life today, had become the assistant pro at the Connecticut Golf Club in Easton. Once he got the job, he could hardly wait to call me and let me know that one of the members was the aforementioned Jim McKay.

Paul told McKay all about his college friend, an aspiring young broadcaster in Houston, who would love to meet him. McKay didn't hesitate to say, "Well, why not invite him up for a round of golf?"

Within days, and with great anticipation, I flew to the East Coast. Paul was working such long hours that he often camped out in the clubhouse. Alas, on the evening before meeting Jim McKay, I spent the night on the floor of the men's locker room.

The club was closed on Monday morning so Paul arranged for us to play at the nearby Country Club of Fairfield. We got there early, and as we waited nervously on the putting green, I conjured up visions of my illustrious hero arriving ceremoniously in a stretch limousine. Instead, to my astonishment, we watched as an old-fashioned family station wagon with wood paneling on the sides pulled up, then out popped Jim McKay himself from the driver's seat. We quickly agreed that McKay and I would play our best ball against Paul's. I got lucky and birdied the first hole. McKay started running toward me and almost jumped into my arms. I'd never expected to see my globe-spanning deity get worked up so quickly. My heart was racing, and I thought to myself, "*Oh my God!* I was just *hugged* by Jim McKay!"

As we played, I had a chance to inquire, at long last, about all those names in the credits that I had long ago committed to memory. "Mr. McKay," I would ask, "what is Roone Arledge like?" And I went down the list: Chet Forte? . . . Howard Cosell? . . . Bob Goodrich? . . . Joe Aceti? . . . and so forth. This was a roll call of names that I knew from decades of watching *Wide World of Sports, Monday Night Football,* ABC's golf coverage, and the Olympic Games.

In each case, McKay talked about them just as he would talk about the athletes in his broadcasts—focusing on what had captured his fancy about their roles as husbands and fathers, or even something as simple as where they lived. McKay had a gift for sifting out one or two personal details that somehow conveyed the essence of who people really were.

I asked about his former colleague the British golf commentator Henry Longhurst, who had passed away a few years earlier. I was always spellbound by the unique way in which the very proper Longhurst would construct his commentary. For example, in describing Jack Nicklaus's famous 40-foot putt on 16 at the 1975 Masters, Longhurst waited for the ball to go into the cup before declaring, "My, my! . . . In all my life, I have never seen a putt quite like that!"

After spending the day basking in Jim McKay's aura and quizzing him about the profession, my career aspirations suddenly seemed attainable. This magical morning had exceeded *anything* that I could have reasonably hoped for. Here was my childhood idol—the person I most wanted to emulate—encouraging me to continue pursuing my dream, and even graciously offering to help in whatever way he could.

Seven summers earlier, back in 1974, Dad and I had stationed ourselves at the base of McKay's broadcast tower at Winged Foot, straining to hear his U.S. Open commentary. Now, if only for this one memorable morning, we stood face-to-face, even though I had at least a foot height advantage; we were professional colleagues, albeit in the broadest sense of the term; and we were partners—well, at least for a round of golf.

The clubhouse was closed, so there was no place to grab a bite to eat or a soda. But I had brought a camera in my bag, and we took a few quick photos before parting company.

Immediately, I wrote McKay a thank-you note, as Dad had taught me long ago never to let the opportunity slip by to promptly express your appreciation for someone's kindness.

Then, just about a week later, I received a package in the mail. Jim McKay had sent me a note saying how much *he* had enjoyed spending time with me. Enclosed with the note was a book—a collection of essays that had appeared in the London *Financial Times* entitled *The Best of Henry Longhurst*. McKay inscribed the flyleaf, "To Jim Nantz, Remembering our day on the windy links of Fairfield."

Interestingly enough, the gift book, which I still treasure, contained only one photo—a cover shot of Henry Longhurst in the tower overlooking 16 at Augusta National. Was McKay prophetic? Or was it simply a remarkable coincidence that five years later I was broadcasting from the very same seat that Henry Longhurst had once graced at the Masters?

CHAPTER THREE

You could rarely catch my dad without a smile on his face. He was always telling jokes, making friends, charming kids, and complimenting the ladies. "Hey there, Madonna!" was how he liked to greet women, well before the singer of that name was born. Although today's society tends to under-value and even mock such genuine jolliness, my father believed that it was a true source of health, prosperity, and other bless-ings. For Dad, life was good, and what's more, it was always just about to get even better. He loved his work—and he loved coming home to his family even more. He awoke happy, and every day dawned on a wealth of opportunities that beckoned his ever-curious mind to visit new places, to meet new people, to discover new adventures.

When Dad learned that the Smithsonian Institution was going to exhibit the rocks that Neil Armstrong and Buzz Aldrin had brought back from the moon, he packed us into

the car and whisked us down from New Jersey to Washington.
While Nancy and I were, regrettably, not mature enough to
appreciate these unique stones for what they represented, Dad,
who was a history buff as well as a patriot, simply gazed at
them in awe. He told us that he would have *walked* the two
hundred miles for such a chance to view these artifacts of space
conquest. His humble roots in small-town, Depression-era Mt.
Holly, USA, provided him with the perspective to genuinely
understand what a "giant leap for mankind" the Apollo program had achieved.

Aiming for the stars is what Dad always encouraged us to do.
He was a big believer in dreaming big dreams, and pursuing
them with passion. "Son, you've got to follow what's in your
heart," he used to tell me all the time, and he meant it. While
Dad actively encouraged us to be as intellectually curious, open-
minded, and well-rounded as he strived to be, he was careful
never to steer our interests in any particular direction. He certainly wasn't like those parents who take infants out of their
cribs and immediately begin trying to turn them into world-
class athletes or musical virtuosos. As long as we gave an honest
effort, played by the rules, and enjoyed what we were doing,
Dad was more than glad to let *our* dreams become his dreams.

I thought of this on Super Bowl Sunday 2007, as I scanned
the field at Dolphin Stadium with kickoff time approaching. I
was struck by how many faces I knew on the sidelines, backstage, and in the stands. This is exactly where I dared to dream
that I would one day find myself—smack in the center of the
sports universe. But as thrilling as it was to be getting ready to
call the Super Bowl play-by-play for the first time, surrounded
by so many friends that I've made over the years, the one face
I would dearly have loved to be able to pick out of the crowd

would not be there. As a result, I could never totally fulfill this particular dream because an essential ingredient was sharing the big moment with my dad.

.   .   .

Houston was a great place to learn the ropes as a young broadcaster in the early 1980s. I was on the fast track, anchoring at age twenty, breaking virtually all the "youngest ever" records, with the exception of the 1974 college-football sideline reporter "talent hunt" that ABC Sports had staged between Jim Lampley and Don Tollefson. Still, I was always looking forward, keeping my eyes firmly fixed on the prize, which for me was to get to the network level—ideally CBS—and I set a specific deadline. If I didn't crack the network by age thirty, I had pledged to myself and to my family that I would move on and help Dad, so that he wouldn't have to work so hard in his office-furniture business. In retrospect, it sounds easy to have made such an altruistic declaration, but I was one hundred percent serious about switching gears if my broadcasting ambitions did not materialize.

The fast track took an unexpected turn one morning in mid-September of 1982, when Don Judd, the sports director at KSL, called me. He wanted to know if I would be interested in flying up to Salt Lake City for an interview at the CBS affiliate there. My first instinct was to respectfully decline. I knew nothing about Salt Lake City, and I couldn't see what would be gained by moving from the nation's fourth-largest TV market to the thirty-eighth. There was one more important fact: I was engaged to my high school sweetheart, Lorrie, who was also living and working in Houston. We were planning an April wedding.

I drove out to my parents' house for dinner and to solicit the family's advice. Naturally, everyone was thrilled that I was living and thriving professionally in Houston. So was there any reason for me to even accept the invitation to visit Utah? Salt Lake was just as much a mystery to my family as it was to me. Mom asked me how I felt about this opportunity, and I told her that I didn't really see any advantages in leaving the setup that I had worked so hard to establish. Lorrie was relieved to hear me say that. But, Dad always had the final say in family discussions, and to him, it was a no-brainer. "Jimmy, I think you should accept their invitation to interview in Salt Lake City." And before I could even muster the words "But, Dad," he added, "And I'll tell you why."

As a businessman, he not only knew how to anticipate objections, but how to take them out of the equation simply by reframing the scenario. "We don't even know if they're going to offer you this job," he began, subtly positioning this as a personal challenge. "Even if they do," he continued, "we have no idea what terms they'll offer. But the one thing we do know is wherever your next job turns out to be, it is going to require that you do well in your interview. So why not let them fly you up to Utah, and if nothing else, the interview itself will be a good learning experience." Well, when he put it that way, how could anyone argue with his logic? Dad was the master at presenting everything as a win-win situation.

I was not prepared for what awaited me in Salt Lake—from the scenic natural beauty of the valley framed by soaring mountain ranges to the state-of-the-art technical equipment at KSL. I could see why they dominated their market. KSL was also the first station outside of New York, Chicago, or Los Angeles to be recognized as the best local news operation in the country. More important from my standpoint, they also owned the broadcast rights to the Utah Jazz, as well as BYU football and basketball. You could tell from the billboards along the highway leading in from the airport that they poured a great deal of money into promotion, and they were building a new facility. Everything about KSL was first-class.

On my way into the studio, I made a mental note of the shiny red Fiat X1/9 sports car in the parking lot. The interviews went well, and I was introduced to sports producer Jeff Gochnour. Then, they surprised me by asking me to go into the studio and audition on the spot. Jeff showed me a package of sports highlights and asked me to go on camera and introduce and narrate them as though I were their sports anchor. After two years of on-the-job training at KHOU-TV, where I routinely worked without a script, this was easy and straightforward.

Paul James, who had been doing BYU radio play-by-play on KSL since 1965, was the established face of the station's sports team. Don Judd was mainly interested in hunting, fishing, and outdoors stories. I would be the number-three man in the sports department rotation, but with Paul traveling to do games, I would see plenty of work.

As Don drove me back to the airport, he told me that I could have the job if I wanted it, and that he would also try to get me some work broadcasting the Jazz and BYU, although he couldn't make any promises. After explaining that the cost of living in Salt Lake was much easier on the wallet than it is in a big city such as Houston, he offered me a two-year deal with a starting salary that was more than the $36,000 I was currently making from all of my various jobs combined. And—not that this is necessarily what clinched the deal—he also said that the

Fiat X1/9 conveniently parked in front of the station would be mine. It was a tough decision, but in my gut I knew I had to take the job.

Ten weeks later, on Thursday, December 9, 1982—overshadowed only by Donny Osmond's twenty-fifth birthday—I made my debut in Utah. In retrospect, Dad knew intuitively that I would never grow personally and professionally without leaving the comfort zone that I had built with friends, family, and colleagues in Houston. It was an important element of decision-making that I would draw upon again and again as opportunities presented themselves over the years.

The first few months at the station proved trying. Jeff Hullinger, whom I succeeded, was a popular guy, and he had his share of fans at the station. And while I understand that it is only human nature for colleagues to miss their buddy and to be wary of his replacement, that doesn't mean that all the whispers I heard about "the new guy" didn't sting. I must admit that, as a defense mechanism, I assumed an I'll-show-them attitude. But, in retrospect, it was a good lesson for a young kid, and my father articulated it well in one of our late-night phone conversations, when he told me, "No matter how much talent you have, Jimmy, you can't expect to walk in to a hero's welcome. You've got to roll up your sleeves and convert the folks to your side. *You've got to earn it!*"

.   .   .

With Paul James heavily committed to BYU events, I landed the opportunity to work the Utah Jazz broadcasts, which were simulcast on KSL radio and TV. Hot Rod Hundley was the play-by-play man while I was cast as the "analyst"—which might have been easier had I played in college or the NBA. Being co-captain of my Marlboro High School basketball team didn't give a twenty-four-year-old quite enough credibility to call out veteran all-stars, such as Adrian Dantley, for defensive lapses, so I stuck to anecdotal material and whatever nuts-and-bolts information Hot Rod left out.

As both a player and a broadcaster, Hot Rod was very much a part of the game's history. He was the NBA's number one overall pick out of West Virginia in 1957 and brought his unique ball-handling skills and showmanship to the Lakers—first in Minneapolis, then in Los Angeles. But where I first knew of him was through watching him broadcast NBA games on CBS with Pat Summerall, Bill Russell, and later Brent Musburger. I also remembered him from when he teamed with Dick Enberg on the TVS college basketball package during the heyday of UCLA's dynasty.

Even though he was twice my age, we spent a lot of time together. It didn't take much to wind up Hot Rod and get him to tell his favorite stories about what it was like working at CBS—and as someone who aspired to work there one day myself, I couldn't hear them often enough. To this day, we remain close, and he tells people that he considers me his adopted son.

KSL was providing me with a nice mix of studio work along with NBA and BYU football play-by-play, where I teamed up with future Hall of Famer Steve Young, and call it blind luck, but in the one season we worked together, BYU, his alma mater, won the national title. Everything was working out well, and I felt happy and comfortable in Salt Lake City.

My work began to draw attention and I received inquiries from other stations around the country, including ones in Phoenix, Denver, Cincinnati, Philadelphia, and even KHOU-TV, my old station in Houston. One of the most intriguing offers came from an independent station, KCOP in

Los Angeles, the nation's number two market. They were will-ing to triple my KSL salary, and they did not air local newscasts on weekends. I thought that would allow me to do some free-lance work on Saturday or Sunday calling games, which would put me one step closer to my dream of making it to the net-work by the age of thirty. Alas, KCOP stood firm. We'll pay you a lot of money, they told me, but we don't want to share you with anyone else.

I wondered whether I might ever receive another offer as lucrative and as tempting. Fortunately, Dad was there to put it all into perspective for me once more: "Son, this is an easy one. You're only twenty-five years old. It's too early to lose sight of your ultimate goal." Not only was my father right, but he saved me from stepping into a kind of trap that would later present itself several times in my career. Bottom line: I didn't want to run after the money at the expense of my dream.

On Thursday, August 15, 1985, I played in the pro-am of the Utah Open at a course called Willow Creek. I was paired with Keith Clearwater, a BYU All-America, who was still try-ing to qualify for the PGA Tour. After finishing the round, I anchored the six-o'clock sportscast live from Willow Creek, then headed back to the station to prepare for the ten-o'clock show. Having been gone for the day, I looked through my mes-sages. Only one stood out. It was from an Ed Goren at CBS Sports in New York. When I returned the call, it was well after 9:00 P.M. in the East. While I prided myself on knowing all the network directors and producers listed in the credits, I had never heard of Goren. Today, even casual sports fans know that he is the president of Fox Sports, which he helped launch in 1994, and is one of the most influential television executives of the twenty-first century.

Goren told me that he was calling on behalf of executive

producer Ted Shaker, whose name I was certainly familiar with from the verbal acknowledgments at the end of every CBS Sports broadcast. They had received my demo tape, Goren said, and liked what they saw. There was only one problem—I had never sent them a tape. I began to suspect that perhaps one of my old college buddies, well aware of my network aspirations, was pulling a prank. But Goren's excited staccato and his New York accent were far too distinctive for any of my old Houston pals to have mastered.

"Of course, you know about the opening we have here," Goren continued. Once again, I had absolutely *no idea* what he was talking about. Apparently, CBS's negotiations with Bob Lobel of WBZ-TV in Boston had bogged down. With the college football season fast approaching, the network had to quickly find an anchor for its scoreboard show. Somehow, I had missed hearing about this job vacancy, which had been noted in *USA Today* and elsewhere.

CBS was holding auditions in New York on August 17, less than forty-eight hours away, and they wanted *me* to fly out and take part in them. I told Ed that I had one serious problem— everyone else at KSL was on vacation. I was the only guy around in the sports department. I told him that I'd see what I could do and raced over to the restaurant next door, where the assistant news director, Ernie Ford, was having dinner. After listening to the whole wild story of the mysterious demo tape that had somehow got me a last-minute network audition, Ernie smiled and told me that, in this business, if you're lucky, an opportunity like this comes around once in a lifetime. "We can always find someone to pinch-hit for you," he said. "You go call back this fellow from CBS and tell him you'll be there tomorrow."

My head was spinning as I went back to the station, where

I quickly phoned Lorrie to brief her on this unlikely development. Then I called Ed back to tell him that I was in. "That's great!" he said. He had already reserved a seat for me in first class on the 8:00 A.M. Western Airlines flight from Salt Lake to JFK. There would be a ticket waiting for me at the airport.

The next afternoon, when I checked into my room at the Parker Meridien Hotel on West Fifty-seventh Street in New York, I found a schedule of events, starting with a seven-thirty dinner with Ed Goren at the Russian Tea Room, an elegant Manhattan restaurant that was famous for its decor and specialized ethnic cuisine. I also noticed that the hotel had set up a videotape machine and a monitor so that I could watch tapes of some of the previous year's shows.

I popped in one of the 1984 show tapes. Pat O'Brien was the host, and as I watched him on one tape after another, I was blown away by how good he was. I thought this was a joke— why would they ever want to reassign him? Then again, I hadn't even been aware that a change was in the offing, let alone that it was a matter of public knowledge.

Also, I was considerably younger than everyone else, and I was also the only candidate who didn't represent a major market. So I just was honored to be here—and as Dad had said about going to Salt Lake three years earlier, the interview and the audition would certainly serve as invaluable learning experiences. I had nothing to lose—and if I hit the lottery here, I'd win the job of my dreams.

As for the bizarre tale of the demo tape, we eventually pieced together what had happened. After the Lobel deal fell through, Ted Shaker asked his new boss, Peter Lund, for suggestions. Prior to becoming president of CBS Sports, Lund was head of the affiliates' group, and he had a strong background in running local stations. One of Peter's go-to contacts was a forward-thinking San Francisco–based TV headhunter named Don Fitzpatrick, who went from town to town video-taping local newscasts. Lund had asked Fitzpatrick for a reel of potential sports-studio hosts—and I happened to be on that tape.

On audition day, I awaited my turn with the other candidates. Jimmy Wall, the veteran stage manager who had played the role of Mr. Baxter for ten years on *Captain Kangaroo*, came over to the makeup area and said, "Young man, it's your turn." He escorted me around the corner, and then—*Wow!*—for the first time in my life, I actually laid eyes on *The NFL Today* set. I was totally awestruck. But at the same time, I felt strangely comfortable. I had over the years spent so much time imagining myself being in this studio that it seemed as if I were walking into *my* living room—and it felt good to be home again. Jimmy held the seat for me, a chrome desk chair with a coarse brown fabric that had seen better days. On the back was a strip of gaffer's tape, and on it, written in black marker, was the name BRENT. Now, I was sitting in Brent Musburger's chair, not the make-believe one I'd used as a kid in Colts Neck.

As I started flipping through the scores and highlights for the audition, they seemed remarkably familiar—as though I had already seen them before. Then I realized that, indeed, I had! To save time and effort, CBS had simply taken the actual game-day results from the previous year, which were already loaded into the computer graphics system. I knew instantly just which Saturday it was—November 10, 1984. It was a day I'll never forget, because on that day Steve Young and I got trapped in an elevator on our way to the broadcast booth and missed the first quarter of the BYU game that we were supposed to be calling. Right after the game, I was helicoptered from Provo back to Salt Lake City. I then caught a flight to

Denver, where Hot Rod Hundley and I called the Jazz-Nuggets contest. Just to complete my broadcast marathon, I also anchored the six-o'clock and ten-o'clock sportscasts live from the floor of McNichols Arena.

What were the odds that CBS would choose as a broadcast simulation the very day that had already tested my ability to think on the run? Just as I began to feel really comfortable, perhaps even a bit cocky, Jimmy Wall came over to address me in that resonant voice. "Young man," he said, "did you bring a wallet with you?"

"Yeah, sure," I replied, reaching back instinctively to check my pocket, which was empty.

"Someone found this in the green room, and I assume it belongs to you," Jimmy said, shaking his head ever so slightly as he handed it to me. "Just a word of advice: This is New York. You don't leave wallets hanging around." How this had happened was a mystery, but there was no time to ponder it.

"*Ten seconds!*" Jimmy boomed out the countdown, his voice stopping at "*Two*" but his fingers finishing the cue. In my ear, I heard the theme music, mixed with the voice of announcer Don Robertson, who was reading the opening billboards. The audio was interrupted whenever Ed Goren pushed down his talk key in the control room. "Energy and warmth," Ed whispered. A moment later, studio director Duke Struck hit his key and said, "Go to work."

"Hello, everyone. I'm Jim Nantz. Welcome to *The Prudential College Football Report*. Let's quickly get you up-to-date on a big day for the Top 10 teams . . ."

We wrapped up the Top 10, and I read the copy leading to commercial: "We'll be back with more scores and highlights when *The Prudential College Football Report* continues in a moment, here on CBS." To give the audition a more authentic flavor, Duke rolled in a sixty-second commercial. Meantime, Ed told me that everything was going well. In segment two, there would be fewer highlights. He wanted to see how many scores we could squeeze in before we had to go to break. In other words, this was the *speed drill*.

"We're back in five, four, three . . ." I took the cue from Jimmy Wall, and it was off to the races. "Welcome back, everyone, to *The Prudential College Football Report.* " I breezed through the next four or five games—my objective was to summarize the headline story in a sentence or two without wasting time on reciting the actual score, which the viewers could always read for themselves over my shoulder. But the control room had planned a little surprise for me. Suddenly, the scores were coming out of sequence. No matter how hard they tried to confuse me, I didn't lose a beat. Finally, I sensed they had conceded that I could handle their fire drill when I heard Ed order, "No more scores, Jim. Get out. Go to commercial." No problem, I thought. I used to practice these scrambles just for fun in my spare time. "Up next, we'll talk about some of the hot topics in college football, when we return in a moment." At this point, according to several eyewitness reports, Struck turned to Shaker and Goren, who were in the back row, and said, "Where did you find this kid? We couldn't shake him. He's pretty darn good!"

While that was transpiring in Control Room 43, and another sixty-second commercial spot was rolling on the studio monitor, CBS Sports' resident college-football expert came out from the side of the set. "I'm Mike Francesa," he said, extending his hand. He was also Musburger's NFL editorial consultant and was there to serve as my interview subject for the final segment of the audition. Little did I know that he would become a close friend, confidant, and ultimately a media star in his own right. I asked Mike what he wanted to discuss, and with no shortage of confidence—then or now—he stared at me as though I was both too polite and too naïve at the same time. "Go ahead and ask me anything you want," he said. "Don't worry, Jim. Ask me anything you want."

I *was* naïve to an extent. After the scoreboard ordeal, why would I have thought that this interview would be relatively straightforward? Mike was actually a co-conspirator with Shaker and Goren—and he was going to be anything but easy to interview. In fact, having watched me calmly quell the fire in the previous segment, he was determined to "break me." First, he answered my questions in a long, leisurely manner that required me to cut him off. Then he shifted gears and offered terse, shorthand responses that left me to fill in the blanks for the non-football insiders. Even with Ed and Duke shouting contradictory instructions in my ear, I managed to find an appropriate zig for every one of Francesa's zags.

"Mike Francesa, thank you for joining us on *The Prudential College Football Report*. Right now, it's game time on CBS. Brent Musburger and Ara Parseghian will be along to call the action for you right after these messages and a word from your local station."

"Good job, Jim," Francesa told me. Just then, Ted Shaker came barreling into the studio. Ted was stocky, with a sense of the dramatic. He always dressed in khakis, a button-down shirt rolled up at the sleeves, and a sweater vest. Like Goren, who followed in his wake, Shaker was also bearded and had roots over on the CBS News side. "My gosh, that was just . . . *incredible!*" Shaker proclaimed. By now, many of the staffers were packing up to go home, but others gathered to hear what their executive producer had to say.

I was pleased with how it had gone. I felt relaxed and totally in control. The words just flowed freely, and it seemed like the easiest thing I had ever done. But now I felt disappointed that this special moment that meant so much to me was suddenly over. The adrenaline rush was abating, and I was in somewhat of a daze as Ted Shaker asked me how old I was. "I'm twenty-six," I said, to his disbelief. Then he inquired whether I felt I could host this kind of program. "Will I have a bit more time to prepare?" I asked. And when he said that I'd have all week, and a full team of researchers, I replied, "Sure, no problem!"

Shaker looked up at the big monitor that was showing CBS's coverage of the Travers Stakes from Saratoga. He pointed at the screen and said, "You remind me an awful lot of *that guy*." I turned to look behind me and saw CBS's horse-racing analyst, Frank Wright, talking on the screen. "I remind you a lot of *Frank Wright*?" I said, drawing a big laugh from the circle of onlookers—and perhaps extra credit for correctly identifying Wright.

Shaker, who has a full-throated and easy laugh himself, was clearly amused. "No, look again!" he chuckled. This time, Brent Musburger, the signature face of CBS Sports, was on camera. "You remind me a lot of Brent Musburger."

"That is a great compliment!" I said, somewhat in shock that Musburger's boss and friend was publicly comparing me to this icon.

Ed Goren was almost giddy as he walked me back to the hotel. He kept recounting how weird the whole Don Fitzpatrick tape episode was, and how it ended up with a network version of a walk-on coming in from Salt Lake at the last moment and taking on the city slickers from the big stations.

Back at the hotel, I clicked on CBS's NFL preseason game—Dallas at San Diego—just as Pat Summerall and John Madden were doing their opening on camera. It dawned on me that I might get to *meet* them. No, wait, there was more: I might actually have the honor of working with them. Was I starting to hallucinate from starvation? Or could this all indeed be happening?

The next afternoon, I was back in Salt Lake, where the anxious vigil began, as I waited—*and waited*—for the phone to ring. By now, I had heard that the choice was down to Roy Firestone, the sports anchor in Los Angeles and host of *Up Close,* an ESPN interview program, and me. I knew that it was a big leap from KSL to the network, and absolutely unprecedented for a twenty-six-year-old, regardless of where he was from. Several days went by without my hearing back from New York. Finally, Ed called and told me I would need to come back quickly to New York to spend a day meeting some of the key decision-makers.

CBS Sports in the early 1980s had four executive producers, which the staff referred to as the "four-corner offense." Shaker was responsible for the NFL and college-studio programming and the NBA; Terry O'Neil was in charge of NFL game coverage and the anthology programming; Kevin O'Malley handled the college basketball and college football packages; and Frank Chirkinian oversaw golf and tennis.

I knew all about Chirkinian, who was widely considered the "father of golf television," and was eager to meet him. Alas, he was in Akron producing the World Series of Golf. O'Malley was on vacation. That left two VIPs for me to meet—O'Neil and CBS Sports president Peter Lund.

My hosts, Ed Goren and Ted Shaker, walked me into Terry O'Neil's office. O'Neil had begun his career as an Olympics researcher at ABC Sports and worked his way up to producing *Monday Night Football.* Terry said that he had watched my audition tape and was impressed. Then he asked me, "By the way, who's the head coach at the University of Pittsburgh?" I didn't know where he was coming from, but I replied, "Foge Fazio," and I pronounced it "FAH-ziyo." He shook his head. "It's pronounced FAY-zio, Jim," he said, adding, "This is the network, not Salt Lake City. You can't make a mistake like that. You'll get a thousand letters." He wished me luck, and it was off to lunch with Shaker and Lund.

We sat down in what was then the U.S. Steakhouse on West Fifty-first Street, around the corner from CBS's corporate headquarters building, Black Rock. We began by talking about the audition and about my interests. They were pleasantly surprised to hear about my golf background. Then it was time to order. Shaker was strictly a steak-and-potatoes guy. Lund ordered the swordfish.

"*Swordfish?* I've never had that before," I said, turning to Lund. "What does that taste like?" It seemed like an innocuous question. Little did I know that it almost cost me my career. Apparently, not since the Marx Brothers' classic *Horse Feathers* had *swordfish* been such a critical password. Years later, Lund and Shaker each related to me that following our lunch, they had actually gotten together to discuss whether my being so uninformed about the fast-swimming *Xiphias gladius* meant that I was too unworldly and unsophisticated to represent the network on the air.

Once more, I returned to Utah to await the final verdict. In the meantime, I could tell that CBS was doing its due diligence and checking me out through every back channel at its disposal. Hot Rod Hundley phoned to say that his old CBS pal Charles H. Milton III had just called to see what I was like as a broadcast partner. One of the grand gentlemen of our business, and the father of our current golf director, Steve Milton, Chuck was legendary for asking entry-level job applicants, "Do you like your grandparents?" He used to say that, depending upon the response, he could always predict what kind of person the prospective employee would be. In this case, he wanted Hot Rod to vouch for my ability to perform under pressure. "What if the scores came in upside down?" he asked Hundley. Hot Rod replied, "My man Jimmy wouldn't miss a beat."

A day or two later, Fred Couples called with a similar story. He was spending a day at the U.S. Open Tennis Championships in Flushing Meadows, New York, and when he went over to the CBS compound to pick up tickets, Frank Chirkinian called him into his office for a chat. "There's a kid named Jim Nantz who is close to being hired by CBS," Chirkinian told Fred. "He claims that he was your roommate in college. Is this true?"

It was now Thursday, August 29. I was back in northern New Jersey to host the pre- and postgame shows for KSL live on the field at the Meadowlands as BYU opened its national-title defense against Boston College in the 1985 Kickoff Classic. On my way out of the hotel, I was handed a message that Ted Shaker of CBS Sports had called. I got to the stadium, set up for the pregame show, then began a desperate search for a telephone. In the runway to the tunnel, I spotted a phone on the wall and told the security guard I needed to use it. This was an emergency.

"Hey, Jim! I'm so glad you called back," Shaker said enthusiastically. "Where are you? It sounds like you're standing in the middle of a marching band."

"I'm in the tunnel at Giants Stadium, getting ready to go on the air," I said.

"Well, I suppose that's the perfect setting for me to say, 'Congratulations!' And welcome to CBS Sports."

Football had taken my father from Mt. Holly and given

him a chance to explore the world. Now, by delicious coincidence, college football was about to take me from Salt Lake
City on a journey to New York . . . and beyond. But as Dad
had taught me, at every stop along the way in life, it's all about
the integrity with which you approach work, the way you treat
people, and the relationships you build. As smoothly as the audition seemed to have gone, the enthusiasm with which my
"references" vouched for me had really sealed the deal.

I reflected on this as I prepared to greet the Super Bowl XLI
audience—as I do at the top of every broadcast—with what's
become my signature line, "Hello, friends!" I consider this
phrase the ultimate tribute to my dad. Once he met you, you
were his friend—and he had *only friends* in this world.

Chapter Four

By chance, right before I flew to New York to launch my CBS career, my old roomie Fred Couples was in Salt Lake City for a golf event. We meandered through one of those marathon catch-up-with-each-other conversations and giggled in great delight at how my dream job—the one at CBS that had been on my radar before I even knew how to shave—was now just a couple of days from reality. With the "countdown to kickoff" under way, I knew that Fred would be the perfect counsel to teach me how to maintain my composure. As one of the most popular golfers in the world, Fred had built a reputation for being the most carefree guy in the universe. But I've always known that, beneath the surface, there was a lot more nervous energy than he ever revealed.

According to Fred, the secret is in learning to manage your own expectations before others can impose theirs. "My advice to you, Jimmy," he said, "is that you just keep telling yourself,

'It's no big deal! . . . It's no big deal!'" It may sound strange, but much to everyone's surprise, I really wasn't nervous during the intense week of rehearsals. Maybe I had already internalized Fred's mantra—"It's no big deal!"—or perhaps I had adopted the philosophy that I had nothing to lose and everything to gain, so I should just have fun out there.

In various Nantz family outposts from Mt. Holly, North Carolina, to Houston, my grandparents, aunts, uncles, and cousins were organizing viewing parties. In Utah, my KSL colleagues reported that it seemed as if the whole state was shutting down to see its "local boy" go national. Meantime, out in Denver, Verne Lundquist and Terry Bradshaw were racing through preparations for the next day's Saints-Broncos game so that, as Verne later told me, they could "see this ballyhooed twenty-six-year-old kid from Salt Lake—and see if he's going to hold up." Back in Houston, my old KTRH radio friends had alerted another alumnus of that station that I was being called up to the big leagues—and I received a gracious, handwritten note from Dan Rather, welcoming me to the network.

Outside of CBS, no one promoted the broadcast with as much relentless enthusiasm as my father, who single-handedly drove up the ratings in the Houston market by telling everyone he knew to tune in. He and Mom watched the show in their den, along with my sister, Nancy, and her husband, Don Hockaday. "We were so excited," Nancy remembers. "We were hanging on to every word that came out of his mouth—and just praying that he wouldn't make a mistake."

The plan was for Brent Musburger to introduce me right before the start of the Notre Dame–Michigan game—and I can guarantee that neither the Fighting Irish nor the Wolverines had prepared as meticulously as our team had in Studio

43. I was going to quickly say hello and hand it off to my partner at the desk, Pat Haden, the former star quarterback. At long last, only one item remained on the weeklong agenda: the final communications check-in with the remote.

"Jimmy, say hello to Brent," producer Ed Goren told me.

"Hello, Mr. Musburger," I said. Moments later, I heard the reply from Ann Arbor in my earpiece: "How'ya doin', kid?"

. . .

"Now it's time to go back to the studio in New York, where the man who's going to be leading the way this year is new to CBS Sports. He comes to us by way of our affiliate KSL out in Salt Lake City. We say welcome to Jim Nantz . . ."

Suddenly, I was "looking live" at Brent Musburger, with one hundred thousand roaring fans behind him. He, in turn, was looking over my shoulder—in more ways than one—as his image projected onto the big monitor. My heart skipped a few beats. With all due respect to Fred Couples, this felt like a *huge* deal! And as for that nervous moment everybody had been clamoring for all week long, well, here it was! My pulse was racing in high gear; I had never encountered such a flash of tongue-tying anxiety before—not even during Mr. Applegate's public-speaking class back in high school. With what seemed like brute-force willpower, I managed to spit out the first words of my opening.

"Thank you, Brent Musburger . . . and here to help quarterback our team is Pat Haden . . ."

A few scores and highlights later, I threw it back to Brent at Michigan Stadium. There was a tremendous sense of relief all around. I didn't think it sounded all that conversational, but it was technically flawless—and that's all that seemed to matter.

Spontaneous applause broke out around the desk that Pat and I were sharing. Teddy, Ed, and director Duke Struck, all grinning broadly, ran out in the kind of frenzied jubilation that's usually reserved for winning a national championship. Believe me, if we had had goalposts on the set, they would have torn them down in celebration.

.   .   .

From day one, Shaker seemed determined to keep a close eye on me. He went so far as to give me "double coverage," assigning two of his best players, show producer Ed Goren and editorial consultant Mike Francesa, to shadow me around.

Fresh out of Syracuse, with degrees in journalism and political science, Goren had started out as a copyboy at CBS News back in 1966. He also had a sports pedigree—his father, Herb, was a sports columnist for the old *New York Sun* and also served as the PR man for the New York Rangers hockey team. Eddie was like a big brother, protecting me at every step. His passion and creativity shone through in the four years that we did *The Prudential College Football Report* together.

In addition to Ed's daily mentoring, Mike Francesa's weekly preparation and on-air coaching were invaluable; he'd stand just outside camera range and signal me—part defensive coordinator, part Paul Shaffer. He did much more than supply statistics and story lines, though—Francesa had a real gift for concisely packaging sports opinions. That skill would serve him well a couple of years later when sports radio, as we now know it, was introduced in New York in 1987. The general manager at the fledgling WFAN was Luke Griffin, whom I had worked for as a stringer back when he was running the sports department at the Mutual Broadcasting System while I was still in college. At Mike's urging, I called Luke and told him, "You've got to put my buddy Mike Francesa on the air. He was born to do this!"

"But, Jim, I met with him last week, and as you know, he has no on-air experience," Luke replied.

"That's why I called. Don't put too much emphasis on that. He's a natural. I'd stake everything I've got on that."

Ultimately, WFAN would transform Francesa into a genuine New York sports icon. One of the keys to that success was the station's decision to pair Mike with Christopher "Mad Dog" Russo, whose excitability and passion were a perfect complement.

.   .   .

Every now and then, through my association with Francesa, I had the opportunity to spend some time with the bigger-than-life oddsmaker, Jimmy "the Greek" Snyder. He always called me Kid—which I regarded in this case as a term of endearment, even though I was never quite sure that he actually knew my full name. (I knew *his*: Demetrios Georgios Synodinos.)

Greek was a genius when it came to grasping the psychological dynamics of men, money, and sports. He was also a pioneer in the art of leveraging the media for self-promotion. Behind every one-man brand, a strong support team makes sure all the machinery keeps rolling smoothly. In Greek's case, he had Francesa ghostwriting his syndicated newspaper column; daughter Stephanie managed the business and philanthropic affairs; and a personal assistant named Terry followed him around everywhere. Often he would suddenly turn around to Terry and say, for instance, "Larry!" And she would dutifully take out a reporter's notebook and write *Larry*. Then, a few minutes later, he'd turn around again and say, "Caesars!" At the end of each day, she'd read back the list, and Greek would expand on what he meant with his idiosyncratic shorthand code.

On Tuesday, January 12, 1988, I interviewed Greek—along with players Harry Carson of the Giants and Todd Christensen of the Raiders—for a preview piece on the NFC championship game between the Vikings and the Redskins, which would air a day before the game as part of our anthology program *CBS Sports Saturday*. When we finished, Greek invited the show producer, David Winner, and me to join him for lunch at one of his favorite "joints."

Even though the Carnegie Deli was only three-quarters of a mile away, Greek insisted that we go by cab. As a taxi pulled up in front of the CBS Broadcast Center, he motioned for David, Terry, and me to jump in the backseat, while he yanked open the door on the front passenger side. The cabbie, looking panicked, desperately tried to communicate using what little English he knew, that Jimmy could not sit there. "No, sir, you're not allowed to sit in front seat," he pleaded. "No, no, no! I get ticket, I get ticket."

The Greek told him, "No, you listen—just go! I'll take care of you."

The driver insisted, "I cannot do. I don't want ticket. Please don't sit in front."

With casual panache, Greek pulled out a wad of hundreds, peeled off a crisp $100 bill, and slapped it right on top of the dashboard. "See that hundred right there?" Jimmy pointed. "That's yours. You can kill the meter."

Greek's offer was for a three-minute ride with a fare, back in those days, of perhaps $2.70. But Jimmy wasn't finished. Now he would flash some of the bravado and skills that he had honed in Las Vegas, where he'd made his name as a legendary oddsmaker.

"Now look," he told the driver almost matter-of-factly. "If you get pulled over, I'll take care of the ticket—*and* I'll pay you fifteen-to-one on the hundred." The driver stared at him for a moment. "Oh, now I know you—Jimmy the Greek. . . . Okay, let's go!"

As we jumped out of the taxi, forty people must have been waiting on line out in the cold to get a seat, but Greek just marched right in. Instead of yelling at him for cutting ahead of the line, everyone started applauding and calling out to him. "Hey Greek, who do you like on Sunday?" was a common question you'd hear shouted out at him wherever he went. All the while, he would keep on turning to tell Terry more things to add to her list, and she would frantically try to get it all down on paper.

"What's the best thing here?" I asked Jimmy. "Get the corned beef!" he said. Being relatively new to the New York deli scene—and always trying to eat healthy foods—I ordered it on wheat toast.

Unlike the swordfish incident that nearly cost me my career, at least I was familiar with beef cured or pickled in brine. I was just unaware that this ethnic delicacy was traditionally savored between two slices of fresh rye bread. David Winner would continue teasing me about that gastronomic faux pas for the next twenty years. As we dined and exchanged jokes, none of us could have imagined that we had just taped what would be the final appearance of Jimmy the Greek on CBS.

Three days later—on Martin Luther King's birthday—Greek was holding forth at an impromptu press conference in a Washington restaurant when he blurted out some offensive comments about black athletes. Once those sound bites made the air, a remarkable career, built on little more than his own creativity, was wiped out.

As this was happening, I was in Hawaii for a presentation to the CBS Affiliates Board. That very morning, I had played a quick round of golf and was now enjoying lunch in the grill room with my foursome. I looked up at the TV behind the bar and lo and behold, there was Jimmy the Greek's photo—in a slide over the anchorman's shoulder. There was no audio, but I stared in shock as they ran what looked to be the kind of grainy file footage they used for obituaries. I dropped my sandwich.

I thought Jimmy had died. Heartbroken, I ran outside to locate a pay phone and call Mike Francesa to find out the details of this apparent tragedy. When he picked up, I frantically asked how our charismatic friend had met his untimely demise.

"Oh, no, Jimmy," he replied. "The Greek didn't die. It's *much worse* than that!"

. . .

By 1989, I was doing all sorts of events for CBS: college basketball, golf, track and field—and I even got my first taste of international competition at the 1986 world swimming and diving championships in Madrid, where the U.S. team was led by Matt Biondi from my old hometown (albeit for only nine months) of Moraga, California. But, I was spending each fall hosting the college-football studio show at the CBS Broadcast Center in New York, so it seemed only logical to find a place to put down roots in the metropolitan area.

"Son, you're crazy!" Dad told me, and he could not have been blunter. "You're buying your first house, and you are spending way over your head!" This wasn't the first time I didn't take my father's advice, but it was one of the few times when my gut feeling would prove to be sounder than his experience-based wisdom (and I will admit that it *was* an ambitious stretch financially).

Moving day was June 28, 1989, and I was surprised to hear the phone ring that very night. Who had our new number?

"Jim, Ted Shaker here," boomed the familiar voice. "I just wanted to welcome you to the Nutmeg State. I also wanted to let you know that [CBS Sports president] Neal Pilson and I decided that we're taking you out of the studio to be our lead play-by-play voice for college football. We know you're only thirty, but we both think it's time for you to take the next step in your career."

"What about Brent?" I asked, still trying to recover from the news that had blindsided me.

"Brent is tired of double duty on weekends. Doing the games and then flying back all night to do the NFL show on Sunday," Teddy tried to reassure me. "Don't worry about Brent. He'll be fine."

As I hung up the phone, I thought to myself, "Boy, I'm sure glad I overruled my dad's advice and overextended myself to buy this house just so I could be close to the Broadcast Center."

While today you can find a college-football game almost every night of the week on just about every network, back then CBS was the dominant carrier in that sport. With producer Mike Burks and director Joe Aceti, we tried to make each contest into an *event*. Each opening tease had that major-motion-picture look and feel. We would say, "We're making a movie."

For me, it was also a chance to continue working with Pat Haden. We'd struck up a close friendship my first year in the studio, and it had continued. Pat was a serious student of the game—you'd expect nothing less from a Rhodes Scholar—who was also a successful attorney and businessman, as well as a terrific family man. Tim Brant, my other college-game colleague back then, was also a class act. I've never forged a friendship on the air faster than the one I was privileged to enjoy with Tim.

We televised some landmark games—classic rivalries, including Miami–Notre Dame, Notre Dame–USC, Oklahoma–Nebraska, and Alabama–Auburn. Virtually every week, the biggest games in college football were ours to document. But even with all these high-profile matchups, the one that resonated the most with me was Army-Navy.

This service-academy rivalry had a certain "purity." These young men were truly America's finest—scholar-athletes in the true sense of the word; they were not playing to impress scouts and enhance their standing for the NFL draft. Their future was already committed; they were destined to defend the cause of freedom anywhere around the globe. Invariably disciplined and well-mannered, they would always finish one of our pregame background conversations by saying, "It's an honor to talk with you, sir." But you could not help but feel that, to the contrary, it was *our honor* to have been with *them*.

On a frigid December day in 1989, Army came into the Meadowlands as a decisive favorite over a struggling Navy squad. In the best tradition of military commanders, Navy's embattled coach, Elliot Uzelac, redesigned his offense for this game. The Midshipmen surprised the Cadets by switching from their usual wishbone formation to the I-formation. Alton Grizzard, the Middies' enthusiastic quarterback, was up to the task. I had met him a few days before the game and knew that I was in the presence of greatness.

Grizzard was arguably the best quarterback to play in Annapolis other than Roger Staubach. "Griz" was Navy's all-time career leader in total offense with 5,666 yards. Thirty of them came on the final drive against Army in 1989, when he drove the Midshipmen into position for a game-winning field-goal attempt. With fifteen seconds left on the clock, Coach Uzelac sent out kicker Frank Schenk, telling him—as captured on the air—that his 32-yard attempt would be a "piece of cake."

Schenk had missed a potential game-winner at the end of Navy's previous game against Delaware, and his coach told him not to worry about it, because he would have the honor of beating Army with a field goal. The Cadets waited for the Middies to line up, then called time out to "ice" the kicker—a psychological-warfare tactic designed to increase the pressure on him.

"Make believe it's a seven-iron," Uzelac told him now. "Hit the seven-iron, and then you and I are dancing and drinking champagne tonight." I found it amusing that the coach would resort to a golf term with a kicker named Schenk, which sounded like the last thing anyone would want to do in this situation—*shank* the ball. Schenk came through, and Navy had its upset. I didn't say a word for the next minute and a half, while director Joe Aceti "cut around" the stadium capturing the emotional highs and lows.

In their glee, the Midshipmen flung their white dress hats into the air. While I was silently watching the shots on the monitor, one of the hats came flying onto my lap. Later, while Army was lining up for its last play, I said, "If there is a Midshipman named Mackowitz out there, I have your hat!" Then, in one of my favorite moments, after sixty minutes of incredible intensity—and days of feverish buildup—the players from the two service academies, many with tears streaming down their faces, locked arms while their schools' alma maters were played. Once again, they were all *brothers*.

Within days, I received a two-page handwritten letter from New York Yankees owner George Steinbrenner, whom I had never met, saying that it was maybe the finest sports broadcast he had ever watched, and that he had been deeply moved by the commentary.

Some fifteen months later, I was invited to speak at the Naval Academy's All-Sports Banquet. So I flew to Annapolis right from Pebble Beach, and I stayed on Captain's Row in the home of the athletics director, Jack Lengyel, who had been the head football coach at Marshall following the tragic 1970 plane crash. After I spoke, they named the Navy "Male Athlete of the Year," and I presented the award to senior Alton Grizzard. He came up, shook my hand, and began sobbing so hard on my shoulder that I feared he wouldn't be able to talk. Eventually he did. He was so proud to be a Navy man. He said he felt so honored to follow in his father's footsteps. His dad was a career navy man—a chief petty officer, who retired after serving for twenty-eight years.

From Annapolis, Grizzard went on to volunteer for training to become a member of the elite U.S. navy sea, air, and land (SEAL) Special Operations Forces. This excerpt from the SEAL creed tells you everything about Alton Grizzard and his comrades:

> I serve with honor on and off the battlefield. . . . My Nation expects me to be physically harder and mentally stronger than my enemies. If knocked down, I will get back up, every time. I will draw on every remaining ounce of strength to protect my teammates and to accomplish our mission. . . . I will not fail.

. . .

Eight years later, I was visiting California's Monterey Bay Aquarium with my four-year-old daughter in tow when a polite young gentleman—holding the hand of his own daughter, who looked to be about Caroline's age—came over to introduce himself.

"Excuse me, Mr. Nantz," he began. "You probably don't remember me. I'm Frank Schenk, and you called the game back in 1989 when I was fortunate enough—"

"To kick the winning field goal to beat Army at the Meadowlands," I jumped in to finish the sentence. "Of course, I remember you, Frank. *'Piece of cake!'*" We both enjoyed a good laugh, and we introduced our respective daughters to each other in what looked like a miniature pregame coin-toss ceremony.

Neither of us said anything as we watched the girls interact for a few moments. My mind flashed back to an awful morning, December 2, 1993, when I had opened *The New York Times* at breakfast only to see the following: "Alton Grizzard, the acclaimed Navy quarterback who set team career records for total offense from 1987 to 1990, and Kerryn O'Neill, a 1993 Naval Academy graduate who set records in women's track, were shot to death by a fellow Academy graduate at a California naval base early yesterday."

Frank Schenk's teammate Lieutenant (jg) Alton L. Grizzard, bound by the SEAL creed to "serve with honor on and off the battlefield," was trying to protect his friend Kerryn from her distraught former fiancé, George Smith, when Smith showed up unannounced at her apartment, then shot and killed both Kerryn and Alton before turning the gun on himself. I can still remember the haunting words in one account of this tragic double-murder suicide case: "The heart can be an enemy of promise, undoing even the most disciplined of lives."

I was crushed. Granted, I had only been involved in Grizzard's young life from the periphery—as a commentator at a couple of his football games and a presenter for a school award. Still, that was enough to get a taste of his brilliant potential. Alton Grizzard could have made admiral one day, maybe even president. To me, he represented every value that my own dad stood for and had striven to instill in his offspring.

Today, when I look back now at this tragic episode, it touches a raw emotional nerve within my own psyche: life's random *unfairness*. Night and day, I struggle with the question, what did my father ever do to deserve his living hell? And now you have an Alton Grizzard, who did very many things right, but had the misfortune of being in the wrong place at the wrong time. As I wrote in a condolence note to Alton's parents, this was not how the final chapter of their son's life was supposed to end.

Frank Schenk and I shook hands, exchanged knowing looks, and moved on. I watched him walk off, talking with animated excitement to his young daughter, and I thought to myself, "*That's* the way life should have been for his old teammate, as well."

· · ·

Over the years, both in the studio and in the booth, I have been blessed to have shared the microphone with wonderful friends and analysts. But I've come to realize that working alongside former coaches—such as Terry Donahue, Lou Holtz, and Ara Parseghian—is different from working alongside former players, whether it's Pat Haden, Randy Cross, or Phil Simms. It's not necessarily better—or worse. It's just *different*. Coaches have a different perspective. They don't view the world through a quarterback's eyes or a lineman's lens. Coaches are teachers, motivators, and role models. They are often cast as surrogate fathers for their players—and they seem perfectly comfortable assuming that role. Perhaps that may be why, sub-liminally, I enjoyed being in their presence. In many ways, they reminded me of my ultimate coach, Dad.

And then, there was Hank Stram. I first worked with Hank, part-time, in 1987, doing NFL games on CBS Radio. When the NFL introduced a Sunday-night package, Bob Kipperman and Frank Murphy, two widely respected and beloved executives who ran CBS Radio Sports, tabbed me to call the games and teamed me with Pat Haden and John Dockery. This radio gig was a subtle, yet I believe, important, career move for me. After two seasons of hosting the *College Football Report*, I began to fret that I might become "pigeonholed" as solely a "studio guy." Second, when Ted Shaker drove home from the studio on Sunday nights after a late NFL doubleheader game, he would hear our radio coverage. What's more, being the lead Sunday-night commentator positioned me to substitute for Jack Buck on those Monday nights when he was doing baseball. And that's how I first came to partner with Hank.

I remember watching the Chiefs versus the Vikings in Super Bowl IV with my parents and a real estate agent in a Howard Johnson restaurant on Route 35 in Middletown, New Jersey. We were moving from California and, at the age of ten, I was already riveted by all things involving the NFL. While the Dallas Cowboys were the team that I rooted for as a boy, my second-favorite franchise was the Kansas City Chiefs—and that was because of Hank, his many innovations, and the classy way that his team presented itself.

In that game, Hank became the first head coach to allow himself to be wired for sound—and NFL Films picked the right person for its experiment. The archival clip of Hank—diminutive and dapper with his trademark red vest and hairpiece—pacing the sidelines, a game plan rolled up in his hand, exhorting his

Hall of Fame quarterback Len Dawson to "keep matriculating down the field," remains a classic. Coach Stram appeared to be in complete control of the situation and of his team, yet at the same time, what is so striking is how much *fun* Hank appeared to be having. Like my dad, he radiated joy.

Unlike anyone else I had ever worked with, Hank would just blurt things out impulsively. In fact, his ability to "predict" plays—"Jim, sweep right coming. If the Bears are lined up like that, it has to be a sweep right!"—was a trademark that endeared him to the audience. From a professional standpoint, commentators are always taught to *wait on* rather than to anticipate the action.

Traveling with Hank was also an adventure. Everywhere we went, he would be introduced as a Hall of Famer, because it was *assumed* that someone who had developed five players already enshrined in Canton would be there himself—but *he wasn't.* Along with others, I wrote letters to the Veterans Committee to make the case for Hank's election. There was no question that he would eventually be inducted, and I was pained by the thought that he might not receive this singular recognition while he was still alive to enjoy it. To me, that would have been the worst injustice.

I was honored to be sitting right behind Hank's wife, Phyllis, and their six grown children when Coach Stram finally "matriculated" into the Pro Football Hall of Fame on August 3, 2003. By then, his health—and his *mind*—had deteriorated to the point where he couldn't stand up and speak at the event. He couldn't even pretape an acceptance. Instead, NFL Films put together a short profile. But he was on the stage in his wheelchair when they played the tape—and that served as his acceptance.

When it came time to have photos taken with the honorees, I leaned over and kissed Hank on the forehead. As I looked into his eyes, I saw a look that, unfortunately, I was familiar with—the same look I have seen in my father's eyes many times: the faint recognition, the happiness to see someone who you know has been a part of your life, and the bewilderment at not being able to piece it all together properly. Somewhere, forever locked inside, were all his memories and stories—alas, Hank no longer had the password to his own brain. Over the years, I had heard many of his tales; sometimes, I heard them two or three times, but that was okay with me.

Hank was eighty-two when he finally succumbed to pneumonia. Stram was a patriot, a veteran, and a classic American success story—so perhaps it was fitting that he left us on the Fourth of July. He passed away eight weeks before Hurricane Katrina devastated his adopted home city of New Orleans, where he finished his career in 1977—as a Saint.

.   .   .

In business, as in life, my father used to say to me, "everything comes and goes in *cycles*, Son." That's why he tried to teach me never to get overly excited by the good news—or overly upset by the bad.

In 1990, CBS Sports had NFL and college football, NBA and college basketball, and Major League Baseball. Then, one by one, many of these properties disappeared, as the NBA went to NBC and the CFA college-football package migrated to ABC. The Major League Baseball package, for which CBS had vastly overpaid in 1988, would vanish after a four-year run.

In late October of 1993, I led a press tour over to Lillehammer, Norway, where CBS would broadcast the 1994

Olympic Winter Games. I returned just in time to call the
Cowboys-Eagles doubleheader game in Philadelphia on a rainy
Halloween Sunday. The previous evening, which is referred to
by some as Mischief Night, we met with Coach Jimmy Johnson, quarterback Troy Aikman, and a few other Dallas players at
their hotel. On the way out, we ran into Cowboys' owner Jerry
Jones in the hallway. "Hey, fellas," said Jones, "here's a little
heads-up for you: You guys at CBS are in trouble with the
NFL's TV contract." At the time, that comment seemed absurd.
CBS had been telecasting the NFL regularly since 1956. Surely,
this was just some trick to try to scare our executives into raising the formal bid. I chalked it up to another Mischief Night
moment.

But as of Friday morning, December 17, 1993, nothing in
our universe functioned according to what we had grown up
believing were the natural laws of sports television. It was as if
the sun suddenly rose in the *west*—where Fox Sports was about
to establish itself as a major player by acquiring the NFL TV
rights—or at least our NFC half of it. To start its Los Angeles–
based expansion team, Fox recruited CBS senior producer Ed
Goren as its first overall draft choice, if you will—and no one
deserved it more. But it was a sad day when Eddie and his wife,
Patty, moved out to California. They had been instrumental in
my career. More important, they were dear friends.

Losing the NFL was not only painful for all of us in the
sports division, where countless jobs disappeared in the down-
sizing that ensued, it was also a shortsighted corporate blunder
of epic proportions. Several network affiliates—including Atlanta, Dallas, and Detroit—defected to Fox. Without the usual
huge late-Sunday-afternoon audience, promoting the fall season's weeknight prime-time lineup was more difficult—and
not nearly as effective. Ratings, advertising dollars, and net-

work profitability all spiraled downward in lockstep. Internally, morale was at an all-time low.

These were dark days at CBS, and it would take *years* for the sports division to recover. Still, there was work to be done—and under executive producer Rick Gentile, we carried on with the NCAA Tournament; the Masters and PGA Tour; the Olympic Winter Games. And just as one door slammed shut, another was about to open: Soon I would meet one of the most profoundly influential people in my life. He, too, was learning to adapt to major change. He had just moved out of 1600 Pennsylvania Avenue.

CHAPTER FIVE

During the summer and fall of 1995, several members of our CBS Sports golf team and I shot scenes for the Warner Bros. movie *Tin Cup*—a romantic comedy that starred Kevin Costner and Rene Russo. The movie opened the following August in Los Angeles with the full Hollywood red-carpet treatment. Although the hotel where we stayed was only three blocks from the theater where the premiere was being staged, the film publicists urged us to forgo the leisurely five-minute walk in favor of a limousine ride. We didn't realize that they would have us circling the outskirts of Westwood for forty minutes until the equivalent of an air-traffic controller cleared us to pull up at the front curb. It was all cleverly choreographed so that when I got out, a young production assistant dutifully whisked me right to the waiting microphone of a celebrity-news correspondent.

"Hey, I saw the movie," he began—a premise whose likelihood ranged from implausible to impossible. "Man, you were *great!*" I thanked him, playing along. "I had no idea that you could *act* like that. Tell me, what was it like?" As I was launching into my answer and making eye contact with the reporter, he stepped back out of the frame, holding the microphone with one hand and motioning to one of the staffers with the other, as if to say, "There's so-and-so, go get him for my next interview." I continued with my earnest appraisal of what it was like to be an "accidental tourist" in the world of filmmaking, all the while disturbed by the interviewer's lack of attention. For all he knew, I could have rattled off all the train stops along the commuter line from New York to New Haven, and he would have turned back to me just as he did and said, "Oh, that's *terrific!* Say, what was it *really* like, working with Kevin Costner?" Clearly, he was just going through the motions, buying time until another "famous" person, hopefully one higher up in America's celebrity pecking order, came his way. In short, everything at this event was predicated on *who* you were, not *what* you were.

Well, there is perceived power and then there is *real* power. It was fascinating to juxtapose the Hollywood scene, with all of its "make-believe" importance, with a more familiar encounter that I had experienced only forty-eight hours earlier on the other side of the country. This also took place in an outdoor public setting—Barnacle Billy's, a restaurant and ice-cream parlor in Ogunquit, Maine—with an individual who had recently truly been at the top of the pecking order as the "most powerful man in the world." And yet, there was George H. W. Bush, the forty-first president of the United States, patiently waiting on line in the noonday sun for an ice-cream cone. "Go on in, Mr. President, it's too hot out here!" people were yelling our way. But he just smiled, almost bashfully, and waved off their offer.

We had taken his boat down the Maine coast for a casual ride and, on the spur of the moment, docked for a midday treat. The wait to get inside was fifteen minutes, and while we stood in line, the former president graciously accommodated every request for autographs and photos. In George Bush's eyes, everyone was equal; there was no hierarchy—of fame, power, money, whatever. Cutting to the head of the line—or pulling rank, as my dad used to call it—was discourteous, inconsiderate, and unthinkable behavior.

Like my dad, the former chief executive never felt that he was better than anyone else, more entitled to anything, or deserving of any preferential treatment. Although they came from entirely different social backgrounds, my father and George Bush share the same *moral* DNA. Their humility, their etiquette, their kindness made them almost brothers. In my imagination, I wondered what it would have been like to have been able to watch these two wonderfully old-fashioned gentlemen, in their physical primes, battling one another over who would pick up the check—or who would get to sit in the *worst* seat.

In 1998, I was invited by the Bush family to a small reception in New York City that would serve as an early "test-market" event for Texas governor George W. Bush's possible presidential run two years out. One of the guests was legendary jazz vibraphonist Lionel Hampton. When I walked over to meet him, I saw that the former president was kneeling on one knee so that he would be able to speak at eye level with the ailing, wheelchair-bound musician. The former president could simply have leaned over—as other guests of similar height did—but this instinctive gesture of dignity and respect was right out of my father's playbook. When CBS was NFL-less from 1994 to 1997, I spent a great deal of time commuting to visit my ailing father in Houston, as well as my "surrogate" father in Maine—and I came to notice many other similarities between the two guiding figures in my life. Beyond their innate decency and generosity, both gentlemen were invariably upbeat, active, and *spontaneous*.

"Well, Caroline," former president Bush said to my daughter one day when I brought her to his Houston office, "I've got to ask you a question: What are you and your dad doing tonight?" She told him she wasn't sure. "Do you like baseball?" he asked, and she responded politely that she sure did like baseball. "Well, then, I don't have anything planned, but I do know that the Astros are in town. Why don't we all go to the ball game tonight," Bush suggested on the spur of the moment. "And let's take a bunch of the Secret Service agents and their families with us." He pulled out his credit card and instructed Tommy Frechette, his personal aide, to purchase some tickets, telling him, "Just get the upper-deck seats. I want to watch the game with the real fans, eat hot dogs and popcorn, and have a good time." Bush could easily have called his friend Astros' owner Drayton McLane for tickets, but that would be "imposing," and that's something that neither the former president nor my father would ever want to do. Having hatched his last-minute plan, he had that same delightfully mischievous, almost conspiratorial, glint in his eye that my father used to get when he'd suddenly stop what he was doing and say, "Oh, to heck with this—let's just go out and have a good time!"

Early on in our friendship, the forty-first president and I were paired together in a round of golf against my college buddy Paul Marchand and another Bush family friend. (Paul has been a wonderful "matchmaker" for me: He arranged for me to meet Jim McKay, then years later brought me together with President Bush.)

We had started the day with the president entering the pro shop, plopping his wallet on the counter, and—despite the shop assistant's offer to waive the usual fees—paying for himself, as well as his guests and the agents.

It was a classic George Bush moment. My father had always acted the same way. He didn't want people to make a fuss about him or to do anything that would make him feel as if he owed them one.

That day at the 15th hole in our match, we had the option of what is called pressing the bet. The president came over to me and said, "Hey, how do you feel about it? Do you want to press these guys?"

I wasn't sure exactly what kind of stakes were on the line, so I asked how much we were risking. "Jimmy, if we lose," he explained, "we'll lose a *dollar*!"

Wanting to be certain that *dollar* wasn't some sort of code for a hundred—or a hundred *thousand*—dollars, I asked him to clarify that he actually meant one hundred cents.

"Yeah, a dollar," he reassured me. "A plain, old American dollar."

"You know what, Mr. President," I responded, "let's do it! Let's be bold! Why don't we just step out there and really challenge them?"

"*Want to?* Let's do it!"

Game on! The president was just so happy. Most people would say, why waste your time for a dollar? But the president, exactly like my dad, loved to create silly contests, simply for the fun of it, and perhaps to satisfy his competitive spirit, although he never did bet more than a dollar. Lord knows, both my dad and the former chief executive have had their respective share of serious decisions to make and crises to endure, yet neither one ever missed an opportunity to try to spice up mundane moments by injecting them with joyfulness. The ability to elevate ordinary situations into special occasions is a true blessing. It makes life so much sweeter.

. . .

The year 1998 was shaping up as a busy one for me, starting with my role as prime-time host of the Olympic Winter Games in Japan. Our anchor location in Nagano was, perhaps ironically, in front of an ancient Zenkoji Temple. Yet in no way did I experience anything remotely approaching the tranquillity of Zen. I was on edge, knowing that my father's situation was continuing to deteriorate, and I was half a world away.

Upon returning from six weeks at the Olympics, we ran right into the NCAA basketball tournament, which culminated with Kentucky, under head coach Tubby Smith, winning its seventh national title. Happily, since the Final Four was in San Antonio that year, I was able to be with my dad again, and in an optimistic moment we decided to bring him to the Alamodome. In retrospect, it was probably a mistake. The noise and the crowds made him anxious and uncomfortable. Whereas Dad used to sit and silently watch me, now we found ourselves having to rotate family members to sit and watch *him*. Assuring the safety of our loved ones and guarding against sudden outbursts that might damage their reputations are among the ongoing burdens that Alzheimer's families, such as ours, must bear. We have to be constantly vigilant.

From the Alamodome, I flew to Augusta for the Masters, which Mark O'Meara captured by sinking a 20-foot birdie on the final hole to defeat my old pal Fred Couples and David Duval by one shot.

Soon the golf summer zipped by, and my focus turned, at long last, back to the NFL. In late 1996, Sean McManus, who had, for years, been on my agent Barry Frank's team at IMG, became president of CBS Sports. Sean was always self-assured, but not cocky. He was quietly confident in his ability to re-build CBS Sports, although both inside and outside the net-work everyone felt that we would never be whole again until the NFL returned. On January 12, 1998, I was in the lobby of the Ritz-Carlton Pasadena when Sean called from New York with the great news that CBS had acquired the rights to the NFL's Sunday-afternoon AFC package.

"Jim, you never lost faith in CBS Sports," Sean told me. "So the choice is yours—do you want to do the games or do you want to do the studio?" McManus dutifully advised me that doing the lead play-by-play, especially in the late-afternoon doubleheader-game window was, by far, the more significant assignment. He quickly crunched all the numbers for me—audience size, ratings, airtime exposure, and so forth. Throughout my career, I had always focused on doing the games—and for all of the reasons Sean was now giving me. But something about growing up with *The NFL Today* was in my blood. This time, I wanted the studio.

On September 6, 1998, I had the great pleasure of wel-coming the world back to the NFL on CBS by narrating an opening tease that paid homage to the celebrated heritage of *The NFL Today,* while also looking ahead to "a new future" for the program. The "new" pregame show was somewhat akin to the expansion Cleveland Browns. After the franchise relocated to Baltimore (as the Ravens), Cleveland was allowed to keep the team name and all the historical statistics, but it had to start from scratch in assembling players and building a winning program. Prior to losing the NFL, CBS Sports was a production, and ratings, juggernaut. But Fox, ESPN, and financial cutbacks caused by corporate chaos had changed the division. Now, new players were at most of the "skill positions"—from executive producer Terry Ewert to the three rookies surrounding me at the anchor desk: Hall of Fame running back Marcus Allen; George Seifert, who was replaced in midseason by our information guru, Michael Lombardi; and Brent Jones, the runaway winner of our preseason talent search, who would eventually become so successful in business that he could no longer "afford" to divert his time to television.

On the whole, 1998 was an exciting and rewarding year, which was capped by my selection as the National Sportscaster of the Year. Within our broadcasting fraternity, this is considered by many to be the highest honor—more so than winning an Emmy.

The annual event is held in Salisbury, North Carolina, home of the National Sportscasters and Sportswriters Association and Hall of Fame. Salisbury is located one railroad stop from the town of Spencer, where my great-grandfather Mark Nantz, an immigrant from Alsace-Lorraine, had worked for the Southern Railway. Salisbury is also less than an hour's drive from Charlotte and Mt. Holly, where my parents had grown up. This was wonderful for all my aunts, uncles, nieces, and cousins from around the area, who were all excited about coming to cheer me on.

For weeks, I agonized about what to do with my dad. I desperately wanted to have him with me, but his Alzheimer's had so progressed that I worried that this might be too much. Yet how could I not allow him to share this special evening after all that he had done to help nurture and develop my career? Ultimately, we reasoned that the dinner would only run for a couple of hours, and that we would indeed go for it.

On a beautiful and festive evening, the guest list of more than three hundred included some forty relatives and close friends, including Billy Packer, Ken Venturi, and Barry Frank. Sean McManus was my presenter, and he surprised me by reading a handwritten congratulatory note from his father, Jim McKay, who had been enshrined in the Hall of Fame there in 1987.

After thanking the committee, as I began to acknowledge the major role that my parents had played in encouraging me to fulfill my boyhood aspirations, out of the corner of my eye I noticed that my father had pushed back his chair and stood up—even though I had not yet introduced him. I just stopped, and the room fell silent for a good four or five seconds. All eyes were on Dad, and no one—least of all me—had any clue what might happen next. My father began waving to the room with dignified gestures. His pride was evident. The guests—most of whom could sense that something was amiss with my father—erupted into applause, and my dad appeared to be pleased as he basked in the ovation. As Mom later put it, with her usual positive outlook, "He just came through for us so well!" I struggled to get the program back on track. "Ladies and gentlemen," I plowed on, "my beloved mother, Doris, is also here this evening—and, Mom, I want to make you proud, as well." This sparked a second standing ovation.

The emotional energy in the room rendered me speechless. I realized that I was squeezing both sides of the lectern with a death grip. As I tried to compose myself, my daughter, Caroline, who was five years old at the time, must have sensed that her dad was having a difficult moment. She jumped out of her seat, maneuvered her way through the maze of tables, and leapt into my arms. All dolled up in an adorable yellow chiffon dress, she was a lemon angel. And she was just what her daddy needed at that moment. If I hadn't been holding her, I don't think I could have finished my remarks.

On a night dedicated to honoring a year's worth of well-chosen words, both spoken and written (Rick Reilly of *Sports Illustrated* received the award as National Sportswriter of the Year), my dad and his precious granddaughter stole the show with their own moving, but unscripted, *non-verbal* communication.

. . .

Six months later, I was invited to speak at a corporate golf event in Bermuda. My sister, Nancy, proposed that we turn it into what we all implicitly understood would be our final "family" vacation. Since she and her husband, Don, would come along, we were all able to take turns "daddy-sitting." By coincidence, Michelle McGann, an LPGA star and a dear friend, was vacationing there with her parents, as well. They had recently lost a family member to Alzheimer's, and so they were well acquainted with the familial stress that is part of the package. As I introduced my father to the McGanns, he blurted out a few disjointed remarks—nothing profane, but still somewhat inappropriate nonetheless. I started to apologize, and they cut me off.

"Please, Jim," Michelle said, "don't give this a second thought. We know exactly what's going on and what you must be going through. Just enjoy your time with your dad. And try to make the most of every moment together." Relieved and grateful, I took her advice to heart, and we tried to show Dad a good time.

On the final night of our stay, I arranged for Dad to be the guest of honor at one of my favorite restaurants in the world, Tom Moore's Tavern. The general manager, Bruno Fiocca, was a prince about this, setting us up at a private table in the back, without a lot of people around. Sure enough, Dad began saying some things to Bruno that made absolutely no sense. Perhaps he thought that he was telling jokes, as he used to do all the time; now he was plagued by neurological disconnects that made it almost impossible for him to properly output his thoughts. Nonetheless, Dad seemed to *think* he had his audience in stitches. Bruno was a perfect gentleman and a good sport. He laughed along heartily—*with* my dad, not at him. This was the type of elegant and relaxed dining experience that I had hoped Dad and I could occasionally enjoy together when I had proposed, years earlier, that my father join me as a business adviser and regular traveling companion. Instead, this evening on the town would mark my dad's final appearance in public. Despite the hardships of the situation, the consensus of the family was that Dad *appeared*—again, that is always the operative word—to be having a grand time.

We returned to the Mid Ocean Club that night on a high. Everyone felt that this final family dinner had proved as memorable, for us at least, as we had hoped it would. When I went back to my room, a voice message was waiting for me with some stunning news. Suddenly, an almost perfect evening got even better. That very day, Houston had beaten out the favored Los Angeles bid and was awarded the NFL's thirty-second franchise. As if that weren't enough, reportedly, Houston would also get to host the Super Bowl in early 2004. Knowing that CBS broadcasts this showcase game every third year, I did the quick calculation and announced to everyone's further delight that this Super Bowl would be a homecoming party for the Nantz family.

I couldn't sleep that night, but in a refreshingly welcome change, for good reason. I sat out on the veranda feeling that the stars above the ocean were aligned positively. I thought about how much Dad loved Houston, and about how good the city had been to him and to his family for almost three decades. Like Dad, I love Houston. I've always been grateful for all the doors that it had opened in my life. Not only did my father always make it a point to repay the kindness of others, but he tried to do so in ways that were uniquely meaningful. Now, I sensed that I had just been handed a rare chance to do something special for Houston on my dad's behalf. While I didn't quite know what form this new project would take, I did know just the man who could help me make it happen— fellow Houstonophile George Herbert Walker Bush.

CHAPTER SIX

Beyond satisfying my decades-old emotional ties to *The NFL Today*, hosting the pregame show had several hidden perquisites. For starters, I was able to spend a chunk of quality time at home with my family. Another was that, during this trying period in my life, I felt as if being on camera made our program into a weekly "visit" with my father. I've never asked for face time, but it came automatically with my role as anchor. Somehow, I hoped that my visibility would create some sort of recognition for my dad; in fact, each time I introduced myself—"*Jim Nantz* here"—I was calling out *his name*, as well. It's impossible to say whether any of these coded attempts to reach Dad ever penetrated his limited consciousness. To me, they were certainly worth a try; ultimately, they were harmless—and until now, no one was ever the wiser.

The show continued to be a work-in-progress. We knew that we needed some strong personalities to create good TV.

So late in the 2000 season, there were rumors—true, as it would ultimately turn out—that Deion Sanders was a candidate to join the pregame show. Jerry Glanville, who was now a cast member seated at the far end of the desk, took the musical chairs metaphor literally. At one point during a show, when I asked Jerry a routine football question, the former Oilers and Falcons head coach said, "I don't know about that, but I know one thing—*nobody's taking my chair!*" With that, he actually picked up his chair and carried it right out of the studio. Those kind of madcap antics were typical of Jerry. He was a brilliant defensive football coach and a total free spirit. Each Sunday, right before we came on the air at 11:59:30 ET, our producer, Eric Mann, would remind everyone, "This will be live, coast to coast, on the CBS Television Network."

"Live? Did you say *live?*" Jerry would scream, and we would all crack up. "*I don't do live!* I only do tape. You told me this was on tape."

I must confess that I loved Jerry's routine so much that I actually expropriated it and pulled it off successfully on several occasions. One of my favorites was the time when LPGA star Annika Sorenstam played in a men's golf tournament, and CNN asked to interview me about her chances.

"Hey, Jim . . . Wolf Blitzer here. Thanks for coming on," CNN's anchor said to me as they ran a routine microphone check during a commercial. "Stand by. We're about thirty seconds to live."

"Wolf, d-d-d . . . did you just say *live?*" I stammered.

"Yeah?"

"Well, I don't do live," I said, keeping a poker face. Although I couldn't see him, I knew that he could see me on some monitor in his studio. "You guys told me this was going to be on tape. Like I said, I don't do live, I only do tape."

"Oh, c'mon, Jim," he said in disbelief. "How do you do all those games?"

"Oh, that's easy. I *record* all my lines, and the producers insert them in the appropriate places. It's all on tape."

With about fifteen seconds to air, I could hear Blitzer frantically asking his producer what he should do. Afraid that I might have pushed them over the edge, I quickly put Wolf out of his misery by explaining that it was all a gag. I'm sure he's filed that episode away and is looking forward to returning the favor with a practical joke of his own at my expense.

. . .

Another retired coach who rotated through *The NFL Today* and provided an engaging on-air presence was Mike Ditka. Like so many others who were in awe of him as a player and a coach, I was initially intimidated by him. After all, he was George "Papa Bear" Halas's anointed son. And then he was deified in the "Bill Swerski's Superfans" sketches on *Saturday Night Live*. ("Who wins in a fight, Ditka versus God? Trick question, Ditka *is* God.") But I quickly found out that Mike was one of the most approachable and kindhearted gentlemen I'd ever met. Ditka's teammates, coaches, and players absolutely adored him, and there's a tremendous two-way loyalty. Mike also felt a special kinship to the old guard at CBS. We had been the NFC network, the TV home of his Bears. He was also fond of our golf coverage and was a friend of Pat Summerall's.

"Da Coach" would fly in on a private jet on Friday afternoons, and off we would go to play a round of golf. Not only would Mike never let anyone else pick up a check, he would never accept any change back. And the only currency Mike seemed to carry was a C-note. So, for instance, on a $3.60 cab ride from the hotel to the Broadcast Center, he'd whip out a

$100 bill—"Keep the change!" Coat check: $100. Stop and buy a beer at the bar: $100. Conservatively, I would estimate that he spent $100,000 over the course of the NFL season—that's five grand per weekend visit. Mike's largesse didn't stop there. He took care of more homeless people on the street corners than all the government programs combined. All you had to do was ask, and a crisp Ben Franklin was heading your way. "Iron Mike" was the ultimate soft touch.

These days, Coach Ditka's generosity has been focused on helping former NFL players who have gotten little or no disability or pension assistance from the Players Association, the league, or the teams themselves. Mike has taken this personal crusade to the halls of Congress, where he testified before a House judiciary subcommittee. In his mind, today's well-paid players and successful owners don't seem to fully appreciate their debt to those players of his generation and earlier who helped build the NFL into the $6 billion entertainment cash cow that it is today.

This cause also touches one of *my* hot buttons, because my dad took countless hits in his amateur and semipro football career. One blow was so violent that it blew out the eardrum in his left ear, which caused him chronic discomfort and periodically had to be drained of fluid. While no one could conclusively say whether Dad's old football injuries at Guilford College had actually triggered or accelerated his Alzheimer's, they had certainly increased the potential risk.

Like Mike Ditka, veteran syndicated radio host Don Imus also straddles the line in the public imagination between irascible curmudgeon and philanthropic entrepreneur. But there's a difference: While Iron Mike is basically an old-school, can-do optimist, the I-Man tries not to allow the good deeds he does to ruin his sardonic mood.

In September of 2000, I played for Don's "team" in a New Jersey charity golf event, the aptly-named Imus Teed Off Challenge. It was only a two-hole affair, and I played awful golf—with one exception. I got lucky and made a 40-foot putt on the last hole to salvage a double-bogey seven. The next day, I was driving up to Maine to visit with former president Bush. On the four-hour drive, I listened to Imus rip me mercilessly. Apparently, in his eyes, I had the ability to sink a 40-footer at will—as though I could have turned it on whenever I wanted to. (Had that been the case, my life might have taken a much different path!) So he spun out this whole preposterous scenario in which I had betrayed him by purposely tanking the match in favor of Mike Francesa's team.

That night, over dinner with President and Mrs. Bush, I proposed that he go on the show and "defend my honor." In typical fashion he said, "It sounds like fun—let's do it!" The next morning, we waited until 9:00 A.M., and then from the former president's office I dialed the inside number at WFAN's studios just outside Manhattan.

"Don, you've been besmirching my good name and character here," I told him on the air. "I've decided that it's time for me to stand up and present somebody who will back my character and clear my good name."

"Well, who on earth would that be, Nantz?" Imus said with his distinctive mixture of annoyance, amusement, and curiosity.

"I-Man, this is George Bush—the father, not the son," the former president jumped in. "Heard about your golf tournament a couple of days ago. I want you to know that I was out playing golf yesterday with Jimmy Nantz, and he shot the smoothest little seventy-one you ever saw in your life. Turned it on when he had to."

Imus was in shock. He was not used to a president calling him on the air. Now that we had Imus rocked back on his heels, we decided to press the bet with some jokes we had worked up over breakfast, starting with a reference to Don's recent horse-riding injury.

"Now, Imus, Bar [former first lady Barbara Bush] and I would love to have you come up to the house up here in Maine sometime," Mr. Bush continued. "You know, we could have some fun. We could go ride some horses together."

In the background, we could hear Imus's sidekicks, Charles McCord and Bernie McGuirk, laughing, so we layered on another level.

"I've got a special horse that we picked out just for you," said the president. "And the horse's name is Sub-lim-i-nal." That was a reference to his own son's stumble over the word *subliminal* in a recent campaign speech that had gotten the candidate widely ridiculed. Now the laughter kicked up a notch.

The president was on a roll and clearly enjoying it. "You know, Don, Nantz just brought up some of this salsa. It's got your picture on it. I had some of that stuff, I-Man. And let me tell you, I don't know what you put into it, but I haven't had a reaction to a meal like that since I threw up in the lap of the prime minister of Japan."

. . .

I knew "W"—the president's eldest son—from my periodic excursions to Maine dating back to the mid-1990s. He's a big sports fan, a former owner of the Texas Rangers baseball club, and a fitness fanatic. We went jogging together a few times from Walker's Point, the Bush family estate, into downtown Kennebunkport, pitched horseshoes, played golf, and, of course, took part in all the usual Bush family diversions. The Governor of Texas, who has a penchant for tagging everyone with a nickname, even began calling me Velcro—because, as he put it, "Every time I see you, you're just sticking to my dad." He's also never failed to express his appreciation for the time that I have spent with his father, just as I've always been thankful that friends and relatives stop by and visit my dad. Every son with a busy schedule is grateful for pinch-hitters who can share some time with and pay a little extra attention to his father.

Just one week after George W. Bush's inauguration, I interviewed him for *The Super Bowl Today* pregame show. Because of his schedule, we had to tape our conversation on the day before the Giants and the Ravens played for the Vince Lombardi Trophy in Tampa. I was on our set, which was on the replica pirate ship in the far corner of Raymond James Stadium. Toward the end of the chat, I asked President Bush if there was a particular play that he would recommend for the Ravens or the Giants. Thirty years earlier, President Richard Nixon had reportedly asked head coach George Allen of the Redskins to call a certain play at a postseason game in San Francisco. Ironically, Nixon wanted an end-around—and it resulted in a 13-yard loss that helped cost Washington the game. President Bush may or may not have been familiar with the Nixon anecdote as he considered his response for a few moments.

"Well, Jimmy," he said finally, "you know, my favorite play is . . . *the bomb*."

Now fans of every political persuasion would agree that a long downfield pass is one of the most compelling plays in football—and knowing the president as I did, I could guarantee that he was totally sincere and straightforward when he answered my question. We chatted for almost fifteen minutes, but this story turned out to be one of several that didn't make the air the next day due to time constraints.

.　.　.

While you don't want the president of the United States to say something that might be misconstrued as provocative, the on-air talent is another story. And Deion Sanders is certainly provocative. CBS had been following Deion Sanders for a while. He was a sharp, contemporary, charismatic two-sport athlete—the only man to play in both the World Series and the Super Bowl—who understood marketing, branding, and communicating. Reserved and reverent in private, Sanders had a high-profile public alter ego, known as Neon Deion or Prime Time, that he had carefully been crafting since his days in school. He was also—and this was often underappreciated—a serious student of the game. We all thought that when he retired as a player, he'd set the world on fire as an on-air personality.

Sean McManus urged me to help recruit Deion. Our first phone conversation lasted at least two hours. I told him every reason why he should come to CBS: our leadership; our vision; the quality of the people; how he could really help us; and so forth. I also gave him my word that if he came to CBS, we would look after him every step of the way.

Deion came on board and was an impact player. His analysis was crisp and original—often challenging the conventional wisdom. He even created his own cast of characters for comedy sketches, including Sanders Claus, who doled out gifts—or lumps of coal—according to which NFL players and coaches had been "naughty or nice."

One Sunday, midway through the 2001 season, Deion had done the show and flown home. I had stayed to do late scoring updates into the doubleheader game, when I received a phone call in the studio. It was Deion.

"I had a chance to do some reflecting," he told me. "I just want you to know that I'm having a ball, and I realized today that I owe you a thank-you because you gave me your word that you'd take care of me. And this has been everything that you promised me it was going to be."

I was touched by Deion's call. It was the kind of courtesy my dad would have done in his day, yet one that happens all too infrequently in this business, where folks are quick to comment in two words, but rarely are they "Thank you!"

.   .   .

The 2002 NFL season marked the debut of the expansion Houston Texans. Now, there were four divisions of four teams each in both conferences. There was also a major realignment on *The NFL Today*. Deion and I welcomed a new pair of cast members—the tenth and eleventh men to share the desk with me since the show had returned in 1998. Coaches and offensive linemen may know as much, or more, football than anyone. But successful NFL quarterbacks bring something special to the table: *star power*. Given that, it's rather remarkable that in its forty-year history, *The NFL Today* had featured only one quarterback, Terry Bradshaw, on the set. Now, there would be two more.

Since CBS was the NFC network in Dan Marino's heyday (and he was an AFC player), I knew him more as a friend than as someone whom I covered. Dan used to come out for the Doral Open when we did the tournament, and he became friendly with our golf crew, especially Ken Venturi. He would sit in the tower with us by day and join us for dinner at night. At Sean's request, I'd coaxed him to fly out to Los Angeles as a surprise guest at our 1998 CBS affiliates meeting. When Dan walked out onstage, the audience went wild.

"Dan, I've known you for a long time," I said. "And I don't know when you're going to retire. When you do, though, I want you to come join me on *The NFL Today*."

"Well, I just might do that," he said to more sustained applause from the fifteen hundred affiliate representatives.

I reached into my coat pocket and pulled out a document on CBS letterhead. "Dan, this is a contract—with terms to be determined later—signed by Sean McManus, the president of CBS Sports. I'd like you to hold on to it, and when your playing career is over, give us a call, and we'll put this into play."

Those "terms to be determined later" played a major role in Marino's decision to join our CBS Sports family, and maybe that little prop planted the seed in Dan's mind that he was coming to a place where everyone looked forward to having him.

Boomer Esiason had played against Dan many times. They were friends and had much in common. Unlike Dan, Boomer had been working on a second career in the media for a while, even as his own playing days were winding down. We shared plenty of goofy moments on the show, and Boomer was always able to take it as well as he could dish it out. If we were in a pinch, I always knew that I could toss it over to Boomer and he could scramble and buy time. But whenever I think of Boomer, I always come back to the enormous passion he has channeled into trying to cure cystic fibrosis, the fatal genetic disorder that affects more than thirty thousand Americans—including Boomer's son, Gunnar. His foundation work defines him to me more than anything else, and I have unending admiration for Boomer for that.

In 2003, for the first time since CBS reacquired the NFL

rights, *The NFL Today* had the same cast for back-to-back seasons. Moreover, America was beginning to discover the chemistry that had developed among Dan, Deion, Boomer, and me. It's amazing what a little continuity can mean. We were having fun each week together, and we began to close the gap between us and our counterparts (and former colleagues) at Fox. Despite my heavy travel schedule, I had been working nonstop for fifteen months to honor the vow that I had made in Bermuda back on October 6, 1999—the day the Super Bowl was awarded to Houston.

As expected, former president George H. W. Bush absolutely loved the idea of a benefit to honor the great city of Houston. Not only did he accept my invitation to serve as the honorary chairman, he also put his considerable local resources at my disposal. We spent days brainstorming what form this event would take. Over time, our thinking shifted from a megaconcert to the first-ever Olympics-style "opening ceremony" welcoming the Super Bowl to town—a concept that NFL Commissioner Paul Tagliabue was quick to embrace. Thanks to a volunteer team that worked thousands of hours to help carry out the dream, everything fell into place with two weeks to go. And now that we knew who the Super Bowl teams were, it was time to get them on board. I called Patriots' head coach Bill Belichick in Foxborough, and I said, "Bill, I need a very special favor." He didn't make me wait. "Jim, for you, I'll be there!" And so was Panthers' head coach John Fox.

As the evening's theme, we set out to recognize the forty-one (in honor of President Bush, who was our forty-first president) greatest Houston sports legends. The gala dinner and the "Salute" featured a concert by Yanni, who flew in his orchestra from around the world at his own expense. The event attracted a capacity crowd of more than six thousand. I personally called all thirty-seven living Houston superstars and walked them through my entire vision of the evening. Thankfully, they all responded positively, and many later said that it was one of the great nights of their lives. Houstonians from Roger Clemens, Nolan Ryan, and Andy Pettitte, to Earl Campbell, Bum Phillips, Clyde "The Glide" Drexler, and Mary Lou Retton, were just a sampling of the stars who took the stage.

My dad would have enjoyed the evening thoroughly, not just for the sheer excitement and fun, but also to see how it brought the whole town together for the benefit of several worthwhile charities. Probably, though, what would have cheered him the most was seeing his son give back to the community that had helped launch his success.

After all the pressure of organizing, choreographing, and hosting the "Houston Salute" dinner and Super Bowl Opening Ceremony, I was actually looking forward to the marathon live telecast of *The Super Bowl Today* a few days later as a welcome relief. Again, there was an interview with President George W. Bush. This time it was *live* from the snow-covered Rose Garden. The plan was to keep things simple—talk football, not politics. (And leave it to John Fox and Bill Belichick to call their own plays.) The president and I spoke about how the Super Bowl had become a national holiday that the whole country stops to celebrate, and he reminisced a bit about his days in Houston after college. Then he talked about loving sports, all sports, including horseshoes, which he noted, he usually won, until *I* had changed the rules one summer in Maine by insisting that you had to win by two.

Rather than explain his comment, I let it go and thanked him, as we were running out of time. By this point, Reliant Stadium was almost filled to capacity, and after nearly four

hours of pregame programming, everyone was itching to get
to the most popular part of the show: the final predictions.
Boldly, I asserted that three things would happen: reserve Carolina wide receiver Ricky Proehl would catch a touchdown
pass; we'd witness the first overtime game in Super Bowl history; and New England kicker Adam Vinatieri would win the
contest with a field goal.

. . .

Our halftime responsibilities were minuscule. All we had to do
was review the highlights, promote the postgame trophy presentation, and tease the entertainment acts that were coming
up: Nelly, Kid Rock, Janet Jackson, and Justin Timberlake.
Frankly, none of them were exactly my cup of tea. But I had a
halftime agenda of my own, and I knew it would be far more
pleasurable.

I took the elevator up to the long and spectacularly appointed luxury box of Houston Texans' owners Bob and Janice
McNair. We had developed a friendship over the past few years,
and Bob was instrumental in helping make the Houston Salute
such a resounding winner. His owner's box at Reliant Stadium
seats 163 people. My mom and Nancy occupied two of those
seats, a few rows behind former president Bush and his wife,
Barbara.

Not only were those of us in Bob McNair's box casually
ignoring the "entertainment spectacular" on the field, but no
one in Reliant Stadium was paying much attention, either—
which is why so many of us who were there missed the infa-
mous "wardrobe malfunction" seen by millions of viewers
around the globe.

Working my way back toward the set through the maze of

CBS trailers, I couldn't quite understand why executive producer Tony Petitti seemed to be embroiled in so much unusual hubbub and why LeslieAnne Wade, CBS Sports' vice president of communications, and her capable associate Robin Brendle, were in full damage-control mode.

When Janet Jackson and Justin Timberlake had gotten to the final lyric, "I'm gonna have you naked by the end of this song," Timberlake pulled off a part of Jackson's costume, revealing her right breast (adorned with a large, sun-shaped "nipple shield"). CBS immediately cut away to a wide shot, but the damage was done. More than two hundred thousand Americans called to express their displeasure, causing the switchboards to melt down. The incident would also have enormous repercussions for CBS, including stiff FCC fines and mandatory delays on live events.

As part of an explosive fourth-quarter scoring surge, Carolina's Jake Delhomme hit, of all people, Ricky Proehl in the end zone to tie the game at 29-all with 1:08 left. I thought, here comes the first Super Bowl overtime—*just as I had also predicted*. Now it was time for some of Tom Brady's last-minute magic. He drove New England down the field, setting up Adam Vinatieri for a 41-yard, game-winning field goal. I may have been wrong about the overtime, but I was right about the margin of victory and how it would happen.

I could see the crowd of CBS people gathering at the center of the compound for the ritual postmortem. But I marched right past them without stopping, and within ninety seconds of signing off to 140 million viewers, I was at my car. A motorcycle cop was waiting for me, as promised. He and I had begun this long day together at seven-thirty that morning, when he showed up, sirens and lights blaring, in front of my mother's house. I had spent the night there, sleeping in my old bedroom, to escape all the tumult downtown. That was one reason to go home; the other was more personal. The view from my hotel room overlooked the nursing facility that my father has called home since 2000. It was a painful reminder, every time I opened the drapes, that he could not be with me on game day.

With a police escort, it took me less than ten minutes to arrive at my father's bedside. My day would not be complete until I shared the celebration with the one viewer I was trying to reach the most. His room was completely dark except for the flickering image of the TV, tuned, as it always was, to Channel 11, KHOU-TV, Houston's CBS affiliate, where I had begun my on-camera career almost three decades earlier. My voice had been emanating from Dad's television set all day, but I will never know if he recognized it.

I reached over and shook him awake as gently as I could. Then, holding his hand, I gently whispered the words that had been circling in my head but had been held for this occasion. "Dad," I said slowly, "I hosted the Super Bowl from right here in Houston!" With kind of a half-smile, half-chuckle, his eyes opened wide and stared right at me. I took it as a sign that somehow, at some level, he had comprehended what I had just told him. A peaceful happiness slowly eased across his face, and that pure look of contentment never waned as he faded back to sleep.

Chapter Seven

When I was a young boy, my bedroom in Colts Neck looked as if it had been personally decorated by Coach Tom Landry of Dallas. There were photos of Roger Staubach, Bob Lilly, Drew Pearson, and my other favorite players, along with pennants, pillows, pajamas, and even Cowboys wallpaper. I was probably the only subscriber to the Dallas Cowboys' newsletter in the entire state of New Jersey—and clearly the youngest. Dallas was not only America's Team, it was *my* team. I was eleven years old on Super Bowl Sunday in 1971—just a tad younger than my daughter, Caroline, is now. As you might imagine, when the Colts beat the Cowboys on a last-second Jim O'Brien field goal, I was so devastated that I begged my parents for permission to stay home from school for a few days. How could I possibly face all those fifth-graders who were going to make my life miserable?

I knew Mom would be sympathetic, and she was. But these

judgment calls were always left to Dad, and there would be no appeal; in our family, he was the Commissioner. Although I presented my case with all the passion that I could marshal, the final ruling was as swift as it was predictable: I would have to bite the bullet, attend classes as usual, and "play through" the short-term humiliation. Little could I have known back then that the lesson Dad was teaching me that day about confronting adversity head-on, rather than running from it, would prove to be so valuable throughout the rest of my life.

. . .

I always made it a point to schedule my calendar so that I could be in Houston with my dad for Father's Day. I especially wanted to be there on that third Sunday in June of 2004, because I privately feared that it might be the last one I would have with him. To mark the occasion, we arranged to take my father from the special-care facility, in which we had been forced to place him four years earlier, to my mother's new house. We engaged a small army of people and special equipment to transport Dad in his wheelchair, and the whole ordeal underscored just how frail, vulnerable, and totally at the mercy of others my father had become. Originally, we had made a point of bringing him across town for major family occasions at least twice a year. Then, it became so difficult and disruptive for him that we cut it down to once a year. Now, it was painfully clear to all of us that this would be the last time his body could handle the strain.

I've learned that reckoning the passage of time by marking the last times a beloved family member participates in treasured family rituals is common for families caring for the terminally ill. First you count down the public appearances: the last time spent together on a family vacation; the last time you went out to dinner at a favorite restaurant. Then you move on to the private ones: the last holiday dinner together; the last family celebration. And so it is with so many aspects of life that you always seem to take for granted until they become precious and nostalgic.

The day after this particularly emotionally draining Father's Day, CBS Sports president Sean McManus tracked me down in Houston. "Jim, we've decided to make a change," McManus told me over the phone, using a phrase that sparked a familiar anxiety from my childhood; my father would always announce an imminent relocation by telling us, "The company has decided to make a change." Sean continued, "You're going to be the new lead guy on our NFL game coverage."

Sean and Tony Petitti had been dropping hints about this for a while, and they had even asked me outright whether I would reconsider calling games. But I told them that I loved doing *The NFL Today*, and all the people I worked with there. What's more, with all the turmoil surrounding my father's health, it didn't seem like a propitious time to start something new, or to give up rare family time at home.

"It's the right move for CBS and for you, Jim," Sean reassured me. "Believe me, you'll thank us later." In retrospect, it *was* the right move for me; and to this day I *do* thank Sean and Tony for pushing me, just as my father had done, for example, by insisting that I couldn't quit my Pop Warner football team after one grueling practice, or that I had to go to Salt Lake City to gain job-interviewing experience.

My new NFL assignment came with a built-in comfort zone, starting with coordinating producer Lance Barrow. After spending two decades together on golf, it may be fair to say that we've enjoyed more meals with each other than we have with our families. Then there was lead director Mike Arnold, another friend and colleague of long standing, who had directed my games the last time I had done the NFL on CBS. I would also be working alongside Phil Simms, whom I had known casually since his playing days as a Giant. Given my admiration for his integrity as a family man and professional, I was looking forward to spending time getting to know him better.

From the outset, two games in particular took on special importance in our minds: Super Bowl XLI, which would take place three seasons down the road in February of 2007, and, not to equate their importance, our prime-time debut, August 20, 2004. It was only a preseason game, but we wanted to create a strong first impression. Toward that end, we gave it special treatment, traveling down four days early to meet with the Eagles and the Ravens.

We were determined to give that first game our best shot, but I had no idea that it would be a *golf* shot. That Thursday, the day before the game, we were traveling back from the Ravens' camp in Maryland when traffic on I-95 northbound came to a complete standstill. Meanwhile, in the opposite direction, the highway was eerily deserted as far as the eye could see. As the third hour of the standstill melded into the fourth, with no word of any hope on the radio news, we decided to get out and stretch. I remarked offhandedly to Phil that I would give anything to hit a few golf balls.

"Hey, Jim. Go ahead, be my guest!" he said, motioning over to the still-barren southbound side.

On a lark, I sauntered up to the car in front of us and knocked on the driver's window. Just as absurdly as though I were about to inquire of him whether I might borrow some Grey Poupon, I instead asked this random stranger stuck in traffic whether he had any golf equipment in his trunk. With my luck, he did—and, upon recognizing me, was only too happy to oblige my bizarre request. Then, I located a crack in the pavement on which to lodge the tee securely, allowing the ball to sit high enough so that I wouldn't scuff up the bottom of the borrowed driver.

My mortified carmates were no doubt silently calculating the potential impact of this stunt on *their* careers. Temporary insanity? Plausible deniability? Surely the CBS lawyers could find an explanation that would mollify the jury.

"You're not really going to do this, are you?" Phil blurted out. "You push this shot a little to the right and you could kill somebody!"

"Don't worry about it, partner," I said, smiling serenely. "I've been *visualizing* this shot for the past two hours."

With that—*crack!*—the driver struck the ball just above the faceplate's equator, directly on the sweet spot. The ball began soaring toward New Jersey with a gentle fade, just enough to carry it over the trees on the far-side shoulder and slowly bring it back in line with the fairway (i.e., I-95), but not oversliced so that it became a danger to the gridlocked gallery. As the ball continued bouncing toward the Delaware Memorial Bridge, I nonchalantly handed the club back to my sponsor and climbed back into our SUV. A stunned silence awaited me, which I broke by proclaiming cheerfully, "Boys, I think we've just started a tradition unlike any other!"

The big story coming into our first broadcast together was Terrell Owens's home debut as an Eagle. Phil and I were prepared to explore it, and so was Owens's new quarterback, Donovan McNabb, who went deep for T.O. on Philadelphia's first play from scrimmage.

"McNabb back to throw on first down. . . . Steps up, and lets it go for Owens. . . . *Touchdown!* . . . Eighty-one yards for

number eighty-one!" The call *felt* as sweet as that golf shot on
I-95—dead-solid perfect. Less than three minutes into the
game, I knew that I was home. I hadn't called an NFL game in
ten years, since the Dallas–Green Bay divisional playoff in January of 1994 (the penultimate game of the NFC era of CBS).
Now I was eager to reestablish my branch on the CBS NFL
play-by-play "tree" that includes Greg Gumbel, Pat Summerall,
Vin Scully, Jack Buck, Jack Whitaker, and Ray Scott.

Scott, the voice of the Lombardi-era Packers, was the master of minimalism, and his work had a profound affect on
Summerall's laconic style. In fact, my Salt Lake City buddy,
Hot Rod Hundley, could have me in stitches at will by slip-
ping into his impression of Pat ordering breakfast à la Ray
Scott: "Two eggs ... *over easy!* ... Bacon ... *crisp!* ... Toast ...
wheat!"

While many have noted that Pat's less-is-more terseness af-
forded John Madden the opportunity to do his thing, the real
secret to their chemistry was Summerall's brilliance as a coun-
terpuncher. John could rant and rave about something and get
himself all worked up into a lather. Then Pat, with impeccable
Carsonesque timing, would casually intone something on the
order of "*Mmm* ... that may be!" It was verbal jujitsu—the
sublime art of rerouting someone else's energy for your own
advantage.

While I try to emulate Pat's economy of words to keep the
play-by-play as succinct and crisp as possible, what captures my
imagination are the stories that define the players and the
coaches and what propelled them to this moment. Each week,
Lance, Mike, Phil, Tommy Spencer (my editorial consultant),
and I spend some private time with each head coach, and several key players. We also watch the closed practices, scour the
Internet and the local press clippings, and study tapes. We want

to know what's "out there" so we don't ignore any obvious story lines; on the other hand, we want to ask probing questions that will produce fresh insights and untold personal narratives.

Over the years, I have found myself especially drawn to stories whose themes reflect the values and perspective that my dad instilled in me—as well as those that simply capture some element of the special bond between fathers and sons that's fostered through a common love of sports.

I remember once asking Pittsburgh running back Willie Parker a seemingly innocuous question: "How did you celebrate the Steelers' Super Bowl victory over the Seahawks?" He told me that he had bought his father, Willie Sr., a new Cadillac and had his brother deliver it to their boyhood home in Clinton, North Carolina. Then, "Fast Willie" called his dad and asked him to open the trunk to see whether anything had been left there. Willie Sr. found a box and opened it at his son's urging. Inside was Parker's Super Bowl ring. That was the *real* gift; the shiny new car was just the fancy gift-wrapping.

"Dad," he said, "this is for *you*. Thank you for always believing in me."

In any sport or hobby, dads who make time to coach their sons or daughters—as my father did for me in golf and basketball—have an enormous impact on their children's lives. When you look around the NFL, it's not unusual to see second-generation football coaches—the Gibbses, the Shanahans, the Phillipses, the Moras, the Kiffins. Mike Nolan wears dress suits on the sidelines as a tribute to his father. Dick Jauron didn't hesitate to say "My dad!" when I asked him who was the best coach he had ever been around.

Longtime Navy assistant coach Steve Belichick taught his precocious only child, Bill, how to break down game films at a tender age. Bill would hang out at practice, watch his father give the scouting report on the next opponent, and catch passes from Roger Staubach. Together, father and son would explore used-book stores looking to pick up inexpensive copies of old football-coaching texts to add to their collection. The elder Belichick passed on his passion for the intellectual elegance and the history of the game to the next generation.

In week seven of the 2004 season, Bill Belichick's Patriots faced the New York Jets with a chance to win their eighteenth straight regular-season game, breaking the NFL record that had been established by George Halas's 1933–34 Chicago Bears. By the time our production team arrived in Foxborough, I was fully prepared to hear Belichick's usual patter about how the streak meant little to him, and that his sole concern was to win the game at hand. This exchange had become so ritualized that Phil found it amusing to watch me keep pressing—and Bill keep stonewalling.

Finally, seeking a new approach, I asked Bill whether he had ever actually met "Papa Bear" Halas. "As a matter of fact, I did," Belichick responded, much to my astonishment. "My father once took me inside the Bears' locker room after a game. I said, 'Congratulations, Mr. Halas.' He then gave me a fresh dollar bill and said, 'Son, I always give a dollar to the first person who congratulates me after a victory.'"

With just over two minutes left in the Jets–Patriots game, New England came up with a strong defensive stand to protect its lead. It was the perfect spot to tell this story that personally connected the greatest coach of the current era with one of the league's founders and pioneers. It was also a window into how a father's simple introduction inspired his son.

. . .

Just as I had been fortunate in Houston and Salt Lake City with the success of the sports teams when I was working there, CBS has been fortunate that the AFC has been the dominant conference since we acquired the broadcast rights, winning seven of nine Super Bowls from the 1998 through the 2006 seasons. Much of the credit goes to Bill Belichick, whose Patriots captured three of those Vince Lombardi Trophies.

Regardless of the sport, every great champion's stature is enhanced when there is a fierce rival to overcome: Muhammad Ali had Joe Frazier. The Yankees had the Dodgers. The Celtics had the Lakers. And New England had Indianapolis. In Tony Dungy's second season as head coach at Indianapolis, the Colts, with prolific Peyton Manning running the offense, met the Patriots in the 2003 AFC championship game, with New England winning in Foxborough. A year later, they met in the divisional round, with a similar outcome. And in January of 2007, it was another Patriots-Colts AFC title showdown for a trip to the Super Bowl.

Much has been made about the differences between Bill Belichick and Tony Dungy, but they share more in common than meets the eye. Both have overcome professional disappointment and personal issues to reach the pinnacle of success, and both have inspired and mentored the careers of others, expanding their respective "coaching trees."

Herm Edwards, now head coach of the Kansas City Chiefs, once recounted to me how he used to sit in Tony Dungy's office while Dungy was preparing his game plan. At the time, they were both bright young assistants, who would often talk about what they would do if they ever became head coaches. They would make some changes: they wouldn't swear; in fact, they wouldn't even raise their voices—this alone was a form of heresy given the macho culture of in-your-face coaching by

fear and intimidation that prevailed in the sport. Then there
was a bigger picture of goals. For Dungy and his disciples,
coaching was more than winning the next game. "If we can't
make our players better men," Dungy would say, "then we
haven't done our jobs." Tony had often told his closest friends
that he wants his players to look at him and his actions and say,
"Now that's a man, and that's how you live a life."

No doubt that's how Tony viewed his father, Professor Wil-
bur Dungy, a career science educator. Now the son was echo-
ing the wisdom that he had learned from his dad's experience
in breaking through social barriers in his own field. Tony's legendary patience, discipline, and faith were put to the test in the
2007 AFC championship contest. When New England raced
out to a 21–3 lead on Asante Samuel's 39-yard interception
return for a touchdown midway through the second quarter,
one could almost hear everyone at the RCA Dome thinking,
"Same old Dungy. Same old Peyton. Same old Colts." In the
waning minutes of the half, the Colts mounted a drive, ending
with Adam Vinatieri's 26-yard field goal, which made it 21–6.
At the time, I asked Phil on the air whether Indy might have
been better served trying for a touchdown. But my partner
was unequivocal: "No, Jim, there's plenty of time. The Colts
just showed that they could move the football. In this case, you
take the points."

Coach Dungy later told me that his thinking was exactly
in line with Phil's. The Colts eventually tied the game at 21-all.
As if this were a heavyweight championship bout, the two op-
ponents kept answering each other's blows. With 2:17 to go,
and New England hanging on to a 34–31 advantage, Peyton
Manning, now oblivious to a painful injury on his throwing
hand, directed the Colts on a go-ahead touchdown drive. Tom
Brady, the NFL's Captain Comeback, still had a minute to march

the Patriots back. Director Mike Arnold caught a memorable cutaway shot of Peyton on the bench, too nervous to look up and watch the unfolding drama on the JumboTron. Just then, Colts' cornerback Marlin Jackson intercepted Brady, and the dome exploded with pent-up glee. This time their beloved Colts—not the Patriots—were headed for the Super Bowl.

As fate would have it, Tony Dungy, who had done so much to advance the careers of African-American coaches in the NFL, was not the first to lead his squad to a Super Bowl. His protégé and former assistant at Tampa Bay, Lovie Smith, had beaten Dungy to it by a matter of *hours*—when Smith's Chicago Bears ended New Orleans's magical run in the NFC championship game. Tony told me that he was thrilled for Lovie when I asked him about it during the jubilant presentation of the Lamar Hunt AFC Championship Trophy.

Like his colleagues Edwards and Dungy, Lovie Smith also credits his father with teaching him that, with big dreams and hard work, nothing is impossible. Lovie's dad battled alcoholism—and won. This victory inspired his son to persist in his endeavors. Lovie confided in me that he had, years earlier, once earned a wristwatch for being selected as a Texas high school all-star, and he gave it to his father as a gift. When his dad passed away, Lovie found the watch in mint condition: his father had taken great care of the precious keepsake. Lovie then began wearing the watch himself on game days, so that in a sense his dad would be with him to share in the important experiences of his career. It was exactly the kind of story that I loved to share with my audiences, and one that I looked forward to recounting on the air should the Bears win the Super Bowl.

Chapter Eight

Over the course of the grueling twenty-week NFL season, everyone on our production team had bonded into a tightly knit, well-oiled unit. For the Super Bowl, however, the core personnel were augmented by scores of specialists from every realm, and the sheer magnitude of the event was staggering. Despite the huge scale of the Super Bowl and the myriad distractions that week, our game plan was to try to maintain our normal weekly preparation routine as much as possible. We also wanted to make it a point to have some fun and enjoy the experience. On Thursday night, the schedule called for Lance Barrow's weekly production dinner, and it was a memorable meal—as they all are at Joe's Stone Crab in Miami. Ed Goren was hosting a table for his Fox colleagues. The CBS *Early Show* cast and producers were there. And on the way over to our table, I spotted Peyton's parents, Archie and Olivia Manning, as well as Peyton's wife, Ashley.

At some point over the years, I had mentioned to Archie that my dad had taken me to old Tulane Stadium on September 17, 1967, to witness the very first Saints' game ever played. Although I was only eight years old, I still have vivid recollections of the cigar smoke and the smell of the hot dogs on the grill. Dad bought me a program, and we sat in one of the aisles. The Saints won the coin toss, and John Gilliam returned the opening kickoff 94 yards for a touchdown against the Rams, who were then based in Los Angeles. Not bad, I thought. The first NFL play I ever witnessed, and the kick's returned for a touchdown. Alas, that would have to suffice as a franchise high point until Archie was drafted years later.

"I never saw such an outpouring of pure joy as I did in Indianapolis after the Colts beat the Patriots," I said to the Mannings.

"Well, Peyton really wants *this one,*" Archie replied.

He didn't have to complete the thought: there would be no vindication, no respite from the critics, unless his son finally won the big one. It was the same unfair and painful stigma that I've seen applied over the years to the likes of golfer Phil Mickelson and Olympic speed-skater Dan Jansen. Silently, it made the fan in me root for their success all the more. As my father used to tell me, "Son, no one ever understands that all you can ask from someone is that he give his very best. What happens after that is often out of his control."

. . .

"Now I'm not going to say that tomorrow we're going to accomplish something that's going to save humanity," Lance told everyone in our final production meeting on Saturday night. "But everyone in this room should feel mighty proud of yourself because, in your chosen field, you are at the top of your profession. Tomorrow, I want everybody in this room to just stop for a little bit, go out on the field, take a moment, and look around. Take it all in and say, 'Boy, I am one blessed person!'"

When it's the Super Bowl, you know *everyone* will be watching. If you play football as a kid, this is the game you dream about playing in. Similarly, if you work in sports television, this is the game you want to broadcast one day. But it is important to keep things in perspective, and Lance followed his own advice. Before assuming his seat in the control truck, he called Chuck Will, the retired former CBS associate director who had given him his first job in television back in the mid-1970s. He just wanted to thank Chuck for giving a nineteen-year-old college student a chance to get his foot in the door. It would have seemed improbable back then, when Chuck hired him as a spotter for Pat Summerall, that he would one day *produce* the Super Bowl. The odds were long, but I, for one, could relate to them, given my own start as a nineteen-year-old spotter for NBC Sports.

Lance's speech, reminding all of us to be conscious of where we were and what this meant, as well as his own expression of remembrance and gratitude, really hit home emotionally in terms of my father's absence. From the time I started college until the time he no longer recognized my voice, I would call Dad virtually every day. I just wanted to check in, share the daily highs and lows, solicit his advice, tell him that I was grateful to him—and that I loved him. On this Super Bowl Sunday, I would've given anything to have been able to pick up a phone, hear the excitement that would have been in my dad's voice, and then say, "Thank you, Dad. I couldn't have gotten here without you."

Nevertheless, Lance was right, and I counted my blessings,

especially for the other individuals whose lives had touched mine. I thought of generous colleagues like Verne Lundquist, who on my first road trip for the network on Christmas Eve of 1985, invited me to join him and his wife, Nancy, for their holiday dinner. This week, as usual, he was one of the first to log in with a good-luck call. I also recounted my early days with producers and directors such as Vin DeVito, Vic Frank, Bob Mansbach, Bob Matina, Steve Scheer, Craig Silver, Doug Towey, and Mark Wolff—and what an amazing ride we'd traveled together at CBS, watching one another's families grow up along the way. And then there were the pioneering women of CBS Sports, who were already on the production team before I arrived and remain devoted to the division to this day: Cathy Barreto, Colleen Kolibas, Joan Papen, Susie Reisinger, and Suzanne Smith. Ted Shaker and Ed Goren, who were among those responsible for my big break, were just two of many who called or e-mailed to reminisce that "they knew me when!" and to wish me well on the big broadcast. Earlier in the week, I had dinner with my old mentor Frank Chirkinian at Rush Limbaugh's estate. I also had a chance to chat with one of my childhood idols, Jack Whitaker, who had called the second half of Super Bowl I for CBS in Los Angeles, the only Super Bowl to be simulcast, by CBS and NBC. (Ray Scott called the opening half for CBS.) When I asked Jack whether he had any advice for me, he chuckled and said, "Just be prepared for the opening kickoff, Jimmy." Then he reflected on his own strange experience at that inaugural Super Bowl. After narrating what he *thought* was the kickoff to open the second half, Whitaker was utterly bewildered to see the officials inexplicably lining up the teams again for a *re-kick*. Only later did he learn that while the CBS crew and the Packers and the Chiefs were ready to go, NBC was still in commercial. So the officials took it upon themselves to order a "do over."

On my way up to the booth, I met Craig Kelley, the Colts' vice president of public relations. On a day when personal nostalgia had become one of the underlying themes, this was yet another quirky turn of fate. Forty years earlier, Craig and I had been classmates in grammar school back in New Orleans; our pictures were in the same row in the school yearbook. Now we were both working the Super Bowl. We couldn't resist taking an updated photo to mark this reunion. Glancing at my watch, I noticed that it was 1:50 P.M.—still ten minutes before we began our rehearsals. But in the television world, we say, "If you're not early, you're late!"

For Phil Simms, who was already in the booth, this game marked the twentieth anniversary of his nearly flawless performance in Super Bowl XXI. As a broadcaster, my partner was just as buttoned-down as he was as a player. When it comes to football, he's all business. And football *is* the Simms family business. One son, Chris, is a veteran NFL quarterback. The other, Matt, is a promising college quarterback.

With all that we had to do, Phil and I agreed that we would not allow any guests into the booth on game day. We'd be like the astronauts locked inside their spacecraft with the hatch sealed, running through the checklists, and waiting for the launch crew to "light the big candle." But when we received word that our distinguished colleague Dick Enberg was on his way up, we gladly made an exception for this beloved grand master. I always find it inspirational to be around Dick, and I knew that even a brief exchange of pleasantries prior to airtime was guaranteed to generate good karma.

Enberg was certainly no stranger to our perch above the

50-yard line in Dolphin Stadium. From this very spot he'd taken advantage of the perfect sight lines to describe Joe Montana's classic last-minute drive that beat Boomer Esiason and the Bengals in Super Bowl XXIII. It was one of eight Super Bowls that Dick called for NBC Sports, including a pair with Phil (and Paul Maguire). As Dick picked his way through the maze of cables, monitors, and lights, I suspected that deep down, in his heart of hearts, he must have longed to call this game himself. Of course, he was far too classy to have ever let on. After a quick round of hugs, Dick turned to me and said, "I'd wish you luck, Jim, but I know you don't need it because you're good at what you do, and you've earned it. So, instead, I'm going to wish you a *close game*, because that's something you can't control."

I was truly touched that a man whom I consider to be one of my "broadcasting fathers" had taken the trouble to come to the booth and offer me his personal blessing. He has no idea how much his thoughtful and generous words energized me.

As a boy, I had grown up admiring not only Enberg, but also the entire generation of pioneering network sports commentators that preceded him. These gifted storytellers created the television magic that mesmerized me every weekend. And early on, I knew that I wanted to be just like them. Within this pantheon of sports television, however, only Enberg and Curt Gowdy had ever handled the network play-by-play assignment for both the Super Bowl and the NCAA Final Four. Now I was about to embark upon an unprecedented broadcasting "triple"—after Super Bowl XLI, I would call the Final Four in Atlanta, then drive across Georgia for the Masters—three of America's premier championships.

This broadcasting first was largely the product of a unique configuration in the television rights-holders' calendar. I had known that it was coming ever since that Father's Day in 2004 when Sean switched me from the studio to the games. But the story didn't become a big deal until mid-January of 2007, when I was out in San Diego to call the Patriots-Chargers playoff game. Larry Stewart, the well-respected columnist for the *Los Angeles Times,* who has followed the evolution of sports broadcasting over the past four decades, set this three-event sequence into historical context. The results of his research appeared under a big headline: NANTZ'S CBS LIFE BECOMES A SERIES OF MAJOR EVENTS. Another TV critic, Norman Chad, put my "championship voyage" into larger historical context and found that it did not make the Top 5 all-time "journeys" when compared with those of, say, Jules Verne, Marco Polo, Alexander the Great, Admiral Robert Peary, or Hannibal and the elephants. "He's not landing on the moon or sailing solo across the Pacific or even flagpole sitting on a windy day," wrote Chad. "He's simply broadcasting three big sporting events over a two-month period." He's right—although I could certainly quibble about Peary.

.   .   .

In my headset, Lance gave a stand-by for my cue to introduce Billy Joel and "The Star-Spangled Banner." My microphone was hot to both the stadium and the worldwide TV audience. Half a dozen F-16 air force fighter jets were already airborne and homing in on the bright lights of Dolphin Stadium. The pilots, members of the elite Thunderbirds, awaited their orders to drop to 500 feet for their flyover. At 450 miles per hour, there was no margin for error. Now that the anthem had finally started, I knew that I had exactly ninety seconds for what has become an important pregame ritual. Whether one would call it meditation or a prayer, over the years I've trained my mind to block out all the excitement and sensory noise so that I can drift into a calming reflective state. This brief respite allows me to focus on the abundant blessings in my life: my family, my career, my friends, and my country. I first began this ritual in 1986, when my mother's dad, Bronze Holland Trull, passed away. My grandfather was a proud World War I veteran, and I thought of him when I looked at the American flag during the national anthem.

After more than two decades, I've long since broadened the scope of what I reflect upon in this brief meditation. On this occasion, with my family in the stands, and my father back in Houston, I wanted to channel a powerfully positive image that would trigger a smile and lead me through the broadcast in high spirits. I flashed back to Father's Day 1974, when Dad had taken me to see the final round of the U.S. Open at Winged Foot. I was only fifteen years old, but I already knew that I wanted to be a network sports commentator—ideally at CBS Sports, because it was the home of the Masters. So Dad and I spent the day working our way from the base of one TV tower to the next, trying to get as close as security would allow, and hoping to hear what Chris Schenkel or Keith Jackson or Jim McKay were whispering to their viewers. Then, with Hale Irwin about to wrap up a historic win, Dad and I looked at one another and spontaneously took off on a mad dash toward the eighteenth green to witness the finish. Running side by side, with the wind at our backs, we laughed with unbridled joy. It was father-and-son bonding at its best, that rare moment when life is absolutely *perfect*.

· · ·

On cue, a formation of fighter jets roared out of the night sky. The rain continued to soak the seventy-five thousand poncho-clad spectators. Almost 140 million "friends" were tuning in at home. Many were families, congregating in their living rooms and dens, just as the Nantz family used to do back in the day.

Lance reviewed the instructions for the next sequence. We would do a brief on-camera just before the kickoff. I took advantage of that opportunity to acknowledge some of the men who had inspired me. I felt their presence on this special night, and I wanted them to know that.

"Welcome back to CBS's coverage of Super Bowl XLI. It's our sixteenth Super Bowl on CBS. We were there for the first with Ray Scott, Jack Whitaker, Frank Gifford, and Pat Summerall. And it's a pleasure to be with you, tonight. . . . Phil, last thought before kickoff?"

"Jim, in a big game like this, where nerves can be a factor, it's always better to start on defense," Phil responded. "So for the Colts, maybe it was a blessing, losing the coin toss."

Then, in exactly the time it took me to say, "This game is brought to you in high-definition television," Phil and I had swung around to face the field and were ready to go. So was Colts' kicker Adam Vinatieri.

"Back is Devin Hester, the rookie who is so dangerous, who went to college here at Miami. He led the NFC in both kickoff returns and punt returns. And the Colts have had a hard time all season covering kicks. . . .

"It's Hester . . . trying to work it back to the middle . . . gets past the first wave . . . and there he goes! . . . Hester inside the thirty . . . Hester is going to take it all the way for a touchdown! And no flag . . . ninety-two yards!"

The narration was spare and clean. It would have made Pat Summerall and Ray Scott proud. But the man who had really prepared me for this moment was Jack Whitaker, when he admonished me, "Just be prepared for the opening kickoff, Jimmy." And for a split second, I was back in New Orleans in 1967; my dad and I are standing in the smoky aisle at Tulane Stadium, wildly cheering on John Gilliam, as he sprints to the end zone with that opening kickoff for a Saints touchdown. My first exposure to the NFL as a kid and now my first Super Bowl call forty years later were one and the same. The personal symmetry gave me chills and made me feel that this was meant to be *my* night. Not only does life work in mysterious ways, but sometimes, it dictates its own story lines.

.   .   .

The game was marred by fumbles, bad snaps, and dropped passes. By the second half, the rain was surprisingly steady and unremitting. The Colts, who had taken a 16–14 lead into half-time, extended it to 29–17 early in the fourth quarter, when Kelvin Hayden returned an intercepted Rex Grossman pass for a touchdown. During a commercial break, I turned to Phil and told him that 29–17 was going to be the final score of Super Bowl XLI.

Simms looked at me as though I was certifiable. "And *how* do you know that?" he asked quizzically, fully aware that just over ten minutes still remained on the clock. I told him I just had a hunch.

After the game ended (final score: 29–17), I asked India-napolis head coach Tony Dungy what it meant to be the first African-American head coach to win the Super Bowl. In typi-cal fashion, he was prepared, humble, and gracious. He may have been the first, he said, but surely others were at least equally qualified and just as deserving. He also said that he was proud of Lovie Smith, not only for what he had accomplished, but for *how* he had done it. Their successes had revived the old Tom Landry paradigm for winning football coaches: a calm and quiet demeanor that promoted success through *inspiration* rather than intimidation.

The stadium, which had been half-empty by the fourth

quarter, quickly became all but deserted. Unlike three years earlier, I was in no rush to leave the field. We had made sure that the television in my father's room was set to Channel 11, and that the volume was cranked way up. However, we were resigned to the fact that this time around he had probably little, if any, recognition that it was the Super Bowl—or that the voice filling the room belonged to his son.

I lingered inside the stadium to revel in the company of my daughter, Caroline, and my nephew Holton Hockaday. As we stood together on the victory platform where the new NFL champion Colts had officially been crowned minutes earlier, I felt as if the generational wheel was turning full circle. From my dad, I'd learned that the joy of sports, and so much of its romance, stems from *how* the game is played, as well as in finding the good people and the good stories behind them. It's about a work ethic, a civility, an honesty. Ultimately, this love of sportsmanship was my father's gift to me. Now, it was my turn to begin passing on these values.

Strangely enough, one of the last players to linger on the field was Indy's Dan Klecko, who also grew up in Colts Neck and, like me, graduated from Marlboro High School. His father, Joe, had been an All-Pro defensive lineman for the New York Jets. But Dan was strictly a journeyman, a reserve defensive tackle, who had come up with the Patriots and was still in the NFL by virtue of *how* he played the game—with hard work and perseverance. He was my father's kind of player. And now, for the third time, Klecko had won what his more celebrated dad could only dream about: a Super Bowl ring.

The kids posed for a picture with Klecko, then it was time to head back over to the compound to bid farewell, and say thank-you, to our crew. Lance presided over our CBS victory celebration in a jam-packed trailer, and he asked me to say a few words. With my arms draped around Caroline, I thanked Sean and Tony for long ago believing that this was my calling and also expressed my gratitude to our entire production and technical unit for three years of excellence on the air and camaraderie off it. Then I took a moment to frame this occasion through my daughter, who, in my mind, represented all the crew's children who were not present. All of us in the room were grateful to our kids for understanding that the demands of our business required us to be away from home far longer than we wished. Now that Caroline was coming of age, at least she could now see for herself how much time, effort, and passion it takes to build a winning team—in any aspect of life.

Lastly, I thanked Phil and told him how much I enjoyed being his boothmate, and that I looked forward to continuing a long and successful run together.

"Phil, you remember when I told you that twenty-nine to seventeen would be our final score?" I said. "And you told me, 'What are you talking about?'

"Well, many of you already know that I found comfort in the coincidence that this was Super Bowl XLI—and that 41 is the identity of the man who has become one of my guiding lights, former president George Bush. Tonight, all the numbers added up, and after I explain this I'm going to have to change the four-digit security code on everything from my private e-mail to by voice-mail password. You see, April 29 is Caroline's birthday, and May 17 is mine. Just keeping them together in this short-hand code makes me feel close to my daughter every time I punch in these numbers, especially when I'm away from home. Ever since she was born, 29-17 has been my lucky number." Sure enough, it came up big on the first leg of my three-championship journey.

CHAPTER NINE

The same gentleman, a medical doctor and Presbyterian minister, who invented the football helmet also created the game of basketball. Dr. James Naismith's charge was to come up with a constructive indoor recreational activity that would fill the time between the outdoor sports seasons during the snowy Massachusetts winters. It's still cold and blustery when the phenomenon known as March Madness tips off, but for the sixty-five teams in the tournament field there is a sense of "rebirth" after their regular seasons and conference tournaments—and hope abounds anew across the land. To me, these are among the welcome harbingers that spring is in the offing.

Unlike the NFL season, which our broadcast team picks up in August and stays with right through to the Super Bowl, my football and golf commitments mean that I have to "JIP" (join in progress) the college basketball season. But we compensate for our late start with experience. Among us, the core CBS production team that worked the 2007 NCAA Final Four—producer Bob Dekas, director Bob Fishman, Billy Packer, and me—embarked upon the road to Atlanta, the second leg of my championship journey, having logged more than a hundred years' worth of Final Fours collectively.

Basketball has been in my bloodlines for generations, dating back to my grandfather Jimmie Nantz, captain of the 1926 College of Charleston team. My dad also lettered in basketball at Guilford, and as a second-generation Carolinian, he grew up with an appreciation for Tobacco Road hoops lore, golf, and NASCAR—although for some reason my family never got the NASCAR gene.

Back in the late 1960s, when we lived in New Orleans, I was still too young to be able to physically shoot a basketball upward at a hoop, so my dad modified the game so that I could shoot *down* at a target on the street outside our home. Here's how it worked: You'd shoot the ball at a storm drain, which served as a makeshift goal, and if the ball bounced back toward you, it counted as a two-point basket. Such were the games created by a loving father trying to foster in his young son an appreciation for a sport that began with Naismith's famous peach basket.

In late December of 1968, my father took me to see my first basketball game. Houston, Iowa, Western Kentucky, and Duke played in what was known as the Sugar Bowl Basketball Classic at the Loyola Fieldhouse. Dad had been impressed by Houston, in part because it had just been to the Final Four in the spring, but even more so because its coach, Guy V. Lewis, was one of the first to integrate sports teams in that region (shortly after his Houston coaching colleague, Bill Yeoman, had broken the color barrier in football). With Duke, a team from my father's home state, and Houston, whom Dad had "adopted" because they had done the right thing in his eyes, we had rooting interests in both games of the doubleheader.

My father's explanation of the social significance of integration, even greatly simplified for a nine-year-old, went way over my head for the most part. But the trademark bright red-and-white polka-dot towel that Coach Lewis carried around that night while he patrolled the sidelines did capture my fancy. What was truly way beyond the grasp of my imagination at that age was that here I was in New Orleans watching my first college hoops game and it involved the school that would one day be my alma mater. Moreover, Coach Lewis would be a pivotal player in my nascent broadcasting career.

One day in 1980, early in my senior year at Houston, I was attending the basketball team's practice when one of the assistant coaches, George Walker, called me over to one of the side baskets. He wanted to introduce me to a promising freshman from Nigeria. "Hello. I am Hakeem," the new player said in a distinctive British accent, then bowed formally. "It's a pleasure to meet you." After we chatted a bit, I watched Hakeem Olajuwon put up soft hook shots with natural ease from both sides. It didn't take long to realize that my new friend was endowed with special gifts. In fact, by the time I got back to my dorm room I was practically gushing with enthusiasm. "Guys," I blurted out to my roomates Blaine and John, and whoever else was hanging around the first floor of Taub Hall. "You're not going to believe this, but I think we're going to the Final Four!"

Hakeem was an integral part of what became college

basketball's greatest fraternity. The Phi Slamma Jamma power-house would make not one, but *three* straight Final Four appearances, beginning the season after my graduation. With another future Hall of Famer, Clyde "The Glide" Drexler, also in its lineup, the 1982 Cougars returned to the Final Four for the first time since that squad I had watched as a boy in New Orleans. This time, Houston was knocked out in the national semifinals by a North Carolina team that went on to win the championship two nights later, when a freshman named Michael Jordan hit the winning basket against Georgetown.

A year later, Coach Lewis's squad was ranked number one. I was already working full-time in Salt Lake City, and I begged my boss at KSL to give me Championship Monday off, so that I could watch my alma mater play North Carolina State for the 1983 national title in Albuquerque. Without a game ticket or credential, I flew to New Mexico and headed straight for the Houston team hotel to join the Cougars as they awaited their seemingly inevitable coronation against Jim Valvano's Wolfpack squad. When it came time to leave for the game, I hopped on the team bus, as if I were still a student—for once, looking so young worked to my advantage!—and we pulled right up to the back entrance of the arena. Wedged between 6'9" forward Larry Micheaux and 6'7" guard Michael Young, I strutted right up the ramp. Then, when the team veered off to the locker room, I went to secure the perfect seat in the stands.

The Pit, as the University of New Mexico arena is more commonly known, seated some eighteen thousand—mostly on benches. I knew exactly where I wanted to sit, so I quickly claimed a spot at the base of the platform that had been constructed as CBS Sports' host position. While the teams were warming up on the court, I could hear CBS's talent go through its complete pregame, halftime, and postgame rehearsals. I was so close that I could reach over and tie Brent Musburger's shoelaces—talk about learning "at the feet" of the master! Several times during the evening I was sorely tempted to reach up and say hello as a *colleague*—after all, I was a sports anchor at the CBS affiliate in Salt Lake. But that introduction would come less than two and a half years later, when Brent himself would introduce me to the nation. And as for that host's chair on the set, I would get to occupy it at the 1986 Final Four in Dallas three years down the road. By that time Brent had moved courtside, where he called the games with Billy Packer.

Dallas is only a four-hour drive from Houston—a relatively quick hop by Texas standards—and so for that 1986 Final Four, my dad came up to take in the open team practices on Friday and to watch me go through rehearsals before hosting my first Final Four. Dad sat and observed from virtually the same seat location where I had studied Brent in Albuquerque. My father was fascinated by all the lighting, camera, audio, and research activities that were buzzing around the set. He was pretty much in awe that his twenty-six-year-old son was in the center of all this attention. (I was still trying to get used to it myself.)

That evening, our illustrious director, Bob Fishman, suddenly turned to me.

"Hey, Jim," he asked, "where's your dad? I didn't get to say hi to him . . . Wasn't he going to join us for dinner?"

"Well, he went home," I replied.

"Oh, that's too bad. I hope everything's all right."

"Yeah, he's fine, Fish. He had a wonderful time, although he probably watched me much more than he watched the teams practice. It's just that he couldn't get a ticket for the games tomorrow, so he drove back to Houston."

"Jim, did you just say what I thought you said?" Fish responded with incredulity, bordering on anger. "What do you mean, 'He couldn't get a ticket'! Did you even ask?"

"Well . . . no," I stammered. "I didn't know we *could* ask."

"Listen, you're at the *network* now! You're hosting the network coverage. Of course, we can get him a ticket. . . . Please, Jim, we always take care of family here. . . . Don't make that mistake again!"

I was duly chastised. Even as I think about it today, I feel pangs of guilt for making my father drive five hundred miles round-trip to and from Dallas in one day because I was too naïve to ask for tickets. Moreover, given his current condition, the mere recollection of that 1986 Final Four could start me welling up with tears. How I would dearly love to have that one back!

. . .

That night, while Dad was returning to Houston, CBS was holding a barbecue-themed reception at the Southfork Ranch, where the popular prime-time soap opera *Dallas* had been set. Billy and Barbara Packer offered me a ride out there with them. By the time we got there, however, every one of the chafing dishes on the buffet lines was empty; there was nary a nacho to be found. So we hopped back into the car and went out together for a leisurely dinner.

From that night on, the Packers adopted me into their family. Although I had met Billy before, this was the first real opportunity that we had to spend time getting to know each other and to begin what would blossom into a lifelong friendship.

I was still in school the first time that I ever ran into Billy Packer. It was at a national championship—the 1979 NCAA *golf* national championship, which was being contested at Bermuda Run in Advance, North Carolina. The Packer home was right on the course. In college golf, only five players from each school enter the tournament. Coach Dave Williams, though, always wanted to have his players paired off in their hotel rooms; he didn't want the odd man out to feel lonely, nor did he want the four who were doubling up to be jealous of a teammate with a single room. So Coach Dave occasionally brought me along to serve as his assistant. He put me to work phoning reports of the team's progress back to the Houston radio stations. He also had me walk the course to encourage our guys, and to brief him on their scores as they made the turn at 9.

At the pretournament banquet, Houston and twenty-nine other college teams were the guests—and Packer was the keynote speaker. Afterward, I rushed up to the podium and introduced myself, eager to tell Billy that I was a longtime fan, and even mentioning that I used to turn my television antenna so that I could pick up his ACC broadcasts. My roommate Fred Couples had already caught Billy's attention by winning the unofficial NCAA long-drive contest. As I walked the course on the first day of the championship, I noticed that I wasn't the only one following Fred around. Billy Packer was in the gallery, with his two young sons, Mark and Brandt, in tow.

It was around the time when Billy's prominence was beginning to spread nationally since he was part of NBC's celebrated Final Four broadcast triumvirate, along with Dick Enberg and Al McGuire. It may have been a generational thing, but I know that Billy looked up to Al and learned a lot from him. To this day, Billy loves to regale audiences with his price-less Al McGuire stories. One of my favorites is the tale of a dinner they once had together at the Russian Tea Room in New York City. The waiter came over to the table to greet them and explain the evening's specials.

"I don't need a menu, I know what I want," Al said in that endearingly distracted, absent-minded professor way of his. "I'm going to have a peanut-butter-and-jelly sandwich. . . . You guys have any strawberry jelly for that?"

The waiter, dressed in a Slavic-style uniform, chuckled and told him that it was the famous Russian Tea Room.

Suddenly, Al was very focused. "You asked me what I want. Well, that's what I feel like having," he said firmly. With that, he leaned back to see what would happen. A few minutes later, one of the busboys came over to the table to unpack a plastic sack full of groceries that he had just purchased at the super-market a few blocks away. With a contented look on his face, Al unwrapped a loaf of Wonder bread and put two slices on his empty plate. Then, while the bemused patrons around him looked up from their caviar, blini, and borscht, McGuire opened the jars of peanut butter and jelly and made himself the dinner that he wanted.

It was a classic demonstration of how Al McGuire con-ducted his entire life. It wasn't so much about doing only what he felt like at the moment—he was hardly a prima donna. Rather, it was about figuring things out and making them hap-pen. He knew that it couldn't be that hard—even for a gour-met restaurant—to provide a hungry customer with a PB&J sandwich. Whether it was a last-second shot that one of his Marquette players had to make to win a national champion-ship or whipping up a favorite feel-good meal, the one answer that Al could simply never tolerate was that something couldn't be done.

I could listen to Billy talk about Al for hours, and he does so with the same zest that he brings to his courtside commentary, always finding something fresh in the commonplace. While Packer has always been an independent thinker, I suspect that the time he spent in McGuire's company validated, maybe even emboldened, his innate nonconformism.

.   .   .

Brent Musburger was the busiest broadcaster in sports. From time to time, when his schedule was overbooked, I would fill in calling the play-by-play next to Billy Packer. For several years, I also did the college basketball halftime shows from the game sites, so Brent, Billy, and I traveled together. By 1990, I was already hosting my *fifth* Final Four, when Georgia Tech, Arkansas, UNLV, and Duke convened in Denver. After the national semifinals, the three of us were taken downtown for a quick meet-and-greet at a CBS Sales gathering, where we were each asked to say a few words to our sponsors. Little did we know what was about to unfold overnight. The next morning was, fittingly, April 1. Our executive producer, Ted Shaker, jolted me out of bed with the shocking news that CBS had fired Brent—or at least that was the upshot of a heated midnight exchange between CBS Sports president Neal Pilson and Brent's brother, Todd, who was also his lawyer and agent. My initial reaction was that this had to be a really lame, tasteless April Fools' Day stunt.

"Jim," Shaker told me, "I know you have to go over to host *CBS Sports Sunday*. Now, if I were you, I would not have a lot to say about this. *You got that?*"

Shaker enjoyed a good prank as much as anyone. But I

could tell by his phone demeanor that this was no joke, and it was confirmed an hour later when I arrived outside the CBS compound at McNichols Arena. The moment I stepped out of the car, hordes of microphone- and camera-toting local news broadcasters engulfed me. They were pushing and shoving and blocking my path, all the while trying to prod me into commenting on this stunning set of events that I had yet to fully comprehend. It must have taken me a good five or six minutes to wade through this sea of reporters who filled the hundred yards between the parking lot and the safe haven of the CBS trucks.

After surviving another aggressive media throng on the way back to the hotel, I called ahead and asked Lorrie to meet me outside, so that we could avoid the feeding frenzy in the lobby and head north to Boulder to regain a semblance of privacy. When we returned that night, I called Dad back in Houston to seek his advice on what had by now mushroomed into the lead national story on the network news.

"Listen, Son," he cautioned me, speaking from experience (a few years earlier, he himself had been forced into early retirement), "remember who you are—and that you are there to do your job. Don't take the bait and get suckered into answering all these hypothetical questions regarding your career. It's not your business, anyway, at least not right now." The next day, bearing Dad's words in mind, I steeled my way through a tense all-hands production meeting, then headed to the arena.

As expected, UNLV beating Duke for the national title was overshadowed by the Brent situation. Not only was Musburger permitted to call the game, but he had also been granted his request for the opportunity to say a few final words. As the consummate professional, Brent didn't speak or even hint of anything but the game itself until it was over and time for his farewell. He briefly thanked his CBS support team, and the viewers, for "a great ride" from "the best seat in the house." Then, one last time, he tossed it back to me on the set to take us off the air.

Having grown up watching Brent, it seemed surreal that it was now my responsibility to bring down the curtain on his CBS career. I read the copy that we had prepared, which thanked him for his many years of service to the network. As though that were not awkward enough, when I looked into the camera, I could see Todd Musburger, leaning forward from just behind the set, anxious to hear what we were saying about his brother.

During that crazy Final Four, I must have spoken to my father at least three or four times. One other piece of his good counsel still stands out: "Jimmy, always remain loyal to your friends!" With that message in mind, several weeks after returning from the Final Four and the Masters, Lorrie and I hosted Brent and his wife, Arlene, for a backyard barbecue in Connecticut.

.   .   .

Next to my dad, I cannot conceive of a traveling companion who would be more entertaining and enlightening than Billy Packer. His gift for rotating ideas in his mind enables him to study all sides of an issue, including many that the rest of us don't see. As a result, Billy often comes up with fresh, sometimes even radical, approaches. Such intellectual agility also makes him a world-class debater who can argue any position with equal persuasiveness. As a natural contrarian, he relishes the chance to adopt whichever position is the least popular.

What really sets him apart, though, is that Billy has never been afraid to go out on a limb to support his convictions; he is never content to be merely a spectator in life. A classic example was his involvement in the Richard Jewell case at the 1996 Summer Olympics in Atlanta. Jewell was a private-security guard who, while on duty at Centennial Olympic Park in the early-morning hours of July 27, noticed a suspicious package and began evacuating people from the area. It was, in fact, a bomb that later went off and killed one person and wounded an estimated one hundred others. While Jewell was initially hailed for his alertness and bravery, law enforcement authorities soon suspected that *he* was responsible for planting and detonating the device, perhaps so that he might be perceived as a hero. Packer was in Atlanta, and a few days later he checked out the scene for himself, including the phone booth from where Jewell was alleged to have called in the bomb threat. One look was all Billy needed to deduce that the FBI's timeline didn't make sense logistically and that Jewell was innocent.

The media, though, had camped out in front of Jewell's apartment and were, for all practical purposes, prosecuting the FBI's lead suspect in the court of public opinion. Meantime, to publicize the other side of the story and to raise money for the legal costs, Billy created the Richard Jewell Defense Foundation.

Three months later, in a rare public acknowledgment of wrongful accusation, federal authorities cleared Jewell of all charges, and in 2005, the real bomber, Eric Rudolph, was apprehended and pled guilty. "I never did meet the guy [Jewell]," Billy told me, but the pride he took in his behind-the-scenes role was evident. This is one story, among many, that has always in my mind closely linked Billy to my father—men who stood up for what they believed, tried to ensure that people were treated fairly, and never sought recognition for performing random acts of kindness.

Billy is also well versed in myriad topics, from sports to politics to art (he's a connoisseur and collector of Picasso plates); however, nothing defines him more than his remarkable business acumen. It would be fair to categorize Billy as the CEO of a midsize conglomerate, except that he never had an office, a secretary, a sheet of stationery, a computer, or even a cell phone. His kitchen table serves as the world headquarters, and he calculates most of his deals on the back of a napkin, preferably a lightly used one.

From that unlikely corporate command post, Billy has brought world-class bicycle races to China as well as Notre Dame football telecasts and college-basketball all-star games to Europe. He's done countless real estate deals, including developing his own golf course, Olde Beau in North Carolina. Anything that remotely reeks of the *possibility* of making money is fair game. And I do mean *anything*.

At the 1995 Final Four in Seattle, we were watching the Oklahoma State team run through the Friday-afternoon hourlong practice, which is open to the public. The old Kingdome was packed, and Billy and I were watching the players from our broadcast position at midcourt. During the traditional layup line, the Cowboys' seven-foot center, Bryant "Big Country" Reeves, came barreling down the lane and launched a crashing thunder dunk. Only a graduate student in physics could tell you why it happened, but upon impact, the glass backboard shattered into thousands of tiny pieces. Shards of glass rained on players and spectators, covering the court. All of a sudden, Billy jumped over the top of the table and started racing toward the ruined basket. I had no idea what was going on. "Where are you going, my man?" I asked him, trying to get a handle on this situation.

"C'mon, Jimmy," he yelled, "there's no time to waste!"

I was baffled and told Billy that they had to clean up the mess. Packer was becoming apoplectic. "Jimmy, that's *money* out there on that floor!" With that, he dashed over and got down on his hands and knees. Working with incredible urgency, Billy scooped up every piece of broken glass he could lay his hands on, stuffing the shards into every available pocket. Finally, one of the NCAA committee officials, clearly amazed by Billy's eagerness to help clean up the court, came over to request that Billy return to his seat.

"Look at them, Jimmy," he gushed, admiring his treasure like a kid on Christmas morning. "They're almost all shaped exactly the same. Now if Oklahoma State wins the national championship on Monday night, we could take these to a good jeweler in Stillwater. He could make Big Country Final Four earrings, necklaces, pendants. This could be worth at least half a million bucks!" With a bit of imagination, the glass shards *did* look like twelve- or fifteen-carat diamonds. And which Cowboys fan wouldn't want an authentic piece of Oklahoma State Final Four history?

As it turned out, Oklahoma State was eliminated by eventual champion UCLA in their national semifinal, so we never did get to take these "semi"-precious stones to market. Years later, I asked Billy what he did with all that broken glass that he thought could be worth $500,000. "Are you kidding me, Jim?" he said. "I threw it all in the garbage the minute Oklahoma State lost. There was no use holding on to that worthless junk—you've got to move on to the next deal." Packer's answer was just what I had expected. He's relentlessly optimistic about opportunities, but he's clinically unsentimental about them once they don't pan out. The bottom line is, Billy's *never afraid to fail*—and that's the key to his genius in business, in broadcasting, and in life.

Since Billy and I don't take ourselves all that seriously as public personalities, we're generally quite relaxed on the road. What's more, barring any unusual circumstances, we enjoy interacting with fans. Every now and then, however, a few unruly individuals take advantage of this accessibility. In February 1991, we were in Fayetteville, where Arkansas was hosting UNLV in a rare regular-season clash between the two top-ranked teams in college basketball.

On the eve of this big game, I was going over my research notes and preparing for the broadcast in my hotel room when I heard this huge ruckus in the room next door. A few minutes later, I began to discern that much of their loud invective was at my expense. "Hey, Nantz," I heard one drunken student scream. "We know you're over there. Why don't you come out in the hall and tell us face-to-face why you hate the Hogs?"

It was nothing new to be accused of partiality. As the old saying goes, "When I hear that *both sides* think that I'm biased against them, then I know I'm doing my job!" I dismissed the incident and went to bed. Unfortunately, the kids in the adjoining room wouldn't let the matter drop—nor would they go to sleep. By the middle of the night, having obviously refueled with several more rounds of drinks, they started pounding on the walls, which were paper-thin to begin with. "Nantz, we hate you!" they shouted, among other less polite taunts. "You're not getting out of here alive. You're not even going to see the game tomorrow. We'll be waiting for you the moment you step out of that room."

Well, that got my attention. When the threats become that personal and that specific, the only thing you can do is call security, which I did. By now it was about three in the morning, and I heard the elevator ding, and the security guard go over and knock on the door to their room. He told them to settle down and headed back to the lobby. "Nantz," they screamed the second the guard left, somehow managing to yell even louder than before. "We can't believe you called security. You are one dead man now!" With that, they actually began trying to physically tear down the wall that divided our two rooms.

By daybreak, and with the benefit of maybe two hours of sleep, I called our producer, Bob Dekas, and told him about my security concerns, and he arranged to have a car waiting for me within minutes. Taking advantage of an apparent lull in the action, I snuck out, got into the elevator, and raced through the lobby and right into a waiting car. The lack of sleep had left me looking and feeling haggard. This was not the way I wanted to approach any broadcast, let alone a game in which number one was pitted against number two. But fatigue was the least of my worries. I confided to Billy and Deke that I feared these crazies might be plotting some deranged attempt at payback.

Dekas spoke with school officials and arranged for extra security around our broadcast location. But I was clearly rattled and anxious by the time we took our positions facing the crowd for our opening on-camera welcome. The national anthem came and went in a blur; I could not will myself into my normal pregame meditational moment. Obsessively, I kept scanning the crowd with my peripheral vision. Sure enough, I noticed somebody hurdling over the press table and racing toward us with what looked like a wild look in his eyes just as we were about to come on the air. Motioning to our stage manager, I covered my microphone and told him, *"Get security!"*

Fortunately, once the broadcast began and Billy and I had to set the scene, this would-be intruder appeared to have calmed down enough for a civil conversation with the stage manager. I exhaled and, per Bob Dekas's instructions, led us to a commercial break. As soon as we were "clear," I made my way over to see who had just created all that commotion and momentarily scared the living daylights out of me. Was it one of those hell-raisers from the hotel? "Hey, Jim, Billy," he rasped. "Terribly sorry if I caused some concern over there. I just wanted to welcome you guys to the great state of Arkansas. I'm Governor Bill Clinton." This would not be the last time that our paths would cross.

CHAPTER TEN

During the open practices at the 2005 Final Four in St. Louis, I was chatting with North Carolina coach Roy Williams, trying to glean some insights into his approach to the next day's national semifinal against Michigan State and then into Monday night's potential national championship matchup versus either Illinois or Louisville. I was also scouting for stories about the Tar Heel players, hoping to find some gem that I could use during the end-of-the-game sequence.

Coach Williams was in his second season at his alma mater and had been lured away from a successful Kansas program by the chance to restore the championship glory to the House That Dean Built. Hall of Fame coach Dean Smith was more than a mentor and an inspiration to Williams; theirs was the strongest surrogate father-and-son relationship that I had ever seen in sports. Roy's own father, Babe, struggled with alcoholism and was estranged from the family. In Smith, Roy found the discipline, loyalty, and respect that he needed to give and receive. Now, returning to North Carolina in the role of his father-figure, it was almost as though Williams couldn't wait to present Dean Smith with a national title, much as I recall eagerly looking forward to presenting my own dad with his first grandchild. I thought to myself if Carolina did win on Monday night, I would punctuate the championship call by proclaiming, "There's a new 'dean' in college basketball."

Just as Roy and I were wrapping up our conversation, my cell phone rang. I saw that it was former president George Bush and excused myself to go take the call in private. "Jimmy," he began excitedly, "I need to ask a really big favor." Knowing him as I do, I've learned that whenever he prefaces a conversation this way, he is about to offer *you* a huge favor. "I'm inviting President Clinton up to Maine as our guest for a couple of days this summer," said "41" (as friends and family call the former president to distinguish him from his son, the forty-third president). "We'll play golf, horseshoes—you know the drill. But I thought it'd be kind of fun to have someone here to mix it up a bit and to make sure he has a good time, so I'd like you to be our 'intermediary.'"

To provide a cover story for this purely social clandestine rendezvous, Bill Clinton's staff booked a speaking/book-signing event in Maine. On the morning of June 27, 41; his personal aide, Tommy Frechette; a Secret Service agent; and I boarded *Fidelity III*, the former president's high-speed cigarette boat. With Secret Service agents in full frogman gear manning flanker boats, our little armada took off into the stormy North Atlantic waters. The high waves kept bouncing the boat up and down, and the undertow exposed the rocky shoals below. The entire coastline was enshrouded in dense fog. Almost an hour into this stealth mission, 41 cut the engines and began trolling toward the eerily deserted harbor. "42 is sixty seconds out," crackled a Secret Service voice over their secure radio frequency, meaning that we were closing in on President Clinton. Moments later, in the midst of the fog, we caught a glimpse of a bright orange shirt. It was Bill Clinton, surrounded by his own protection detail. We jumped out onto the dock, shook hands all around, and piled into the SUVs for the inland ride back to Walker's Point.

We gathered for dinner at a local seafood restaurant that evening, and President Bush's chief of staff, Jean Becker, came over to see how I thought things were going. Jean had been a reporter for the then-fledgling *USA Today* and was on track to become their White House correspondent, when she was unexpectedly invited to become Mrs. Bush's deputy press secretary. Her dad, a lifelong Democrat, convinced her to accept. "You've been offered this fabulous job," he told her. "You can always go back to journalism." Among her many other skills, Jean has also mastered the arcane world of diplomatic protocol, and she suggested I offer a toast.

I hadn't planned on making any formal remarks, but something about this occasion touched me more than I could have anticipated. A few friends meeting for golf and dinner may not be anything out of the ordinary. However, when two of those friends happen to have been presidents of the United States— and from opposing political parties, no less—that is quite *extraordinary*. The two presidents were chatting about their respective libraries. When I sensed a momentary lull in the discussion, I stood up, clanked my glass, and addressed our party of nine:

"Many Americans, I suspect, may be surprised when word

of this gets out. But I, for one, have been struck by all that you two men truly share in common, starting with your love for this great country and your deep-seated desire to help people around the globe. But beyond all that, nothing could send a better message to the rest of the world about the spirit of America than the civility, respect, and friendship that you two have for each other."

The social summit was so successful that a sequel the following summer was inevitable. Meantime, the two former chief executives had added a domestic cause, Hurricane Katrina relief, to their ongoing humanitarian efforts to help the victims of the devastating tsunami in Southeast Asia. In May of 2006, 41 called to request another "favor." This time, though, there was a bit of a twist. "Jim," said the former president, "we're thinking of June fifth and sixth." I told him that sounded good for me; I'd be willing to clear anything on my schedule to assure my participation in Bush/Clinton Summit II. "But [Cape Arundel golf pro] Ken Raynor has a charity obligation," 41 informed me. "Can you think of somebody who could round out our foursome, someone who might make it even more special for President Clinton?"

I blurted out, "How about . . . Tom Brady?"

"You mean the Patriots' quarterback?" 41 said, almost giddy with excitement. "Do you really think there would be any chance that he would come up and play golf with us?"

"Hmm, would he want to play golf with two former presidents of the United States? I don't know, sir. But, well . . . I kind of like our chances."

So 41 gave me the go-ahead to invite him. Brady was awestruck when I phoned him to extend the president's invitation. But he needed Bill Belichick's blessing to work around a

Top: My brother-in-law Don Hockaday, my sister Nancy, Mom, and I looked on as Dad met George Bush, who would later step in as a surrogate for him.

Above right: The first day that I met Jim McKay of ABC Sports in 1981 was memorable. Our round of golf sparked a very special friendship.

Above left: Mom and Dad have been the driving force behind my success—and I've always tried my best to make them proud.

Left: President George H.W. Bush, a wonderful source of fatherly advice for me, joins me at our "Houston Salute," the Opening Ceremony for Super Bowl XXXVIII.

Top left: A last-minute, Super Bowl–winning drive and a chat with me were all in a day's work for Tom Brady at Super Bowl XXXVIII.

Top right: Indianapolis Colts' head coach Tony Dungy is one of the most principled men I've ever met. Even moments after winning Super Bowl XLI, he never lost sight of his larger perspective on life.

Left: After three years together, director Mike Arnold, Phil Simms, coordinating producer Lance Barrow, and I huddled in Miami days before Super Bowl XLI.

Below: The Colts' Dan Klecko, a fellow Marlboro High School alumnus, shared a post–Super Bowl celebration with my nephew, Holton Hockaday, and my daughter, Caroline.

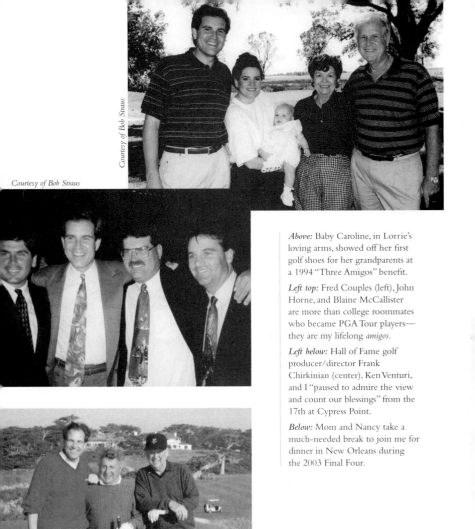

Above: Baby Caroline, in Lorrie's loving arms, showed off her first golf shoes for her grandparents at a 1994 "Three Amigos" benefit.

Left top: Fred Couples (left), John Horne, and Blaine McCallister are more than college roommates who became PGA Tour players— they are my lifelong *amigos.*

Left below: Hall of Fame golf producer/director Frank Chirkinian (center), Ken Venturi, and I "paused to admire the view and count our blessings" from the 17th at Cypress Point.

Below: Mom and Nancy take a much-needed break to join me for dinner in New Orleans during the 2003 Final Four.

Above: Although I've never had the destiny of the free world on my shoulders, as of June 27, 2005, I could say "I was in the same boat" with a pair of former presidents.

Right: For President Bush's eightieth birthday, Paul Marchand and I surprised him with his own putting green at Walker's Point in Kennebunkport.

Below: Sharing a few laughs at Bush–Clinton Summit I in June 2005. A year later, Patriots' QB Tom Brady would round out our foursome.

Top: In a one-show special, I was able to realize a dream by co-hosting a broadcast from Augusta with Jim McKay.

Above: Nick Faldo (left) has surprised viewers with his humor. Meantime, a comment that I intended as a serious compliment to Clint Eastwood backfired into a memorable punch line.

Left top: Like Billy Packer, Ken Venturi, who sat by my side in the tower at 18, shares my dad's principles, values, and grace.

Left bottom: I grew up listening to Billy Packer, never imagining that one day he'd be my broadcast partner for college basketball—and close friend all year round.

Above: It was a proud day when two dear friends, Ken Venturi (center) and Paul Marchand, guided the U.S. team to a landslide victory in the 2000 Presidents Cup.

Right: Gene Sarazen, dapper at ninety-seven, shared a stock tip moments before hitting the ceremonial first tee shot at the 1999 Masters.

Below: Jack Nicklaus, always a larger-than-life figure to me, became my good friend after "coming out of hibernation" at the 1986 Masters.

Right: 1992 Masters champion Fred Couples and I embrace in Butler Cabin after the hardest—but most fulfilling—broadcast of my life.

Below: The historic colorization and rebroadcast of the 1960 Masters in 2007 endeared Arnold Palmer to a new generation.

Bottom: Tiger Woods joined me after his record-shattering performance in the 1997 Masters. It wouldn't be his last visit to Butler Cabin.

Right: By the time of our final vacation trip in October of 1999, Dad—who used to adore the beach—had become terrified of the water.

Below: We could always count on Holton and Caroline to cheer up Dad, even after he was placed in a special-care facility in 2000.

Bottom: In Dad's last hours, he and I played one last "virtual" round on the Monterey Peninsula, where he had visited with me in 1990.

scheduled quarterback mini-camp. Tom made the necessary arrangements, and after finishing his afternoon passing drills, he boarded a helicopter to take him the 125 miles from Foxborough to Kennebunkport.

After dinner, the Bushes retired to their room, and President Clinton held court, teaching us his favorite card game, Oh Hell, a variation on Spades. 42's energy was impressive. He regularly jumped out of his seat to advise those of us who were new to the game how we could improve our hands. With a little leap of imagination, you could just see him hopping into your cabin at Camp David, looking over your country's strategic assets during multinational negotiations, and saying something like "Hey, have you guys thought about moving that border a little to the south?"

The main event, though, was the next day's golf. We divided the morning into a round-robin of three six-hole matches, rotating players and teams. Brady and I were paired together for the final six. "Hey, Tom," I said, as he jumped into my cart on the way to the 13th tee. "Forget all those Super Bowls that you've won. Now you've got a chance to do something truly historic. This is the first time in the history of our country that two presidents have ever teamed up in a match against another duo. We may not look like Gorbachev and Yeltsin, but I think we could be worthy adversaries. Are you up for it?" Brady didn't even bother to answer. He didn't have to. His body language shifted perceptibly. The giggles and smiles disappeared, replaced by a look that he gets when New England has to come from behind in the fourth quarter.

My motivational ploy unleashed a shot-making machine. Tom fired a near-flawless 73 on the day and carried the Brady/ Nantz pairing to a landslide five-up victory over Bush/Clinton.

In fact, walking up the 18th, President Clinton called over to us, "You guys sure don't take it easy on a couple of old presidents, do you?"

"Welcome to the NFL, Mr. President," I responded.

After the round, we headed over to Barnacle Billy's for lobster-roll sandwiches and ice cream. Sitting with Tom in the back of 41's boat, I could tell he was just glowing from the experience. As one of America's most-eligible bachelor-athletes, he has had to learn how to adapt to celebrity, wealth, and power, which have obvious pluses, but also carry disadvantages that the public rarely sees or understands. "If you think everyone always wants a piece of *you* because of who you are," I said to Tom, "just hang back and watch what happens whenever people get around these two guys. I'm always blown away by how their energy is always switched on. They never say, 'Oh, gosh, not another autograph or photo. What do they want from me now?'"

As if to underscore my point, while we were having lunch on the sundeck overlooking the harbor, word circulated quickly, and the inevitable throng of onlookers assembled below. Beaming radiantly as they made their way out of the restaurant, the two former commanders-in-chief bantered with their fellow citizens. It was an idyllic snapshot, a scene that resonated with the respect and warmth with which my father treated absolutely everyone he met from all stations in life.

As I watched President Bush escort President Clinton to his car, I couldn't help but think that had my dad's life not taken the turn that it did, he, too, would eagerly have filled the days of his later years traveling, golfing, shaking hands, and laughing. It's quite a stretch to say that my father would have followed 41's lead and gone parachuting out of an airplane well past his eightieth birthday—but, come to think of it, part of me could at least envision the former president trying to convince my father how much fun it would be.

When the presidential farewells were finished, it was time for the rest of us to return to Walker's Point. I noticed that Brady was relatively overlooked in the rush of the crowd—in the heart of Patriots Nation—as he strolled back to the boat. I had to think that New England's star quarterback found it refreshing that, for once, *he* got to see how the blitz is handled at the highest level.

. . .

Tom Brady hadn't yet arrived at the University of Michigan when a group of freshmen, who were dubbed the Fab Five, took college basketball by storm in 1991, with their hip-hop swagger and baggy shorts. Billy Packer and I had our first chance to see these phenoms in person that December.

"Hey, Jim, see that kid over there?" Billy whispered as we sat in the bleachers at Crisler Arena watching the Wolverines prepare to host the newly crowned national champions from Duke.

"Ray Jackson?" I asked, referring to one of the recruits in a harvest that was unprecedented in its bounty.

"Watch him take this shot," Packer said. "His right foot is on the line."

Jackson took several jumpers, each time catching the ball and stepping into his shot in kind of a pigeon-toed motion. Invariably, his foot was *on* the three-point line as he jumped, making the basket worth only two points. I told Billy that you would think that one of those assistants out there, maybe even a teammate, would pull him over and say something to him. "Meantime, he's reinforcing bad habits," Packer remarked. "It's all muscle memory, but he's one inch away from that shot being worth one more point." During the next two seasons, we must have attended at least a dozen Michigan practices. Each time the Wolverines went into their perimeter-shooting drills, we'd see Jackson continue to practice what he thought were three-pointers, but were clearly twos. Through the years, Billy has noticed this happen in college gyms around the country, and he calls it "the dumbest shot in basketball."

Jackson and his classmates Chris Webber, Jalen Rose, Juwan Howard, and Jimmy King, became the first, and only, freshmen quintet to start an NCAA national championship game. However, they finished as runners-up to Duke in 1992.

That summer, Lorrie and I were touring Europe with our parents, my sister's family, and a group of friends, including Ed and Patty Goren. One afternoon, we were visiting the Louvre, admiring the *Mona Lisa*, when I looked down the corridor to my right and did a double-take. Someone who looked exactly like Juwan Howard was approaching us with a cadre of kids who looked like stunt doubles for the Fab Five.

Then, from behind, I heard a familiar voice cut through the hushed polyglot babble in English. "Jim Nantz, what in the world are *you* doing here?" barked an excited Michigan head coach Steve Fisher. I told him that we were on vacation and asked him what *he* was doing there.

"We're playing a few exhibition games," he told me. "You don't think I'm going to bring my team to Paris without giving them some exposure to culture?" I introduced our traveling party to the Michigan basketball delegation, and I could tell that Fisher had already earned a spot in my dad's heart for making the extra effort to bring his squad to this famous gallery. Dad just loved the intellectual stimulation that these opportunities provided, and he was constantly challenging his family and friends to seize every opportunity to broaden their horizons. "*Wow!* Make sure you guys thank your coach," my dad told the players huddled around him. "I'll bet you, most coaches would have brought their teams to France, taken them to McDonald's for meals, kept them locked up in their hotel, and just focused on the games. Trust me, you guys will remember this experience for a lifetime."

That season, the Fab Five made it back to the national championship game, this time against North Carolina in New Orleans. Now, they were the only school in NCAA history to start five sophomores in the title contest, and in a lesser-known footnote, the only squad to have been addressed by my father in front of Leonardo da Vinci's masterpiece.

With under a minute remaining in a tight contest, Michigan kicked the ball out to Ray Jackson on the right wing. He stepped in to catch it, went up for a jumper, and made it. *"A huge three!"* I said on the air, as director Bob Fishman cut to a shot of Tar Heels coach Dean Smith with his arm out and two fingers up to signal that it was worth only two points. "They call it a two now. *My goodness!*" I updated the situation.

From the truck, producer Bob Dekas confirmed that the replays clearly showed Jackson's right foot grazing the line, exactly as we'd witnessed so many times in practice. It proved to be one of the pivotal moments in deciding a national championship—and Billy had seen this one coming for sixteen months.

Moments later, with the clock ticking down, Jackson's teammate Chris Webber rebounded a missed free throw and raced down the court with a chance to tie or win the game. But a pair of Tar Heels pinned Webber into the far corner by the Michigan bench. Webber called for a time-out, but Michigan had none left, which resulted in a technical foul. That mistake, with eleven seconds left, cost the Wolverines a pair of free throws *and* possession, all but sealing the championship for Carolina.

While the Fab Five never achieved a national title, they did have a major impact. For better or worse, they accelerated the introduction of much of the NBA culture into the college game. Part of that is the notion of the transient mercenary athlete. Talented players come and go, and now, the very best are "one and done," leaving after their freshman year to play in the NBA. (Carmelo Anthony, we hardly knew ye!) As a result, the days when you could build rivalries around, say, a Bill Walton era or an Oscar Robertson era are long gone. The only constant in college basketball is the coach who builds and runs the program. Today's teams are often referred to as Jim Calhoun's UConn Huskies, Lute Olson's Arizona Wildcats, or Jim Boeheim's Syracuse Orange.

North Carolina will always be synonymous with Dean Smith, who was at the helm in Chapel Hill for thirty-six years. Smith had played his own college ball at Kansas under the tutelage of Phog Allen, who, in his student days, was coached by James Naismith himself. So there was only "one degree of separation" between Smith and the legendary physical-education teacher who *invented* the sport in 1891.

On that first Monday night in April 1993 in New Orleans, Smith had won his second—and final—national championship. Not only had this Hall of Fame coach created many of the offensive and defensive sets used to this day, but like Guy Lewis at Houston, Smith was at the forefront of the movement to racially integrate sports at major universities in the South. In his coaching, recruiting, speaking, and community work, Dean Smith met thousands of people each year. Yet every time he saw someone, he could make him feel as if he really knew him. My dad, who didn't run into a fraction of the contacts Smith had, used to refer to this remarkable recall as "the salesman's gift."

"Jimmy," Dad would say, "when you remember someone's name, you make him feel special. But don't stop there—try to pick up something that's of interest to him, or that sets him apart."

Dean Smith was a whiz at storing and retrieving salient personal details. Suppose that he and I hadn't seen each other for a while. I could count on the coach to greet me with something along the lines of: "Hey, Jim . . . what's the latest on your father's health? . . . How's Freddy [Couples] doing? . . . Have you run into my Carolina boy Davis [Love]?"

How his brain is able to file, store, and update so much highly specialized data remains a mystery to me, but it's easy to understand how this knack helped make Smith such an icon in his profession.

That evening, while the North Carolina faithful were toasting another national title for Dean Smith and the Tar Heels, CBS Sports held a post–Final Four party of its own. I was making the rounds to celebrate with everyone when I ran into Mike Krzyzewski, who had served as our guest analyst on the set with Pat O'Brien. I was eager to get his insight on the unexpected ending that had taken place earlier that night. "Mike, what happened with that time-out?" I asked.

"Jim," he replied, "one of the players on the Michigan bench saw that Webber was trapped in the corner. Probably thinking that he could help Chris, he yelled to him, 'Call time-out!'"

"So you're saying that a sub, daydreaming on the bench, cost the Wolverines a shot at the championship?" I asked, seeking to confirm that Coach K didn't think Chris Webber should shoulder all the blame.

"Jim, I guarantee you that's exactly what happened." Then Krzyzewski added, "That's one of the reasons why I grade my players on their bench decorum during time-outs." If I didn't know Mike as well as I did, I would have thought he was pulling my leg. "During time-outs, I have my video guys record our team," he explained. "And we watch to see what every player is doing. If I see guys looking up into the stands or not paying attention while I'm going over the strategy with the five on the floor, well, they're going to suffer some consequences. I want every last person to be on the same page."

Coach K is from the school of coaches who maintain that no detail is small enough to be left unattended, and that any technique that could potentially give your team an edge is worth trying. He's always eager to learn from everyone and then to adapt what management consultants call "best practices" to his own needs.

At one memorable dinner that I hosted at Michael's, my favorite restaurant in Las Vegas, Coach K was enthralled by what Phil Simms had to say about fitness and preparation from the perspective of an NFL player and broadcaster. For his part, Phil was fascinated by Coach K's approach to basketball and life—so you can imagine how this philosophical cross-pollination lasted more than *seven* hours!

One of the stories from that evening that made a lasting impression on Simms involved one of Krzyzewski's best players, Grant Hill. Once, Coach K told us, he tried a little experiment: He told Hill that the next four minutes of the game were going to be "his." He wanted Grant to just go out and do some things on the court that he'd never imagined he could do—whatever he wanted to try would be perfectly fine. These unusual instructions had to be pretty jarring for Hill, as they had come from the West Point graduate who'd made the Duke program synonymous with a disciplined team-first focus. "Don't worry about it, Grant," Krzyzewski reassured his star after virtually ordering him to go one-on-one as if he were on the playgrounds. "Just go out and *have fun*. Then we'll look at the tape and see what you did that we might be able to work into our offense."

Krzyzewski's outside-the-box tactic came up recently when my football broadcast partner and I were reminiscing about that marathon dinner conversation. "As good as Grant was, Coach K thought he could take his game even higher," Simms recalled. "He wanted to help him find his true greatness, and, you know, I've never heard of a coach willing to try that." Hill's talent and leadership helped the Blue Devils win their first two national titles in 1991 and 1992, then led them back to the championship game in 1994, which they lost to Bill Clinton's beloved Razorbacks.

Coach K would not earn his third crown until 2001. In typical fashion, he pulled out every motivational trick when he got to Minneapolis that March. He calculated roughly how long it would take the team bus to drive from the hotel to the Metrodome. Then, at the appropriate time on Monday night's ride to the arena, Krzyzewski stood up, took the driver's microphone, and told his players he had something he wanted them to see. He had prepared a compilation of that season's highlights, and they were set to CBS Sports' inspirational college-basketball victory anthem, "One Shining Moment." When the video ended, the bus had rolled to a stop at the Metrodome, whereupon Coach K told his squad that they'd hear the same song played again later that night—only then they'd be standing on a victory platform as the new national champions.

Nine months later, Billy and I were back in Ann Arbor to

do another Duke-Michigan game—ten years after the Fab Five Wolverines had played the Blue Devils. By this time, I had developed a friendship with a CBS "colleague" who lived in the area. Although he logs only three minutes of airtime on our network annually, his work touches many people profoundly during that 180-second stretch. His name is Dave Barrett—the musician and lyricist who composed "One Shining Moment."

During the warm-ups, I went over to Krzyzewski's assistants and said, "See that guy making his way up the stands? He has an indirect tie to your program; he's 'Mr. One Shining Moment.' You ought to go tell Coach K that he's here." As expected, word came back from the locker room that Krzyzewski would love to meet Barrett after the game. Rarely have I seen Coach K as effusive as he was with Dave. "You have no idea how much this song means to all of us at Duke," Mike said, before introducing him to his players inside the locker room—most of whom had heard Dave's famous song before *and* after the championship game the previous spring. "We talk about things that are important to us," Coach K told the Blue Devils, who had circled around him. "Excellence, integrity, and doing things that are memorable for the right reasons. Now I'd like you to meet someone who embodies that kind of spirit."

Barrett could hardly believe that Coach Krzyzewski was making such a fuss about him; nor could he understand the adulation that he received from the players. As the song says, "And all the years / no one knows / just how hard you worked / but now it shows." The defending champions had accorded the man who penned those lyrics with "one shining moment" that he'll certainly never forget.

·   ·   ·

I'll never forget that day, either, but for a completely different reason. It was the day my mother reached an emotional overload.

Two weeks earlier, I was co-hosting CBS's coverage of the 2001 Macy's Thanksgiving Day Parade with Julie Chen, followed by *The NFL Today*. That weekend also marked my parents' fiftieth wedding anniversary. Unfortunately, no handbook provides children with any guidance for situations such as this, when both halves of a remarkable couple are alive, but only one partner is functional, aware, and active. At best, this milestone would be bittersweet. In the thirteen months since we had made the agonizing decision to move Dad into a special-care facility, his mental acuity had so diminished that he hardly recognized his spouse and children—and even then, for only a fleeting moment.

My sister, Nancy, and her husband, Don, and Lorrie and I spent months brainstorming about how to make this occasion special for Mom. The one thing we all knew for certain was that Dad himself absolutely would have insisted that we celebrate—and make his Doris Jean happy—even if he couldn't join us.

We decided to take advantage of the excitement in New York during the holiday season. The change of scenery, we reasoned, would do Mom some good. If nothing else, it would provide a break from packing as she was preparing to move into a new home in another part of Houston. Reluctantly, Mom agreed to fly to New York. We put her up in the Presidential Suite at a hotel and sent her a bouquet in Dad's name. She sat through the unseasonably cold weather to watch the parade with her grandchildren, Caroline and Holton, then mingled with my colleagues at *The NFL Today* studio. At the anniversary dinner, I proposed a toast to Mom, and to Dad, who was represented by a symbolic empty chair:

"Thank you for serving as such wonderful role models in

our lives: as individuals who strive to do the right things . . . as spouses totally dedicated to each other's health and happiness . . . and as loving, nurturing parents who've demonstrated how we want to raise our own children."

We were all pleased, and greatly relieved, that Mom appeared to have had a good time that weekend. But we hadn't realized that significant emotional and physical issues were percolating. Sure enough, they surfaced two weeks later while I was preparing to go on the air in Ann Arbor.

"Jimmy, I hate to call you right before a game," Nancy said, catching me on my cell phone as I was going over some notes with my statistician, Pat McGrath, two hours before tip time at Crisler Arena. "Something's wrong with Mom!" she continued. I was clearly taken aback. When I recognized her number on my caller ID, I feared that perhaps the worst had happened to Dad. It never occurred to me that the call could be about my mom.

"Don and I knew that she was up all night packing," said Nancy. "But when we came by this morning, she was so delirious she didn't even know who we were. We took her to the emergency room, and they admitted her right away. She was suffering from exhaustion, dehydration, and pneumonia."

I was so shaken by this unexpected development that I wasn't sure I could go on the air. As a longtime confidant, Bob Dekas realized that something was amiss. He quickly came out from the production truck to sit with me in the still-empty stands. As always, I could count on Deke to lend a sympathetic ear and a comforting shoulder. He told me to take as much time as I needed to sort out my emotions and regain my composure. "We had absolutely the best intentions in the world," I started explaining, as much for my own benefit as for Bob's. "We thought a new house would symbolize a fresh start."

This was all part of the game plan that the social worker at Dr. Appel's office had outlined on the day years earlier when the diagnosis of Alzheimer's was confirmed. Mom and I had traveled to North Carolina together to handpick the furniture. Together, we worked out every detail, down to the color of the grout for the bathroom tile. It was all done to provide her with a therapeutic escape from the relentless pain and pressure that confronts caregivers. We suffered through a few anxious days while Mom was treated in the hospital. It took more than a week of bed rest and fluids before she bounced back.

In retrospect, buying and decorating the new house turned out to be the best thing that could have happened to our mother; it's rewarding to see how she's thriving in her new neighborhood. We also learned some valuable lessons the hard way: All transitions in life—big or small, sad or happy—involve stress. Nancy and I underestimated what it meant for Mom emotionally to have to say good-bye to a house where she had lived for nearly a quarter-century; in her mind, she could relive vivid memories in every nook and cranny.

It's never easy for people to close the door on the past—even when it's for their own good.

.   .   .

That college basketball season ended in Atlanta with a surprise team making it to the 2002 Final Four—Indiana. The Hoosiers were coached by Mike Davis, who had been promoted, a year and a half earlier, to replace the fired legend, Bob Knight. At practice before their national semifinal game against Oklahoma, several of the Indiana players confided in me that they were disappointed not to have heard from their former head coach, who had recruited twelve of the thirteen men on the roster, and to whom they were all still devoted.

Once it became clear that Indiana was going to advance to the national championship matchup against Maryland, I remarked on the air that it was "regrettable" that Bob Knight apparently hadn't yet wished his former players good luck. As noted earlier, college coaches often become father-figures for their players. In this case, these kids were raised on Hoosier basketball lore, hoping they'd be good enough to one day play for Coach Knight. They would naturally clamor for his approval.

"Who the hell does Jim Nantz think he is?" and "What the hell does Jim Nantz know about college basketball?" were some of the *kinder* quotes that Coach Knight responded with in the media the following day. He went so far as to say, "I played golf with Jim Nantz, and after seeing him play, I don't know how much he knows about that sport, either." *Ouch!*

"Son, take a deep breath—and then just drop it" is exactly how I envisioned my dad counseling me. But I don't think that Dad himself would have been content to walk away from the situation once and for all. He would have filed it away mentally under "Unfinished Business," and then returned to resolve the matter once cooler heads had prevailed.

I always liked Bob Knight—and I still do. About a month after that Final Four, I sent him a note trying to explain the genesis of this whole incident. "Perhaps you didn't take it this way," I told the Hall of Fame coach in my letter, "but, to put it all into a larger context, I was trying to pay you a compliment. You're a great part of who these kids are and what they've accomplished. They wanted to make you happy." Then, I added that should he find himself in our area recruiting for Texas Tech over the summer, I'd love to have him as my guest for a round of golf at Winged Foot. Several weeks later, I received a brief reply, which said, in essence: Thanks for the invite, Jim, but I won't be in New York anytime soon—and by the way, you're *still* wrong!

Sometime later, a mutual friend provided a cogent analysis of how Coach Knight was caught in a classic no-win situation: If he had made contact with his former Indiana players and they won the title, it might have looked as though Knight was taking credit for their success; on the other hand, if he reached them, and they lost (as they did), he could have been accused of causing a distraction, or even tampering. So Knight elected to wait, certain that, somewhere down the road, he'd find an opportune time to tell these kids how proud he was of their scrappy run to the Final Four.

Well, when it was put to me that way, it made perfect sense, so much so that I was disappointed at having let my heart get the better of my head on the air that night. Sometimes, though, even the best of intentions are not good enough; I should have figured out these end-game scenarios on my own, and I should not have hung Bob Knight out to dry as I did. I can't say that this was the first, or last, such error of my career. But I did learn from it. I'm a lot more inclined now to give people the benefit of the doubt—especially when I'm talking about them to 25 million people.

CHAPTER ELEVEN

"Oh, c'mon, ref! He was traveling! Everyone in this whole gym saw it but you!" I was eleven years old, and I had never seen my father as angry as he was that moment, coaching my sixth-grade sports recreation league basketball team in Colts Neck, New Jersey. "What's the matter? Are you too chicken to blow the whistle?" Boy, was Dad ever hot—and I was absolutely stunned; this was just so completely out of character. He was the most patient, relaxed, good-humored, and *nonconfrontational* person you'd ever want to meet. "That's a *technical foul*, Coach Nantz!" the referee said, pointing to my dad. "One more outburst and we'll have to ask you to leave."

As we sat down around the kitchen table that night, Mom asked cheerfully how things had gone at the game today. "Oh, Doris, I'm afraid I embarrassed myself in front of Jimmy and his teammates, and some of the other parents," Dad began to confess. "A kid on the other team had a blatant walk, but the ref just swallowed his whistle. For some reason, I lost it. I said some things that I had no business saying—after all, the poor guy is only a volunteer, like the rest of us. . . . Let's enjoy dinner, and then I'll call him to apologize."

As great as my dad was, and as much as everyone loved him, he would be the first to admit that he was neither perfect nor a saint. He was human, and as prone to having bad days or making mistakes as we all are. I vividly recall that vignette from my youth, watching Dad grapple with his actions for the rest of the day. Who hasn't experienced those moments when we wonder: What was I doing? Why did I allow myself to lose control? We're constantly evaluating our behavior, educating ourselves, and trying to grow. What we really hope is that when a similar situation comes up again, we will have learned enough to handle it better.

One of the more recent regrets that I've had professionally was the way the selection show prior to the 2006 NCAA basketball tournament took on a much bigger life of its own than it should have. And I deserve a good deal of the blame.

The NCAA Division I Men's Basketball Committee, chaired that year by University of Virginia athletics director Craig Littlepage, spent four days sequestered in an Indianapolis hotel analyzing data that would enable it to finalize the tournament field and determine who played whom—and where. The results of these deliberations were then announced live on CBS Sunday night, following the Big Ten conference championship game.

Billy Packer and I had less than half an hour after calling the game to study the seeding brackets before Greg Gumbel, who was hosting the selection show from New York, tossed it out to us. As I raced through a recap of the brackets, I noted that a pair of "midmajor" conference teams, Bradley and George Mason, were among the thirty-four at-large teams invited, while major conference teams Michigan and Maryland, with similar résumés, were left out.

Billy and I asked Craig Littlepage, via satellite, about the basis for these and one or two other decisions, hoping that he could provide some insights about how the tournament field was shaped. Most fans watching the program thought that we were doing our jobs; alas, others felt that I was too aggressive in demanding an explanation as to how the ACC and the Big Ten, with their track records of success, had ceded tournament at-large bids to the unproven Missouri Valley Conference and Colonial Athletic Association. To those viewers, it appeared that I was being churlish and publicly undermining the prestige of the committee.

At the end of our discussion, Craig paused for a full second or two in the middle of one of his responses. The added two-second satellite delay made it seem to me as though he had finished his answer, and since I couldn't *see* him in real time, I had no visual clues that he was merely pausing. After a couple of awkward seconds of "dead air" passed, I thanked the Chair, wrapped it up with Billy, and sent it back to Greg in the studio. Unfortunately, it came across to some as though I had cut Craig off rudely, which, as anyone who knows me would attest, is the last thing on earth that I would ever do.

Instead of fading away, as I had expected would be the case, the whole incident picked up momentum in the media. All of a sudden, I found people critiquing everything from my manners to my knowledge of the game. Distressed that Littlepage and his committee had been dragged into this firestorm, I called Craig to apologize, and I promised that I would make amends.

Meanwhile, the story was also continuing to snowball on the court. Bradley, one of the last teams to make the field, knocked off high seeds Kansas and Pittsburgh. George Mason, the school that I had really singled out as an example on the selection show, was pulling off a string of stunning upsets, toppling Michigan State, defending national champion North Carolina, Wichita State, and number-one seed UConn.

Within days, George Mason had become not only a household name, but one of the all-time Cinderella stories in tournament history—and most deservedly so. Still, as we headed back to Indianapolis for the Final Four, Billy and I found that, in some quarters, we had been cast as the haughty stepsisters who thought that the fairy-tale heroine had no right to be at the royal ball.

Shortly after landing in Indianapolis, I went right over to the venerable St. Elmo Steak House—my "local office"—where three weeks earlier, Billy Packer, Bob Dekas, Bob Fishman, research maven John Kollmansperger, and I had spent hours devouring the famous shrimp cocktail while poring over background data in preparation for that now-infamous selection show. In the course of our dinner discussion, we expressed qualms about a statistical model used by the selection committee and how it ranks every school according to a variety of differently weighted performance factors, including strength of schedule. We began to question a few of the underlying assumptions—especially strength of schedule—that were baked into the RPI (Ratings Percentage Index) formula. As such, we suspected that some of the midmajor conferences had "cracked the code" on how to spike the computer ratings.

"Hey, Jim, welcome to the Final Four," said Chris Clifford, the general manager at St. Elmo. "Sarge says your steaks are almost ready, but I thought you'd like to know that one of the teams is here tonight. George Mason is downstairs. They just finished dinner and they're getting set to leave." Although I didn't think it would happen this quickly, I knew that there would be a point when I'd have to confront the George Mason team and explain what really happened with regard to the selection show.

As we entered the basement dining room, where the Patriots' players, coaches, and administrators were scattered around four circular tables, I could hear the buzzing, as if to say, "What are *they* doing here?" Head coach Jim Larranaga, who had vowed to "have the most fun of any head coach," hurried over to greet us warmly, and to make sure that there were no awkward moments. I congratulated him and asked if I could say a few words to his squad.

"You guys have every reason right now to look at us with suspicious eyes, to think that we're your enemy, that we're not rooting for you, or that we have some ulterior motives," I began. "All of that is very understandable, which is why I appreciate Coach allowing us to share the story from our perspective with you directly."

After explaining how, strangely enough, we had been in this very room less than a month earlier preparing for the selection show, I told everyone, "Whatever we may have said on the air that Sunday night had absolutely nothing to do with the committee, for whom we have the utmost respect. And any comments that may have been taken as critical had nothing to do with George Mason, or with any other school. It was about the way *the computers* were programmed to rank the teams. That was our focus—we thought *the system* had some flaws. I've been around for a while now, and this is one of the greatest stories I'll ever have a chance to cover in my career. We're here in the heart of Indiana, the Hoosier State, and what you've accomplished to get here is better than the script for the movie *Hoosiers*. So, please, don't ever think that you can't go out and win two more."

My remarks were received with some reserved applause, which picked up a little steam. Then it was Billy's turn.

"Does anyone in this room know what this tournament is really all about?" he asked them. "And if you think the answer is basketball, then you're wrong! This is about the great American dream. It's someone saying, 'All I'm asking for is a *chance!*' Well, you guys have gotten a chance, and you've made the most of it. Now, enjoy what you've earned. Make sure you take it all in these next few days." With that, we went over to each player, shook hands, and wished him well.

· · ·

The next afternoon, I was over at the historic Murat Theatre, rehearsing for that night's NCAA opening ceremony, which I'd hosted annually since 1991. As I was trying to gather some introductory thoughts, I had an inspiration. Melissa Miller, my indispensable assistant, looked at me warily when I approached her with the words "I've got an idea!" She's heard that one enough to make her apprehensive. "What would you think about bringing in a 'mystery guest' to help welcome the teams? You used to live here when you were the marketing director for USA Track & Field. Who's the biggest name in town?"

"It's got to be Peyton Manning," she replied.

We called Peyton's cell and reached him while he was playing golf at Wolf Run Golf Club. As expected, he had been watching the tournament and rooting for his home-state school, LSU. When I broached my last-minute idea, his only real question was "Do I have to make a speech?" When he was assured there would just be a few spontaneous questions, he was more than eager to volunteer.

We didn't tell the NCAA or CBS. Melissa was waiting to meet Peyton in the back parking lot when he pulled in at seven o'clock on the dot. Backstage, we had the audio technician fit him with a microphone just as I was being introduced onstage. I began, "What a magnificent tournament this has been, one filled with many surprises. In fact, since that's been the main theme of March Madness this year, what better way to begin this opening ceremony than with another surprise. Ladies and gentlemen, to officially welcome everyone to the great city of Indianapolis, say hello to . . . *Peyton Manning!*" The building, packed with an overflow crowd some two thousand strong, was shaking as Peyton took the floor. He was his usual humble, gracious, knowledgeable—and *funny*—self.

His appearance made the night special for the kids, no one more so than Florida's sharp-shooting guard, Lee Humphrey, who'd grown up in the shadows of the University of Tennessee, where Peyton had played college ball. Humphrey was just about quaking as he met his hero for the first time.

After Manning finished his bit, I wrapped up that portion of the program with a comment that proved a lot more prescient than my remarks about George Mason on the selection show: "Peyton, thanks for getting this Final Four off to a memorable start. I look forward to sharing the microphone again next February fourth in Miami, when you are on the victory stand at Super Bowl XLI on CBS!" With that, the Colts fans in the audience exploded in glee.

Then, we introduced the players one at a time. Each came

up and shook hands with Craig Littlepage and NCAA president Myles Brand. Not long ago, these opening-ceremony events were "grown-ups only" affairs. But at the 2004 Final Four in San Antonio, I persuaded UConn Coach Jim Calhoun to bring his players. He did, and they won the title—which proved that it wasn't a distraction. Now there's even a pre-event dinner where all the players from the four teams meet one another and mingle—just like it was at that 1979 NCAA golf championship banquet where I first met Billy Packer.

To introduce the George Mason team, I echoed some of the sentiments that I'd expressed the night before down in St. Elmo's about how this state was the home of the celebrated underdogs from Milan High School—and this was college basketball's version of it. I added that I wouldn't be surprised if, one day, their story might also be immortalized by Hollywood.

·   ·   ·

Sometimes, no matter how hard you try, you can't please everyone. That was my reaction on Sunday morning, the day after the national semifinals, when I saw some of the accounts of Florida's easy win over George Mason. The clock had finally struck midnight for the Cinderella Patriots. One of the Gators' stars, Joakim Noah, vented to the media that he had attended the banquet the other night, and "some guy"—that would be *me*—talked about how they might make a movie about George Mason's Final Four run. Noah said that he had taken that remark as a sign of "disrespect" to his team, although I never saw a hint of that from anybody else.

Noah was one of three "famous sons" on the Gators. His dad, Yannick, was a Hall of Fame tennis star in the 1980s; Al Horford's father, Tito, and Taurean Green's dad, Sidney, had both played in the NBA. During Florida's tournament run so much had been written and discussed about that trio and their gene pool that I made it a point before the Gators' championship matchup with UCLA to find out details about the not-so-famous fathers of the other starters. Lee Humphrey's dad was a middle-school teacher in Maryville, Tennessee, just outside of Knoxville. Corey Brewer was also from Tennessee; he grew up in Portland, a rural town just north of Nashville. His father, Ellis, grew tobacco and soybeans, and he had implored his son to get an education and learn how to use computers so that Corey wouldn't have to make his living in those same tobacco fields.

On the eve of the title game I approached Corey at the RCA Dome. "Corey, I know you love your father as much as Joakim, Al, and Taurean love theirs. Could you tell me a little bit about your dad, and perhaps we can show him in the stands tomorrow night cheering you on? Is he going to be here?"

"No, Mr. Nantz," Corey, who is one of the most polite young men you'll ever find, replied. "He has some health issues, so he really can't travel."

"Well, I'll try to mention his name on the air."

"Thank you so much. That would mean the world to me, and I know he'd appreciate it."

After the Gators defeated UCLA for the national title on Monday night, and we had finally signed off, I saw the Florida sports information director, Fred Demarest, and I asked him, "Fred, would you please do me a favor? Please give this to Corey Brewer." As I quickly unknotted my championship-game necktie and handed it over, I said, "Tell him we talked about his dad on the broadcast and I just wanted him to have this tie as a memento in appreciation for the time he spent with me the other day."

Despite the American workplace revolution that began with Casual Fridays and inexorably led Business Formal to the brink of extinction, there's still something to be said for neckties. Though nonfunctional adornments, they foster personalization. When you're wearing a business uniform, whether it's a charcoal gray suit or a navy blue CBS Sports blazer, the fashion detail that allows you to make a statement is the tie. Even the word *tie* connotes a special link. And one of the informal boyhood rights of passage is having your dad teach you how to tie your tie. It's always one of those Kodak moments when father and son stand together in front of the bedroom mirror.

Early on in my CBS career, I once went over to my colleague Pat O'Brien during a break in rehearsal and told him that the back of his tie was longer than the front. "I do that on purpose," he replied. Now, Pat has a great sense of humor, and I thought he was setting me up for a punch line. He was, but it was not intended to be funny. "Back home in Sioux Falls, South Dakota, my dad, Joe O'Brien, used to tie his ties that way," Pat told me. "And I do it that way to remember him. And when people come up and ask me about why the back is longer, I get to talk about my dad—just as I'm doing now." Each of us looks for meaningful ways to stay connected.

. . .

UCLA, the runner-up to Florida in 2006, had made it back to the Final Four in Atlanta in 2007. As usual, Bill Walton was on hand to cheer for his alma mater. One of the greatest legends in college-basketball history, Walton shows up each year at the Final Four on his own dime and goes to every event on the program. He sits in the stands with his wife, Lori, and doesn't screen himself off from the public—no security, no posse.

My father had taught me to appreciate people who didn't have false pretenses and weren't caught up in their own success. In Walton's mind, he's still just part of the team, sitting on the bench for Coach John Wooden—only now that bench is up in the stands. Watching Bill have so much fun just shows how much many former players still relish their college basketball experience.

What's especially admirable, and inspirational, about Bill Walton is that he has become a successful broadcaster despite a major stuttering problem that he has had to overcome. Back in 1989, Bob Dekas and I were dispatched to Los Angeles to audition Walton for a spot on the CBS Sports roster. When we returned and hand-delivered the tape to then–executive producer Ted Shaker in New York, he watched and listened for about two trips back and forth down the floor, then decided to hire him. As we left Shaker's office, Bob and I kind of looked at each other as if to say, "Why would he fly us all the way out to California and back if he wasn't going to watch more than two minutes of the tape?"

Since our first encounter as potential colleagues, Bill and I have become good friends. As soon as you enter his world, you are struck by his deep love and devotion to Coach Wooden, who mentored him at UCLA. It reminds me so much of the deep affection that I felt for Dave Williams, my college golf coach at Houston. Bill calls Coach Wooden every day and tells him that he loves him. It's a type of father-son relationship that is so profoundly beautiful it can bring tears to your eyes. What's more, as Walton's own sons have grown up in life and on the court, Bill made sure that the Wizard of Westwood became a part of their lives as well, extending this special relationship into the next generation. In doing so, I believe that Walton has helped to keep Coach Wooden, a national treasure, active and alive.

. . .

The Florida Gators had made a unique commitment to one another after winning their first crown in 2006. They realized that they could continue to have fun and refine their skills by staying in school. To be sure, a few of them were gifted enough to have been able to jump to the NBA, but somewhere along the line, they received some wise advice about not rushing life. Slowing down and savoring it is often the better option.

The strategy paid off for Florida. Billy Donovan, the scrappy Gators head coach, whom I had first covered when he led Rick Pitino's Providence Friars to the 1987 Final Four as a player, sought advice on how to repeat as a national champion. And the man he turned to for coaching wisdom was Bill Belichick, who was in the stands at the Georgia Dome on Championship Monday 2007. Whatever motivational ploys he shared certainly worked, as Florida routed Ohio State, becoming the first repeat champions since the Duke teams in 1991 and 1992.

During the victory interview, I chatted with Corey Brewer once again. "Corey," I told him on the air, "congratulations not only on another championship, but on being named the Most Outstanding Player. I know how much you wish your dad could have been here tonight. Anything you'd like to say?"

With that, Brewer looked right into the camera and told his father how much he loved him. As for the Buckeyes, their two precocious freshmen, Mike Conley Jr. and Greg Oden, were soon to follow the money to the NBA—one-and-done. Somehow, though, I suspect that they may wake up one day a few years from now with a sudden longing for something that money just can't buy: the rich college experience that they had mortgaged away.

·   ·   ·

At the 1986 Final Four in Dallas, I had learned about passing up life's precious quality time when I failed to get tickets for my dad. Since then, I've made it a point to try to create meaningful father-and-son experiences for others, since this was something I could only enjoy vicariously. In most years, my boyhood best friend Cliff Pyron and my godson Cliff Jr. have shared this magical weekend—and I can hardly express how much satisfaction I've gotten from watching the two of them bond. Once when they couldn't make it, I caught a glimpse of a random father and son outside the Alamodome in San Antonio. I went over and offered them my tickets. That was almost ten years ago now, and each year they still write to tell me how much that spontaneous gesture has meant to them.

The 2007 Final Four marked the first time that I was on the other side of the parent-child dynamic. After looking up to my dad all those years, here was my own daughter looking up at me. We went to the NCAA Hoop City together, shot free throws, and tried many of the games and contests. Then on Monday night, we did something that I had always envisioned over the years. After the game, as the latest incarnation of "One Shining Moment" was beamed around the world, and onto the JumboTrons at the Georgia Dome, I stood at midcourt with Caroline by my side. In the truck, Bob Fishman noticed us on one of his monitors and asked the tape operators to record it. It's a digital keepsake that I will always cherish.

Dave Barrett's magical song was played that night for the

Florida Gators, the winners and still champions, who cheered wildly with every passing image. To the chagrin of the press, and perhaps a few CBS executives, this time around there was no Cinderella at the Final Four. For a change, that didn't matter to me. After all, who needs a fairy tale when you're holding hands with a real-life princess of your own?

CHAPTER TWELVE

Years ago, someone posted a *New Yorker*–style cartoon outside our control room at the CBS Broadcast Center in New York. It showed a team of brain surgeons sweating as they deliberated over their patient, who was lying on the operating table. The caption read, "Relax! . . . This isn't *live television*!"

While the outcome of what we do does not involve holding someone's life in our hands, what we share in common with, say, brain surgeons is the intensity of concentration and the lack of margin for error. In live television, commentators don't have a "backspace" key that we can hit when we'd like to pick a stronger adjective or rephrase a sentence. The producer is constantly providing instructions in one ear, and through the other side of the headset we hear the ambient noise, which allows us to modulate and project our voices accordingly. It's all about disciplining yourself to concentrate on Point A without letting your mind wander off to Point B. All the while, you're trying to tell a cogent story, project positive energy, *and* make everything look *easy,* even though it rarely is.

Performing at such peak intensity for a sustained period can be incredibly draining. When you do finally take off your headset, you're often in a daze, as if coming out of a long hypnotic trance. Paradoxically, you feel both exhausted and wired at the same time. Frank Chirkinian once labeled this state the Blue Funk. It's broadcasting's version of postpartum depression. Like deep-sea divers, who need to make decompression stops along their way back up to the surface, you can't just walk away from a live broadcast without a proper period of separation—usually with others who have also been subjected to that same crucible.

NCAA Championship Monday represents more than an individual broadcast. It's the culmination of a *month-long* national extravaganza in which our team winds up broadcasting fifteen games (including the Big Ten conference championship, which precedes the NCAA Tournament) in four cities in twenty-four days—plus the selection show, the NCAA Final Four opening ceremony, and all the media interviews in between. The tournament takes on a life of its own, and it takes over *yours.*

Long after the revelers have retired to bed, our core production team goes out and bids farewell to the college basketball season in our own way. In San Antonio, for instance, we walked along the River Walk in the wee hours of the morning; in St. Louis, we walked to the Arch, kissed it for good luck, and spit into the Mississippi River for even better luck. This time, we walked through the deserted streets of downtown Atlanta. Nobody would confuse it with General Sherman's march through Georgia, but we did end up at Pittypat's Porch, a landmark *Gone with the Wind*–themed restaurant.

It was a short break, though, and within seven hours Barry Frank, my longtime mentor and agent, and I were in a car bound for the Masters. Jack Nicklaus, Lee Trevino, and Gary Player were set to meet me there at noon to tape a couple of new episodes for the series *Talking Golf,* which Barry had created. Fortunately, this year's road *from* the Final Four was the shortest route I've ever had to take: Augusta National is only 150 miles due east on I-20. In every other sense, however, it is worlds removed.

In TV terms, when a cameraman pivots around so quickly that the images become jarringly blurred, we call it a swish pan. That's exactly what it felt like to suddenly turn from a team sport played at a breakneck pace with in-your-face intensity by college kids with whom you have only a passing acquaintance to a measured, nuanced, tradition-bound game pursued by grown men you've befriended over many years.

The atmospherics, too, seem like polar opposites—from the relentless sound track of a raucous arena to the serenity of Bobby Jones's private garden paradise. While we were cooped up inside airports and climate-controlled Teflon domes, Mother Nature had been busy applying the colorful finishing touches to the latest edition of her masterpiece known as spring. Although I usually feel wiped out physically when I reach Augusta, the moment I walk through those gates, spiritually it's like receiving a jolt of vitamin B_{12}. That rapid transition from "madness" to majesty is complete, and it's time to move on from the Blue Funk to the Green Jacket.

Now, less than a week remained on my ultimate sports road trip as I eagerly anticipated the third and final leg of this journey. The Masters is a constant in a sea of change, refreshingly old-fashioned in its adherence to tradition—and that's what makes this tournament, as we say, "unlike any other."

Billy Payne was also making a transition from Atlanta, where he lived and worked, to Augusta, where he was beginning his tenure as chairman of both the Masters and the Augusta National Golf Club. Payne had convinced the International Olympic Committee to stage its centennial Olympic Summer Games in the capital city of his native Georgia. Now he coaxed Arnold Palmer into hitting Thursday morning's ceremonial first tee shot as the honorary starter. The four-time Masters winner didn't disappoint the early-morning mustering of Arnie's Army, as he pierced the chilled air by launching a solid drive with a slight draw.

The glorious custom of beginning golf's first major of the year by honoring a living legend dates back to the early 1960s, but it really gained popularity in the 1980s, when Gene Sarazen, Byron Nelson, and Sam Snead shared the tee box. Slammin' Sammy had been the last to do the honors in 2002, six weeks before he died. I had met Snead many times before, but I'm sorry to say that I didn't really know him nearly as intimately as I knew the other two golf immortals.

On Wednesday afternoon before the Masters, the "big course" is closed off in order to direct attention to the annual Par 3 Tournament, and to let the main course "breathe" after four days of practice rounds. One of my treasured pre-Masters rituals is to walk around the Cathedral of Golf, reacquainting myself with the aesthetic genius of fabled course architect Alister MacKenzie, who, in 1930, gave life to Bobby Jones's vision of creating his dream course on the site of a dormant nursery. MacKenzie died during its construction and never got to see Augusta National in its full splendor.

On one such stroll in 2003, I walked to Amen Corner, and stood in solitude on the 12th green. When I turned and looked back up the 11th fairway, I saw a couple walking over the hill. The man was clutching the women's arm with one hand, and leaning on a cane with the other. From a distance, they looked just like Byron and Peggy Nelson, and much to my pleasant surprise, as I made my way there, that's exactly who they were. Byron explained that he had gotten a lift to the 11th hole and wanted to take Peggy to see the bridge over Rae's Creek that had been named in his honor back in 1958; she had never seen it before. About a hundred yards away on the 14th green, one of our virtuoso cameramen, Davey Finch, was shooting "beauty" shots; I hustled over to him and said, "Hey, we may have a special moment here that we should record for posterity."

Part of golf's great allure is a reverence for history, and with the Nelsons' blessing, we taped the sweet scene that unfolded as the ninety-one-year-old Byron gingerly made his way across his bridge, slowly leaned over with Peggy's support, and touched his hand to his lips and then to the commemorative plaque. Back at the CBS compound, I passed the tape along to Dick Enberg, who built a touching essay around it, one Hall of Famer paying homage to another.

Nelson was a deeply religious and humble man, who often said that he only wanted to be a professional golfer long enough to earn the money needed to buy his ranch in Roanoke, Texas. Once he saved up enough, he'd retire from playing full-time on the PGA Tour and true to his word, that's exactly what he did at the age of thirty-four in 1946.

In December of 2005, Lance Barrow, who is CBS's coordinating producer of golf, as well as the NFL; Tommy Spencer, my editorial consultant for both sports; and I were invited to visit "Lord Byron" and Peggy out at the ranch. The Barrows and the Nelsons were both active in the same church, and

Melissa Barrow, Lance's wife, and Peggy sang in the choir together.

It was through their church affiliation that Byron had met Peggy. Since they had married later in life, they decided that rather than celebrate their wedding anniversary yearly, they would celebrate it every *month*—which they did for their nearly two hundred anniversaries together.

Driving up the gravel driveway past the simple mailbox, we approached the modest ranch house, which had, over time, become enveloped by industrial neighborhoods. What a stark contrast to the palatial mansions in gated communities that house today's premier players on the Tour. On this afternoon, we sat around the dining room table, seemingly transported back to another era as Byron presided over the discussion. Peggy had fixed his favorite lunch: chili dogs and potato chips. Well into his ninety-third year, he enthralled us by recounting stories from a remarkable career that included the greatest year that any golfer has ever enjoyed: In 1945, Nelson won eighteen tournaments, including an unmatched eleven in a row.

He told us that in the early days of commerical aviation he was invited to South America to conduct a month-long series of golf clinics—all for $1,500. There were no runway lights back then, so one could fly only during the daytime—and only in favorable weather. It took Nelson and his party a full seven days to reach their destination in Argentina. Such was the kind of wear and tear that these pioneers of the sport accepted in order to pave the way for today's Phil Mickelsons and Tiger Woodses, who travel privately—often on jets that they own and sometimes even pilot.

Inevitably, our conversation came around to the Masters. Nelson played in twenty-nine of them, winning in 1937 and 1942. He vividly recalled playing Augusta National for the first time in 1935, in the second year of the tournament's existence. "When I was playing seventeen on Sunday," he told us, "Gene [Sarazen] was playing fifteen. Our drives had left us separated by about twenty yards, each heading in the opposite direction, with a little gravel path in between. I told Gene, 'You go ahead and play first.'"

As he prepared for his second shot on the par-5 15th, Sarazen was 235 yards out, and he trailed Craig Wood by three strokes; the winner's check, had, reportedly, already been prepared with Wood's name on it. Sarazen hit a four-wood that miraculously found its way into the cup for a rare double-eagle—or *albatross*—in what became known as "the shot heard 'round the world" and helped put the Masters on the map. As Nelson recalled the moment for us, we realized what a rare honor it was to be visiting with a man who may well have been the last surviving person to witness one of the most important shots in the history of golf.

I had the privilege of being in Gene Sarazen's company on several occasions, thanks to Ken Venturi, his Marco Island, Florida, neighbor, and my longtime CBS partner at 18. My favorite time spent with Sarazen was at a 1999 charity event that Kenny had organized to build the Beau Venturi Home for Abused Women and Children. Greg Norman, Nick Price, David Duval, and Ernie Els were among the golfing royalty on hand to help Venturi raise money—along with Sarazen. The event featured a "shotgun" start, where every player begins his round at the same time but at a different hole. So I had the precious opportunity to spend the afternoon chatting with Sarazen while we waited for all the groups to work their way around to number one, where I interviewed the golf pros, along with Kenny and Gene, as each foursome came through.

I vividly remember how struck I was, looking at Sarazen

that day, by the contrast between the physical stamina and mental agility of this ninety-seven-year-old marvel and the fragility and disorientation of my own father, who was a quarter-century his junior. While Sarazen was spry and self-sufficient, by then, back home in Houston, my dad had to be dressed and helped down the stairs by my mother; Dad's life options were becoming more limited by the week.

"Jimmy," my mother would say to me plaintively on the phone, "your dad's upset again today about the whole driving issue. He's insisting that he wants to take the car and drive down to the supermarket. Do me a favor. I know you've already done it twice this week, but please get on the phone and explain to him why he can't?"

"Hey, Son," Dad said in frustrated tones. "Your mom is hiding my car keys, and she won't tell me where she's put them. You know I'm a good driver. Heck, I was just out running errands around town yesterday."

"Dad," I'd then tell him, as though he were a child, "I just don't think it's a good idea today. Why don't we talk about this tomorrow, okay?" He was totally unaware of his Alzheimer's, and time was a concept he could no longer grasp; he would forget within minutes that the matter had even been discussed. At the time, Dad hadn't been behind the wheel in two years—ever since he had gotten lost trying to find our house and ended up in a minor fender-bender. That's when we began the cat-and-mouse game of hiding the car keys from him.

And so it was with total awe that I sat with Gene Sarazen that day, admiring how he remained in full control of all his faculties. We talked about his family, his career, and various other aspects of his life. At one point, just out of curiosity, I asked him to walk me through the details of his daily routine.

"Oh, I'm afraid it's not very interesting," he replied. "You know, every day is pretty much the same, Jim. Every morning I shower and shave between eight and nine. By that time, the housekeeper has let herself in, and she puts breakfast on the table, which is a little cup of fruit, half a glass of orange juice, and coffee. It never varies." I asked him what he does after that, and he said, "I take a nap."

Sarazen told me that after a little rest, he sits out on his balcony watching the people on the beach or the construction workers at a neighboring high-rise. Then he'd have a cup of soup for lunch. By this point, I thought I understood the rhythm of his day.

"I suppose you take another nap after lunch?" I inquired.

"Oh, no! Done with the naps," he said. "I watch CNBC. A long time ago, I learned that if you want to learn about the world—*watch the money!*" So I asked him if he was a big stock guy.

"Actually, I haven't owned a stock in *seventy years*," he said, setting me straight. "One day, I was taking the train home and one of my old rivals, [U.S., British, and PGA champion "Long"] Jim Barnes, was in the car. I hadn't seen him in a few years, and he was working as a broker, so I asked him if he had any tips for me. 'Yeah, Gene,' he said, 'I've got a tip—if I were you, I'd sell everything I owned *immediately!*' I went home and thought all night about what he said. We weren't close, but there was something about his tone that made me feel I needed to cash out, which I did the next morning. Five days later, the market crashed. I had all my money out, and that Jim Barnes—why, he saved my life!"

I left Eagle Creek that day vowing to Sarazen that I would come out early the following month to visit with him at the 1999 Masters, where he, Nelson, and Snead were to be the honorary starters. I arrived early at the first tee at Augusta

National to check in on Sarazen, just as I had promised. All
dressed up in his tie and knickers, "the Squire" was as dapper as
ever as he sat in a golf cart and called me over to update me on
a sudden change in his financial approach. "Hey, Jimmy," he
said with a tone of urgency in his voice on that April morning
in Augusta. "Remember, a few weeks ago in Florida, when I
told you I hadn't bought a stock in seventy years? Well, I just
bought one." Then he added conspiratorially, "And *you've* got
to get some of it, too!"

When he stepped out of the cart at the first tee, Masters
chairman Hootie Johnson introduced him, and thousands of
people applauded. The first fairway was lined on both sides as
golf fans tried to catch a glimpse of the man who won the
second Masters, sixty-four springtimes ago.

As Sarazen prepared to hit his ceremonial tee shot, I was
amused to see that the Squire had a graphite shaft in his driver;
here was the man who'd invented the sand wedge still on the
prowl for every last advantage. You can imagine that a ninety-
seven-year-old gentleman cannot generate all that much club-
head speed, but even with his age-slowed swing, Sarazen still
made flush contact. The ball traveled 75 yards in the air, but
with a perfect trajectory and a slight draw. I will remember it
as one of the purest strikes and most beautiful shots I've ever
witnessed. For me, being privileged to stand inside the ropes
was truly a moving experience. As soon as the ceremony concluded, I headed back to the CBS compound to call Dick Ma-
digan, my financial manager. "Dick, I don't care what the
research says," I told him. "All I know is that Gene Sarazen
waited seventy years to buy the right stock. We're getting in!"

What I didn't know that morning was that I was also a party
to something even more rare than a Gene Sarazen stock transac-

tion: I'd witnessed the final golf shot of the Squire's long and fabled life.

.   .   .

Five weeks later, I was in Dallas to call the Byron Nelson Classic—the same tournament where, two decades earlier, I had gotten my first paid experience on the golf tour, earning $60 for the week as a spotter for NBC Sports. On the morning of the first round, Ken Venturi, my longtime partner in the 18th tower, and I were scheduled to tape an interview with Byron for his archives.

"I've got some sad news, Byron," Kenny told Nelson when we met him that morning. "I got a phone call from [Gene's daughter] Mary Ann Sarazen a few hours ago. She told me that Gene died last night." Venturi is an emotional man. I was not at all surprised to see tears well up in his eyes as he informed Nelson. What stunned me, however, was the latter's reaction.

"Gene Sarazen was the best ball-striker I ever saw," Nelson intoned, lapsing almost matter-of-factly into what seemed like a canned sound bite. "No one ever made a better transition from hickory-shafted clubs to steel." Perhaps it was the contrast to Kenny's overt grieving that made Nelson's stoic response so remarkable. A few weeks later, I happened across an article that shed some interesting light on Nelson's reaction to Sarazen's passing. The author theorized that one of the secrets of longevity is the ability to emotionally detach oneself from death, especially in an age group when it becomes relatively commonplace among peers. It could also have been that given Nelson's religious convictions, he believed Sarazen was headed for a "better life" after this one.

The day after Byron's tournament ended, I wanted to fly

from Dallas to Marco Island to attend Gene Sarazen's funeral on Monday, May 17. The services for Sarazen happened to fall on my fortieth birthday, and since I had a strong "hunch" that Lorrie had set up a surprise party for that occasion, I missed the funeral. By coincidence, earlier that same day, my friend Tom Penders—now the basketball coach at the University of Houston—had invited me to visit him while he played a charity event at Brooklawn, a Bridgeport, Connecticut, course, where Sarazen had caddied as a young boy. I took Caroline along with me, and we walked a few holes with Tommy. The clubhouse was closed that Monday, but the pro, Brad Worthington, who was on the Houston golf team with me, got us into the Sarazen Room. It's a small, ten-by-twenty-foot chamber, filled with Gene's memorabilia—and what a career those souvenirs celebrated! Sarazen was one of a handful of golfers to ever capture all four legs of the grand slam.

As I walked around and tried my best to explain to a five-year-old what all these medals and clubs meant, I could envision Ken Venturi at that very moment delivering his eulogy during the services taking place a thousand miles to the south. Although I'm quite certain that this rare opportunity to memorialize this great man was lost on her, she could plainly sense that I was getting all choked up in what, for me, was tantamount to conducting my own private service.

When I took her to the Sarazen Room at Brooklawn, Caroline was about the same age that I had been when my parents took me to a golf course for the first time. Not only did I quickly take to playing the game, but early on I became infatuated with the PGA Tour. Every spring, during school break, Mom and Dad would take us to Florida, and our destination was dictated by where the Tour was playing. One year, we went to the old Greater Jacksonville Open; another time we watched the Jackie Gleason Inverrary Classic; and in 1976 we drove all the way down to Miami Beach because the schedule coincided with the Doral-Eastern Open.

"Son, I'll see you back here at six sharp," my dad told me as he dropped me off right at the front entrance of Doral—everything was much more casual back then, including security. Mom and Dad were taking Nancy to the beach, which was *her* idea of a perfect vacation day, and my parents were always eminently fair about giving each of us quality time.

"Thanks, Dad," I said, hustling out of the passenger seat. "Don't worry, I'll be there at six. I promise!" With eager anticipation, I raced over to watch the early players tee off at number one. In my hand, I was clutching a brown paper bag containing the lunch that Mom had prepared for me: my usual peanut-butter-and-jelly sandwich, a bag of potato chips, and a can of soda that she had frozen overnight and wrapped in aluminum foil. It was only 10:00 A.M., but already it was getting hot in the South Florida sun. The soda was thawing out and starting to sweat through the paper bag, causing the bag to disintegrate. I knew I had to find a place to store this meal. I saw a grove of ficus trees between the 1st and the 18th holes, and I thought, "Bingo!" So I climbed up, found a hollow, and placed the bag in there for safekeeping. Then I came down and spent the afternoon following the pros, including Tom Weiskopf, my boyhood golfing hero, who was near the top of the leaderboard coming into the final round.

A few hours later, when my stomach started growling, and Weiskopf was having his problems, I scurried back up the tree to raid my refrigerator—and I found my lunch untouched and perfectly chilled. Leisurely, I sat down at the base of the ficus, enjoyed my sandwich, and watched the players finish the tournament at 18. Let me tell you: When you're a teenager and you've fallen hopelessly in love with golf, life doesn't get much better!

In 1986, I returned to Doral, and as I revisited those friendly ficus trees, I had a wonderful feeling that I was blessed to be coming back. Only this time, instead of climbing into a tree to stash my lunch, I would be climbing into a tower at the 16th hole to make my debut with the CBS Sports golf team, where I was paired with another rookie, Gary McCord. Through four rounds, Andy Bean and Hubert Green were tied at 276. Bean and Green then matched each other shot for shot in a playoff that began on our hole and proceeded to 17 and 18. They worked their way back to 16 to continue until the tie was broken and the title settled. In other words, Bean and Green were playing number 16 for the *third* time that afternoon. Meanwhile, the late-running golf had spilled over into *CBS Sports Sunday*, which featured a championship boxing match. That left the two (of four) executive producers, Frank Chirkinian and Terry O'Neil, to battle it out for airtime. "Let me take it *for two*," O'Neil told Chirkinian over the phone from Control Room 43 at the Broadcast Center in New York. Whether it was intentional or just a misunderstanding has long been a subject of internal debate, but what quickly became apparent was that Frank thought it was two *minutes,* while what Terry had in mind were two *rounds*.

By the time golf came back on the air, Bean had already birdied 16—the fourth playoff hole—to win the tournament. "Now listen to me, Jimmy and McCord," Frank Chirkinian instructed through our headsets. "We're going to roll the tape, and you guys voice it over *as if it were live*." Even though this was my first CBS golf assignment, I could sense trouble the minute Frank cued us. Gary couldn't resist predicting what was going to happen on each shot. Needless to say, with the benefit

of hindsight, McCord's prognosticative powers were tremendously heightened.

"Jim, I think Hubert Green is going to hit it right of the
flag, two bounces and a stop. I'll say about eighteen feet from
the cup." I shot Gary a look as if to say, "Are you trying to get
us both fired? You can't pretend you don't know what's going
to happen!"

"That was good, but I think Andy can do better. . . . I like
Bean to leave this one about eight feet below the hole, where
he'll have an easy uphill putt for the win—and he should
make it."

Walking back to the compound afterward, I told him, "Gary,
what are you, *nuts*? You can't do that!"

"Oh, Jimmy, come on," he replied. "Who'll ever know the
difference?"

"Well, for starters, the reporters in the pressroom. They
were already interviewing Bean while you were on the air predicting he'd win."

Fortunately, Gary didn't get us fired—although Frank took
him to task with a lecture that was blistering enough to uncurl
McCord's handlebar mustache.

· · ·

I was absolutely floored when, weeks later, Frank Chirkinian
mentioned that he was "considering" putting me at the 16th
hole at the Masters. When I arrived at Augusta, I walked to my
assigned hole, climbed into the tower, and just sat there trying
to absorb everything. This was the same tiny perch from where
British journalist Henry Longhurst had shared his erudite ob-
servations—the same Henry Longhurst whose book of golf
essays Jim McKay had once given me.

In reality, the vantage is not as wide and expansive as it appears on television. The green is right below you, so close that you feel you can reach down and touch it. This proximity is why golf commentators speak in hushed tones—because, yes, the players *can* hear them.

Although I had worked on a variety of events in my first year at CBS, having the opportunity to call the Masters was the ultimate realization of my childhood dream. Like the kid who grew up wanting to play center field for the New York Yankees and then found himself wearing pinstripes and batting cleanup for the Bronx Bombers, this was *the* sport, *the* network, and *the* single event that I had locked onto in my teens—and now, well . . . *I was there!* Was I nervous? *Beyond belief!* But similar to that comforting feeling of familiarity that I'd experienced upon seeing *The NFL Today* set for the first time, I was also strangely at home in Augusta.

.   .   .

On Sunday morning, I came out to the course early to check the hole location at 16. It was set back left, just as I had suspected, so I knew that it would be vulnerable for the final round. "Frank," I wondered aloud in Chirkinian's office, "I hate to ask, but what would I say if someone made a hole in one? How should I handle it?" He looked at me incredulously. "You say . . . *nothing!*" he barked. "This is a *visual* medium, you idiot! Now get the hell out of my office, make sure you're in your tower in time for rehearsal."

It was one of the first of many doses of "tough love" that Frank would administer—although in those days, I wasn't seeing much of the love part. Licking my wounds as I headed out of the compound, I bumped into a friendly face, David Winner, who is not only a gifted producer, but also a Masters history buff.

"Hey, Jim," he reminded me. "I know you know this, but remember, if Nicklaus does something on your hole today, he's got plenty of history at sixteen—the birdie back in '63, when he won his first Green Jacket; then in '75, when he beat [Johnny] Miller and Weiskopf, he made that famous forty-foot putt."

I thanked David and headed for my post at 16 thinking that I'd never need his impromptu briefing. Nicklaus wasn't even on the first two pages of the leaderboard when we hit air. What's more, the "Golden Bear" was *forty-six years old.* If anything, he was more likely to fade even further back into the field than to make a dramatic charge.

At the turn, Nicklaus birdied 9, 10, and 11. He hit a speed bump with a bogey at 12, but when he bounced back with a birdie at 13, a story that had seemed too far-fetched to imagine suddenly had the whole place abuzz. From my tower at 16, I had a bird's-eye view of the 15th green. When I saw Nicklaus eagle 15, I got chill bumps that somehow defied normal physiology and stayed with me for the next hour. The crowd roar sent a shock wave rattling across the famed course.

This was *ridiculous,* I thought. Jack hadn't won a major in six years since the PGA Championship at Oak Hill in Rochester, New York—and back then, everyone thought it was a total anomaly that he could capture it at age forty.

"Jimmy," Frank bellowed. "When we come out of commercial, it's all yours, Son."

As much as I'd like to think that I had always been preparing myself for that moment, I must confess that I was so nervous my teeth were involuntarily chattering. I'm just grateful that I didn't have to be on camera to paint this picture. As it was, I worried that the noise from my clicking molars would be picked up by my open microphone.

While the great Nicklaus readied himself at the tee, I set

the stage by recounting a chronology of Jack's past successes at 16. My remarks were instinctively timed to finish just as Jack was ready to strike the ball—one of Frank's rules was that we never "talked over" someone's swing, just as you wouldn't if you were on the course playing.

Then Jack backed off to confer with his son, Jackie, who was caddying for him. Nicklaus tossed a few blades of grass into the air to gauge the wind. That was all fine, except that I had "emptied the bucket" on my material and was now faced with more time to fill. I decided to "toss it" down to Tom Weiskopf, who was periodically commenting from Butler Cabin.

"Tom Weiskopf," I asked hopefully, "you've known Jack Nicklaus for a long time. He's making an unbelievable charge. What is going through his mind right now?"

"Jim," he said, "if I had any idea what Jack Nicklaus was thinking, I'd have won this tournament a couple of times myself."

In lieu of a nice, leisurely twenty-second fill that I was hoping for, Weiskopf, a four-time Masters' runner-up, came up short. But given the drama, a few seconds of silence played even better. When Nicklaus finally hit the shot, I could tell while the ball was in the air that the trajectory was dead-on. "Get close!" Jackie Nicklaus exclaimed. "It *is*!" replied his father, as he nonchalantly leaned over to pick up his tee while the ball he had struck so purely was still in flight. When it landed, it began trickling off the slope, making a beeline for the cup. It took a peek at the hole before settling about three and a half feet away. Nonetheless, I played it the way Frank had told me to treat a hole in one: I said . . . *nothing!* Frank stayed on Jack, following him as he strode all the way to the green. All the while, I maintained my silence. Then, with the excitement building to a fevered crescendo, Jack knocked in his birdie, and I blurted out my summation:

"No doubt about it: The Bear has come out of hibernation!"

As we went to commercial, I had an awful feeling in the pit of my stomach, as if I'd been sucker punched right in the gut. How in the world did I come up with *that* line, I asked myself. Don't tell me I heard one of my colleagues use it earlier in the show! Why, I continued berating myself, at such a critical moment, did I ever say something so *un*-original? Maybe I really *am* in over my head—a twenty-six-year-old kid who just is not worthy of occupying Henry Longhurst's old seat.

Jack Nicklaus did go on to win, and to my enormous relief, I *had not* recycled someone else's comment. Emotionally, I felt as if I'd just been granted an eleventh-hour death-row reprieve from the governor. To this day, people still come up to me to comment on how they remember that one ad-lib—and when they do, it still triggers that same sequence of emotional reactions: self-doubt, relief, and satisfaction.

When the tournament was over, I chose to stay in my tower to watch the Butler Cabin interview and Green Jacket ceremony. Then I climbed down and began walking back to the compound as Ken Venturi came by in his golf cart. "Hop in, Jimmy," he called over, "I'll give you a ride." Venturi, who finished second at the 1956 Masters—as an *amateur*—was clearly still trying to get his mind around the remarkable events that had just transpired before our eyes. "You know, I've been coming here a long time," he said. "But I'm going to predict something right now: You may be the first person to ever broadcast fifty Masters. If you do, you'll never live to see a greater day than this around Augusta National."

CHAPTER THIRTEEN

Augusta National is one of the most beautiful courses ever created by man. But God's gift to golf can be found on the Monterey Peninsula with a pair of classics: Pebble Beach Golf Links and Cypress Point—separated by only three miles. There is no more breathtakingly scenic spot on this planet than this corner of California real estate. As one whose livelihood depends on his ability to paint pictures with words, I could no more describe the stunning seascape of Pebble Beach than I could do justice to a perfect sunset. Something about this section of the Pacific coastline profoundly stirs my soul: Each new seedling and every old piece of driftwood seems to hold a special sanctity within the Del Monte Forest.

Each February, after the Super Bowl and the grueling twenty-week grind of the football season, I come to Pebble for renewal and spiritual replenishment. Weary though I may be from the travel, I put the time change to good use, waking up before 6:00 A.M. most mornings to slip on my running shoes and jog the course. Following the cart path in pitch-darkness, I work my way out to the tee at 7. There, I sit in silence on the wooden rail fence, waiting for the dawn to break and unleash its dramatic palette of colors on the sky, the 7th green below, and Carmel Bay off in the distance. Minute by minute, as the sun wrestles with the low-lying fog, the hues change—blending, intensifying, even vanishing—with mesmerizing mystery.

When the unfolding panorama of a new day stabilizes, I conduct my annual one-man "Board of Directors" meeting, taking stock of my life and my career. Although I give thanks daily, something about this awesome spiritual setting especially inspires me to prayerful introspection.

Along this same jagged shore, I had often sought insight and inspiration as I thought about my dad. In one period before his illness, for instance, I was plagued by a sense of "success guilt." How, I wondered, could I enjoy the affluence of The Lodge at Pebble Beach, while at the same time Dad was driving all around Texas trying to develop a customer base for his office-furniture business? That was when I began to develop the idea that my father would travel with me and help me in *my* business.

Sadly, before that dream could become a reality, it was overtaken by the unanticipated and unremitting nightmare known as Alzheimer's. It was on the Monterey Peninsula where I had grappled with the traumatic decision regarding my father's transfer to a private-care facility. Balancing the emotional ledger, Pebble Beach was also where I shared a wonderful father-and-son road trip. Back in 1990, I had the privilege of bringing my dad out to watch the AT&T Pebble Beach National Pro-Am; he sat with me in the tower and walked the course, and on the day after the tournament we played Pebble

Beach Golf Links together. For someone who enjoyed the game—and adored the beauty of nature—as much as he did, it was, he claimed, the greatest round of his life.

Although I was never able to duplicate that wonderful experience with my own father, I did relive it vicariously through CBS Sports executive producer Tony Petitti. He and his dad, John, a twenty-two-year New York City police officer, loved golf. On weekends, they would drive out to Long Island's famed public course in Bethpage, arriving at 4:00 A.M. to reserve a tee time and then sleeping in the car. In 1999, Tony brought his father out to play Pebble Beach and Cypress Point. John Petitti passed away five years afterward, and to this day, like me and countless others, Tony says that he cannot go back to Pebble without thinking of his dad and the warm memories of their special rounds together.

Cypress Point Golf Club is where I met Jim Langley, their retired head professional and a saintly man who, above all others in the sport, epitomizes the highest virtues of the game. He's one of the special individuals whom I would choose to include in my "dream foursome." Actually, since I'm making the rules here, it would be a *fivesome,* including my dad; former president George H. W. Bush; Ken Venturi; and Eddie Merrins, the renowned "Little Pro" of Bel-Air Country Club in Los Angeles, who, like Langley, brings a transcendent dimension to the game. For my part, I would gladly *walk* alongside the five of them to keep score as they played—just as I used to do for Coach Dave Williams in the late 1970s, when Fred Couples, Blaine McCallister, and John Horne were on the course competing for the Houston Cougars golf team.

Langley was a member of Pete Newell's University of California–Berkeley basketball team that defeated the Jerry West–led West Virginia Mountaineers for the 1959 NCAA national championship, but golf was his true calling. For more than three decades until his retirement at the end of 2005, he served with distinction as the head golf professional at the Cypress Point Golf Club.

In 1987, Jim's life changed in an instant. He was pushing his car off the road after running out of gas on Highway 101 when he was struck by an oncoming car and thrown two hundred yards in the air. Miraculously, he survived; but this gifted athlete permanently lost the use of his right arm. Rather than let that near fatal accident embitter him, Langley claimed that, like everything else in life, it was "for the best"—providing him with a chance to learn more about himself and life. Like John Wooden, Tony Dungy, and Dave Williams, Jim has such deep faith that it seems as if he's operating on a higher plane than the rest of us. Cypress Point has long been considered "the Sistine Chapel of golf," so it seems fitting that, in Jim Langley, it had more than a world-class instructor running the pro shop, it had a genuine spiritual leader, a man who embodies selflessness, integrity, honesty, and humility—virtues that are rooted in golf, but transcend the sport.

Jim was the one who showed me a plaque to the right of the tee at the 17th hole, which hugs the rocky coastline. The inscription reads, "I suggest that we pause for a moment, admire the beautiful view, and count our blessings. Very few of us are privileged to pass this way." A club member, Clark W. "Boney" Bearden, used to recite those words as he and his fellow players came upon this point in their round.

I was deeply moved by the custom created by Mr. Bearden, a man I never met. I, too, have always believed one should ritualize moments of reflection—whether at sun-up over the seventh hole at Pebble or during the singing of the national anthem before a game. In Tony Petitti's case, every time he returns to Cypress and steps up to the 17th right by Bearden's plaque, he leans over and scratches with his golf tee his father's initials—J.P.—into the sandstone below. Quietly, he memorializes his dad and one of the greatest days they ever shared together. These are all critical reminders that life should not be taken for granted; indeed, we never know if we will be privileged to pass this way again.

. . .

Beginning in 1947, when Bing Crosby first brought his show-business pals north from Hollywood and entertained them at his annual "clambake," the popular conception of celebrities casually at play began to take root at Pebble Beach, and the event was covered by society columnists as well as sportswriters. The first year that I came out to Pebble for CBS was 1986. At one point, Frank Chirkinian assigned me to interview some of those celebrities on Saturday as they came through at 17. I remember going to Frank's office to confide in him that I didn't feel totally comfortable about it.

"What do you mean you don't know what to ask these guys?" he thundered at me with seismic volume. "For God's sake, they're playing a golf tournament. You ask them about *golf*! Son, you see that lake out there?" Frank pointed out his trailer window at the Pacific Ocean. "If you ever come in my office again and ask me another stupid question like that, I'm going to personally pick you up and *throw you* in that lake!"

The good news is that I was a quick study. So, in relatively short order, I learned a pair of important lessons: the diplomatic art of asking non-professional golfers about their swings, and that maybe it wasn't such a great idea to "confide" in Frank on the morning of a broadcast. Eventually, I came to enjoy meeting such show-business legends as Vic Damone, Jack Lem-

mon, Burt Lancaster, Robert Wagner, Phil Harris, Kevin Costner, and Bill Murray.

One of my biggest thrills at Pebble was when I got to meet
a star who was one of my non-sports heroes. Chirkinian was
hosting a dinner at The Lodge in 1988, and the evening was
running late. Realizing that he had made an early-morning
golf commitment for the next day, he asked me to play for him.
When I showed up at the appointed hour at the Cypress Point
Golf Club, I learned that I would be joining Howard Keel and
Sean Connery.

As the latter climbed the hill to the tee box on the par-3
7th hole, the cinematic idol of my youth inquired in that familiar Scottish inflection: "Who has the *ah-nuh*?"

"You do, sir," I said, which would have been perfectly fine
had I stopped right there. Instead I blurted out, "Go ahead,
play away . . . Mr. Bond!"

Instantly, I felt everyone's eyes boring in on me with laser-
like intensity. I tried to steal a glance at Connery, who had assumed one of his trademark smirks. "Well, it is *number seven*. So
it should be kind to you, sir," I muttered, desperately trying to
recover and hoping that I hadn't just compounded the felony.
Connery ignored my feeble comeback and hooked his tee shot
into an unraked sand dune 20 yards short and left of the green.
I thought to myself, "I've rattled the legendary actor and I'll
never hear the end of this from Chirkinian and the rest of the
CBS golf crew."

Now if Connery got away with some implausible escape
stunts as 007, what he did with his second shot defied even Ian
Fleming's imagination. Connery scooped the ball out of the
unsavory lie and somehow guided it through the sloping rough
to the edge of the green, leaving him with a 40-foot putt to

save par. Then, to my further astonishment, he calmly knocked in the 40-footer for a three.

As Connery bent over to retrieve his ball, he pointed his finger at me and flashed that "Do I look like the sort of man who'd make trouble?" grin. *"Number seven,"* he said, milking the moment. "Why, you were right!" You cannot imagine how relieved I was to see that the great Connery had only been stirred, not shaken, by my faux pas. Alas, there was a sequel to my adventure with Mr. Bond, and as usual, the stakes were raised by an order of magnitude.

When we finished our round, Connery asked if I would mind giving him a lift back to The Lodge. *Would I mind?* How could I resist the chance to spend more time with a man whose lines I could recite by heart? Although my rental car was hardly the sort of vehicle he'd use on the big screen, the trunk easily accommodated all the golf bags. Then, as I made my way back around to the driver's seat, I noticed that the rear door was open, so I gave it a good shove. That, to my horror, elicited an instantaneous howl.

"Oh, my [*expletive*] leg!" Connery screamed.

Failing to notice that his left leg was still outside the car, I had slammed the door right into that tender spot where the ankle meets the shin. His pants were torn, and blood was starting to trickle through. My immediate reaction was "Oh, boy, now I've *really* done it!" I envisioned that Connery, after flying halfway around the world just for this tournament, would have to withdraw due to my carelessness. But that fear was soon supplanted by the spectre, if you will, of a weirdly perverse thought: I had managed to do what neither Blofeld nor any of 007's other cinematic adversaries had ever achieved—I had bloodied the invincible James Bond!

Fortunately, the gash *looked* worse than it was, and after he flashed his legendary powers of recovery, we enjoyed lunch together at Club XIX at The Lodge. When the day was done, he graciously invited me to play golf at Valderrama should I ever find myself near Marbella, Spain, where he was living at the time.

"How would I find you?" I asked incredulously.

"Just look me up in the phone book, Jim," he said. "It's listed under Connery . . . Sean Connery."

. . .

Another silver-screen action hero, Clint Eastwood, has ties to the Pebble Beach tournament that go back to the 1960s. He's been the chairman of the Monterey Peninsula Golf Foundation, as well as one of the principals of the group that owns the Pebble Beach Company. Eastwood was even once elected as mayor of neighboring Carmel-by-the-Sea. While Clint hasn't played in the celebrity pro-am for a number of years, he often comes up to join us in the 18th tower, provides some commentary, and talks about the charity components.

All of the PGA Tour events are operated as major fundraisers by nonprofit philanthropic groups. In Phoenix, for instance, the tournament is run by the Thunderbirds; in Hartford, it's the Jaycees; in Dallas, the Salesmanship Club; and at Pebble, it's the Monterey Peninsula Golf Foundation, whose 2007 tournament generated more than $6 million in charitable contributions. For all the talk about the game's alleged elitism, the PGA gives more to charity annually than Major League Baseball, the NFL, and the NBA *combined*. This doesn't even include individual contributions by the pros through their own foundations and their support of other charity events throughout the year.

On the final Sunday of the 2003 tournament, Eastwood

was with me and my partner, Lanny Wadkins, in the tower as Davis Love III was putting the finishing touches on his second Pebble Beach victory. Before releasing Eastwood to go down to the 18th green to participate in the check and trophy presentations, I went on camera to thank him.

"Clint, I'm sure you'll be pleased to know that Davis Love grew up as a huge fan of yours because his dad thought you were the greatest. In fact, the first time Davis's dad ever took him to see an adult film, you starred in it." I thought this compliment was going to make his day. Instead, I felt the temperature suddenly plummet by about twenty degrees as Eastwood looked at me with that Dirty Harry glare.

"Jim," he said, "I have never made an *adult film* in my life!" Every time I see Clint he still chortles about what may have been my all-time on-air blooper.

.   .   .

Along with my college amigos, Fred, Blaine, and John, Dad's favorite golfer was Davis Love III, a fellow Tar Heel by birth. Only four days before he came into the world, his father, Davis Jr., delivered a 69 at Augusta National to share the first-round lead at the 1964 Masters with Arnold Palmer and Gary Player, among others. Davis Jr. was a protégé of University of Texas golf coach Harvey Penick and became a highly regarded golf instructor. He built his son's game, and did an outstanding job teaching him how to become both a gentleman and a winner.

Davis and I were both rookies in 1986, when he almost won the Buick Open on our air. In 1987, he broke through and captured the Heritage at Hilton Head. Eighteen months later, Davis's dad died in a plane crash; he was only fifty-three, and at that special point when both father and son were enjoying the peaks of their respective, and intertwined, careers.

It took Davis a long time to regain his personal and career equilibrium following that tragedy. But by the summer of 1990, he had restored his game to its earlier level, and he was in contention to reclaim his spot as one of the brightest young stars on the Tour. His first win without his father's direct guidance came at the International at Castle Pines in Colorado.

As we waited together on the 18th green during a commercial prior to the winner's interview, Davis, a soft-spoken man of few words, just looked at me. The expression on his face seemed to be begging, "Please . . . don't ask me *about him!*"

"I know he's on your mind," I said sympathetically, "but if you don't want to go there, we won't."

"Please don't. I don't think I can handle it."

"It's *your call,* Davis."

We were almost back on the air when he drew an audible deep breath and exhaled slowly. "You know what? I *would* like to say something. It would be the right thing to do. Just please, make sure it's the last question." After congratulating the new champion, I asked him a few innocuous questions on camera about the tournament and his victory.

"Okay, Jimmy," Frank told me from the truck, "one more, and then wrap!"

"Finally, Davis," I said, "I know this is not going to be easy for you, but how much was your dad on your mind today?" You could feel him steeling himself for the moment. Fighting through tears of sorrow mixed with joy, Davis made a valiant effort to get out a few coherent sentences about how much he loved his father and how this victory was dedicated to him.

Davis went on to further successes, most notably, winning the 1997 PGA Championship at Winged Foot. The PGA of America (as opposed to The PGA Tour) is an organization of some twenty-eight thousand golf-teaching professionals, and there was no better way for Love to honor his father, who was such a distinguished student and teacher of the game.

I'll also remember that major at Winged Foot because it was the last golf tournament that my own father ever attended, an occasion that lent if not closure then symmetry to our blissful romp at the 1974 U.S. Open there. At Winged Foot in 1997, Nancy was nearing her due date with her son, Holton, but she was there, along with her husband, Don, and my mom, to provide "team coverage" for my father. Just before Davis's final putt at 18, a spectacular rainbow arose to the west. Steve Milton, our ace director, instructed Davey Finch to take his handheld camera to the other side of the green to frame the shot so that the cup would appear to be the pot of gold at the end of the rainbow. It was one of those magical visuals, so rich with symbolism, that comes around only a few times in a career's worth of tournaments.

Not only was Davis Love skilled with his golf sticks, but he also proved to be a solid knife-and-fork man. In 1994, when we were in Miami for the Doral, Davis joined Lance, Fred, Paul Marchand—Couples's instructor, and our dear friend and college teammate—and me for dinner on Saturday night. Most of us had already eaten at Joe's Stone Crab so many times that week, we felt as if we were beginning to generate claws. Fortunately, Lance—who coined the immortal admonition "Sometimes, ya gotta eat hurt!"—always kept current on his gastronomic options. He had a Cuban hideaway down on Calle Ocho that was next in line on his restaurant depth chart. Since we were all younger and hungrier, so to speak, back then, our game plan going into the meal was for each of us to order a double entrée; we wanted both quality *and* quantity, and that may have been a huge mistake. The next day, Davis shot a bloated 77. Meanwhile Fred, who was in fourth place on the leaderboard, and well-positioned to win, was even less fortunate.

"Jimmy," Frank Chirkinian said as we were a few minutes into our rehearsal, "something's happened to your boy, Freddy, out there on the driving range, and it doesn't sound good. Now listen, you climb out of that tower and go check up on him. Take as much time as you need. I don't care if you miss the first part of the show. You need to be there for him."

By Doral that year, Fred already had two second-place finishes—all this despite the fact that his heart was with his mom, who was back home in the Pacific Northwest, fighting an uphill battle against cancer. By the time I caught up with him in his room, he was lying on his back in tremendous pain. He had been loosening up on the driving range prior to his round, and Paul had come out, as he did in those days, to coach Fred with everything from his swing mechanics to his tempo. Suddenly, out of the clear blue, Fred hit an eight-iron and the lower part of his back "snapped," leaving him frozen in his finish. While he had already withdrawn from the tournament, Fred didn't want his mother to hear about that from the broadcast. Since he had an aversion to telephones, I explained the problem to her, just as I had in college, when I served as "the official spokesman" to his parents, filling them in on his weekly activities.

Even back then, in the days before e-mail and cell phones, Violet Couples organized Fred's life for him by long distance from Seattle. Fred's father, Tom, worked for the Seattle Parks and Recreation Department. When Fred was in his midteens, his parents knew he had a special gift. So Mrs. Couples worked overtime in an office job at Boeing so that they could afford to send their golf prodigy to compete against the best juniors on the amateur circuit each summer.

Just two months after Doral, Violet Couples succumbed to her illness on Mother's Day 1994. Later that fall in Houston, Fred created a cancer-research fund in her memory and tearfully told the audience at our "Three Amigos" charity benefit, "Somebody once said that God takes away *only the most special moms* on Mother's Day."

At about the time Fred's mom had passed, Lorrie and I were blessed with the birth of Caroline. Of all the many thoughtful and beautiful gifts that we received, one was especially poignant. A package from Seattle arrived at our Connecticut home, and inside was a matching set consisting of a little baby cap, a sweater, and a baby blanket. Each of these adorable items had been lovingly hand-knit for the occasion by Mrs. Couples.

If any solace was to be found, it had to be that Violet Couples lived long enough to see her son become recognized as the number-one player in the world. In 1992, Fred had won three tournaments and finished second in two others as he approached the Masters, where he was a favorite to capture his first major.

But first, there was the NCAA basketball Final Four, which fell on the weekend before Augusta. On an impulse, Fred and Blaine McCallister decided to join me in Minneapolis at the Final Four. No tickets, no hotel rooms, *no worries!* They slept on the sofa in the lounge on the concierge floor of my hotel and "earned their keep" as my "runners." Just to make it official, as I walked the half mile from the hotel to the Metrodome, Fred and Blaine took turns, block by block, carrying my briefcase. Once inside, Billy Packer and I made sure that CBS would get its money's worth from the $50 fee it was paying each of its millionaire gofers. Billy and I kept our special assistants on the go chasing down interview transcripts and refilling our refreshments. Columnist Mitch Albom thought it strange to see two high-profile golfers trying to balance four Cokes on trays.

"Hey, don't strain yourself too much, Fred," I told Couples as I tried to keep a straight face. "You're going to win the Masters next week. We don't want to see the dream ruined here and now."

That dream dated back to 1977, when we were freshmen in college. Just for the fun of it, my roommates and I would sometimes play-act the scene from the Butler Cabin at the Masters. I would pretend that I was hosting the Masters for CBS and interviewing Fred, who, in turn, made believe that he had just won it. Obviously, talent and good fortune are the key elements of success—but imagination also plays an important role in mysterious, subconscious ways. Sure we were college kids throwing up career Hail Mary passes, but defining a desired end is a good way to assure that all roads will lead there.

Each of our Taub Hall foursome has fulfilled his long-standing ambitions. In addition to Fred and me, Blaine enjoyed a prosperous twenty-five-year Tour career, winning five events; John Horne, too, played on the PGA Tour in the 1980s—and now holds the ideal position in his second career as head golf professional at Plainview Country Club in his old hometown in West Texas.

In retrospect, much of the success that we've enjoyed has come as a result of our lifting one another upon our shoulders and having our inner beliefs emboldened by the knowledge that our best friends had complete faith that we could each pull it off. Despite the astronomical odds stacked against, say, Fred winning the Masters one day and me being there for CBS to present the Green Jacket to him, it was all so remarkably vivid that seemingly all we had to do was wait for real life to follow our detailed script.

With Fred at Augusta in 1992, you could just feel it coming together. All of his God-given golf gifts were finely honed, as usual, by Paul. Fred was confident and relaxed, even by his own standards. You could see him on those first three days of the tournament reminding himself, just as he had counseled me to do before my CBS network debut seven years earlier, "It's no big deal! . . . It's no big deal!"

We all arrived early on Sunday morning to watch the completion of the weather-delayed third round. As play progressed, I just *knew* that this would be Fred's big day. And while I was hoping it would happen, nonetheless I began feeling tremendous anxiety—nervous about being able to make it through an interview that we had rehearsed long ago and far away as a pair of wide-eyed eighteen-year-olds in our dormitory.

On that surreal afternoon time seemed to be flying by while Fred was cruising on the second nine—and yet, as Raymond Floyd made a late run for me, I wished that I could somehow speed up the clock even more. With Fred at the 15th hole, my colleague Ben Wright brought me in—much as I had deferred to Tom Weiskopf back in '86.

"Jim Nantz, you're down there in Butler Cabin," said Ben. "What's it like for *you* right now?"

"Well, Fred's always talked about winning this tournament. This is his favorite course," I said, worried there might be nervousness in my voice. "This has always been his biggest goal." After I tossed it back out to Ben, I gave myself a little talking-to: "Hey, you've been coming to this cabin for years now. You're a professional, and this ceremony is going to be fed out to one hundred and eighty countries around the world. Take a deep breath! Remember: *It's no big deal! . . . It's no big deal!*"

I'd interviewed Fred on camera a number of times at CBS.

The first few of them were awkwardly amusing for us, and we had trouble making eye contact because both of us were afraid that we might burst out giggling. This time, when Fred came into the cabin after signing his scorecard, we again did not look each other in the eyes—but not for fear of laughing.

I thought back to my Davis Love interview after he had won the 1990 International. Only now, the parties on *both sides* of the microphone were emotionally vulnerable. I asked Fred about a couple of things that had happened, such as how his ball had stayed up on the bank above the water on 12, then we showed his second shot to save par. Slowly, like picking our way through a psychological minefield, we recapped his final round.

When I received Frank's cue for the last question, I knew that under these unique circumstances, I could not, as professional commentators are trained to do, simply take my personal relationship out of the story. How could I treat one of my closest friends as if I didn't know him? "Fred," I said, "I think back to our days at the University of Houston. And guys like John Horne, Blaine McCallister, and Paul Marchand—we all said, 'One day, you're going to wear the Green Jacket.'"

Fred shielded his eyes; his head was turned ninety degrees away from me. "I always thought it was a good course for me," he muttered, trying not to invest any emotion in his generic reply. "It's always been my favorite tournament. . . . They do things right here." He never alluded to our special connection. Everyone could tell from his body language that the fear of losing his composure prevented him from offering a heartfelt answer.

"Mr. Stephens," I said, "it's time for the Green Jacket."

Augusta National chairman Jack Stephens motioned to

defending champion Ian Woosnam, who placed the Green Jacket on Fred's shoulders. The sleeves barely made it down past his elbows. Nonetheless I said, "*It's a perfect fit!* . . . Fred Couples . . . Masters champion."

My voice was aquiver, and I was still not letting go of my congratulatory handshake with Fred as I signed off:

"For all of us at CBS Sports, Jim Nantz saying good night from Augusta, Georgia."

I turned and gave Fred a hug, which became a genuine deep embrace, with both of us sobbing on each other's right shoulder. Frank had gone straight to the credits, but he did record our quiet moment of celebration together, and it's another treasure in my personal archives. As Fred went off to be feted at the annual Sunday-night dinner in honor of the new Masters champion at the Augusta National Golf Club, a group of us congregated back at his house to welcome *our* champion. Finally, at about ten o'clock, Fred came in, and we all wanted to hear about his day and night.

Paul, who had walked the course with Fred each day, had set the VCR at the house to record the CBS broadcast. We watched the opening and the Green Jacket ceremony, only this time, instead of being on edge, we were all positively giddy.

"Hey, anybody here want to try on the Green Jacket?" Fred blurted out. "Mr. Nantz," he said in the direction of my father. "How 'bout you first?"

Now if the jacket was too small for Fred, you can imagine that it looked like a little boy's confirmation coat on my father. But everyone cheered, and Dad was clearly moved. He beamed with parental pride as one who loved Fred, and all my friends, as if they were his own children. It's one thing to be a fan, a journalist, or even a casual acquaintance. It's quite another to be part of the inner circle, and to finally be able to say, "I knew him when!" after so many years of saying, "One day you will!"

In terms of sheer golf drama, Fred's victory did not approach Jack Nicklaus's 1986 Augusta miracle, which, as Ken Venturi predicted, may remain unrivaled for another half century. Nonetheless, I cannot imagine ever witnessing a moment that will touch me more deeply than this perfect fulfillment of a glorious dream that had been shared for so many years by intimate friends.

CHAPTER FOURTEEN

In a scheduling rarity, the calendar worked out so that the 1991 Final Four ended a full week before the Masters. That gave me the opportunity to go down to Augusta early and leisurely begin gathering information for our broadcasts. After checking in late Sunday afternoon, I took my first stroll along the course, and I spotted a group playing on the 9th green. Although I had not met him before, I could tell that one of them was Phil Mickelson. Although he plays left-handed, Phil is really a righty; like so many kids, he first learned his swing by imitating his father's, only Phil internalized it as, in essence, a mirror image of what he saw Phil Sr. doing. Mickelson was twenty years old and still an amateur, but three months earlier he had grabbed the golf world's attention by besting a full field of pros to win a PGA Tour event, the Tucson Open. Phil was just finishing up his junior year at Arizona State, and you could see that he was a bright young man with a hearty, engaging personality.

At Phil's invitation, I walked with him the first time he ever played the famed second nine at Augusta National. The reigning U.S. Amateur champion tackled Amen Corner with almost childlike exuberance, practicing shots that he'd seen on TV growing up. He had always heard about how some players try to "skip" balls across the water on the par-3 16th—hydroplaning them to get them to land on the green. Phil pulled off that trick shot on his first attempt. He was having so much fun that I felt bad knowing that he had already become the latest in a line of players who were saddled with the label of being "the next Jack Nicklaus." It was such an unfair burden of expectations. Becoming "the first Phil Mickelson" would have done just fine, thank you, especially after his auspicious Masters debut as low amateur, which earned him a visit to Butler Cabin, where I interviewed him on the air the following Sunday.

After graduating with his degree in psychology, Phil turned pro in 1992, but he really came of age in 1996, winning four events, including the prestigious World Series of Golf. Yet on that very same Sunday, August 25, 1996, as Mickelson was in Akron, wrapping up his most significant Tour victory to date, Tiger Woods was outside Portland, claiming his third straight U.S. Amateur championship, a feat the likes of which golf had not seen since the days of Bobby Jones in the late 1920s.

Following our broadcast, as I made my way back to the CBS compound, I noticed that a nearby maintenance shed was bulging with people as members of the greens crew, volunteers, and staff personnel—anyone with a sense of golf history—were riveted to the television, watching Tiger pull out a win on the 38th hole. Just minutes after Mickelson's impressive three-stroke triumph on Firestone's demanding course, his feat had been totally overshadowed.

Four years into his promising pro career, Mickelson no longer had to try to live up to the pressures of being anointed the heir to Nicklaus's throne; that spot was usurped by the twenty-year-old Woods, who had turned pro within days of his stunning amateur finale at Pumpkin Ridge—less than fifteen miles from the world headquarters of Nike, the global marketing giant that would secure Tiger's financial future within a matter of pen strokes.

Instead, Mickelson would eventually be given a new media moniker: "the best player to have never won a major." It was a left-handed compliment born out of his six second- or third-place finishes in the majors from 1999 through 2003. While Woods amassed a startling eight major titles, including three Masters and the "career grand slam," Phil had become golf's version of Ernie Banks, Patrick Ewing, and Jim Kelly. He was another guy with loads of ability who just couldn't win the big one.

In this regard, Mickelson was fortunate to have learned a valuable lesson at an early age from his father. One day, during a round at Balboa Park, a municipal course in San Diego, Phil Jr. hit an errant shot and in his frustration threw a club.

"Hey, this is supposed to be *fun!*" Phil Sr. instructed his angry prodigy. "Put your clubs away for a while until you're ready to enjoy the game; then you can play."

Dutifully, Mickelson the younger walked with his father, a commercial airline pilot who loved his hobby so much that he built a putting green and sand trap in his backyard. After two or three holes of watching, but not playing, the son begged his father to commute this harsh sentence.

"Dad," he said remorsefully, "I promise, from now on, I'm going to have fun."

What's more, Phil told me, from that afternoon on, he kept the game in perspective—even though he was unmercifully reminded of his serial disappointments in the major championships.

Mickelson's patience and his promise to have fun at golf were especially tested in 2003. He did not win any events and went 0-for-5 in his Presidents Cup matches. Meantime, his wife, Amy, suffered through a difficult labor before delivering their third child, Evan.

Our families had begun exchanging annual Christmas cards, and knowing some of the difficulties that Phil and Amy had gone through that year, the spirit of Santa prompted me to sign their card, "See you at Butler Cabin. April 11th. Around 7:00 P.M. . . . Merry Christmas!"

On the appointed second Sunday in April, Phil birdied four of his last six holes and came to 18 needing one more birdie for a breakthrough win. As his epic duel with Ernie Els reached its climax, Mickelson stroked his decisive 18-foot putt. "Is it his time?" I wondered aloud on the air as the ball made its way to the cup. "Yes—at long last!" Phil leapt into the air, and pranced around the green looking for people to hug. It was a tremendous release of emotion. Finally, he had captured the biggest one of all.

From the truck, Lance and his production team led us through a spectacular sequence of replays that showed the historic putt from every conceivable angle—and how it just caught the lip on the low side and somehow curled in. Phil later said that he felt as though his grandfather, who had died that January, was looking after him from above and had helped knock that ball into the hole to give him the win. One remarkable slow-motion replay focused on Mickelson's eyes as he tracked the path of the ball without blinking. Just before the ball rolled in, I commented, "Watch his life change right here."

Ten months later, Mickelson dominated the AT&T Pebble Beach National Pro-Am from the outset, when he shot a course-record 62 at Spyglass Hill. On Sunday, as Lefty strode up to the 18th green to finish off his four-stroke victory, I noted that his grandfather, whom Phil had credited with helping him win the Masters, had once traversed these very fairways at Pebble. As a young man, back in the 1920s, Albert Santos had caddied, earning twenty-five cents a day for his labors. Now, more than three-quarters of a century later, his grandson found himself also working on this celebrated course. Only for his efforts, Phil would receive a prize check worth $1 million.

. . .

In the spring of 2006, Mickelson came to Mamaroneck, New York, to prepare for the U.S. Open at Winged Foot. Phil was determined to get to know A. W. Tillinghast's challenging West Course, and he came out on three separate occasions. While other players took the more expedient route of scheduling through the USGA, which was overseeing the tournament and had an office on site at the club, Mickelson always took the extra step of personally calling Winged Foot's esteemed general manager, Colin Burns, to find out whether it would be possible to play at a certain time. After Mickelson finished playing the course, walking the course, taking notes, charting the contours on the greens, and practicing wedge shots on his final pre-Open visit, he asked Colin if he would mind taking him to thank the staff. It was a Monday, so the club was closed and the employees were gathered for a low-key lunch in their downstairs dining room.

"Hey, I know you're all eating," Mickelson told them, "but

I just wanted to thank you guys for making me feel so at home here. It's an honor to play at this historic club, and I just hope I can come back, compete well, and maybe even win the U.S. Open." Phil's thoughtfulness won over the staff and the membership in a manner that no one at that club had ever before seen—and at the time, Winged Foot's West Course had been the site of five men's majors. Mickelson had the whole place rooting for him to win. And it looked as if he would grant them their wish, as he entered the final round tied for the lead.

The Sunday of the U.S. Open was oppressively hot and humid, fitting conditions for what turned out to be a painful meltdown for Mickelson as an excruciating double-bogey on 18 turned a one-stroke lead into a heartbreaking loss to Geoff Ogilvy. This time, no rainbow graced the final hole at Winged Foot, as one had for Davis Love III at the 1997 PGA Championship.

Instead, the shell-shocked Mickelson cleaned out his locker, gave the clubhouse attendants the biggest tip of all the players, and headed home. The following day, Jose, the head locker-room attendant, was summoned to the phone.

"Hi, Mr. Mickelson," said Jose, anticipating a familiar scenario. "Did you leave something here by mistake?"

Instead, the runner-up replied, "No, I'm afraid that I *didn't* leave something there by mistake. I just wasn't thinking clearly and I don't think I left a big enough tip for you and the locker-room guys. So just be on the lookout, there will be something extra coming in the mail in the next few days."

.   .   .

While Phil Mickelson and Tiger Woods grew up with greatness indelibly stamped on them, Tom Pernice Jr. has always had to scrap to get by. Tom and I are contemporaries, and when I was in college, I knew about him at UCLA, where he had to compete with the likes of Corey Pavin and Duffy Waldorf to make the top five and represent the Bruins in tournament competition. Likewise, early in his pro career, it was always touch and go whether he would earn or keep his Tour card. Pernice had won only one Tour event in ten years when he came to Castle Pines for the International in August of 2001. He was the second- and third-round leader, and on the Sunday morning of the final round, I learned from Tom's fitness trainer that Pernice's two young daughters, Kristen and Brooke, would be in the gallery that day, I passed that information along to Lance Barrow and Steve Milton in our production meeting, in case Tom was on the brink of victory at the end of the day.

At 18, Pernice needed to two-putt from 40 feet out for the win. In my headset, "Miltie" confirmed that he had located Tom's daughters and he had isolated one of his cameras on them to capture a reaction shot. The first putt brought the ball to within about two feet. Steve cut to a brief glimpse of the Pernice girls waiting hopefully for their dad to make that final putt. When the ball rolled into the cup, Kristen, age seven, held six-year-old Brooke's hand as they raced onto the green and into their father's arms. Brooke, who was born with a genetic eye disease, Leber's congenital amaurosis, which rendered her legally blind, began running her fingers over her father's face; she was trying to determine how happy he was at that moment by *feeling* how big his smile was.

After I explained the significance of Brooke's loving touch, my partner, Ken Venturi, unaware of the young girl's plight, just lost it emotionally. "Jimmy, in thirty-five years on the air," he said in between sobs, "I've never seen anything more beautiful than this. That poor child—that *beautiful* child—God bless her!"

I came home from the tournament moved by what we had experienced, and I related this story to my own daughter; it quickly became one of her favorite bedtime stories of all time. Not only did it have a positive message, but at the end of this inspiring tale, when Caroline would ask, as always, "Daddy, did that *really* happen?" for once I didn't have to invoke parental literary license.

As for the "living happily ever after" part, despite her impaired vision Brooke Pernice surfs, skis, and takes singing lessons. The girl who had moved us to tears that day seven years ago when she measured her dad's smile to gauge his happiness has recently released a CD of spiritual songs, aptly titled *Help from Above.* Unlike his PGA Tour colleagues such as Fred Couples or Phil Mickelson, who were once golf prodigies, Tom Pernice may one day become better known for being the *father* of a unique musical prodigy.

.   .   .

As you may have surmised by this point, Ken Venturi is an extraordinarily *emotional* individual. That, in my opinion, was one of the major reasons for his tremendous success and longevity as a broadcaster; he didn't—or *couldn't*—hide what he was feeling, so he radiated the joy or the disappointment of the moment. While his reverence for the game's history and his technical knowledge of golf are second to none, his expressive empathy was what made him so beloved to our viewers.

With the Tom Pernice scene at Castle Pines, for instance, Venturi could have discoursed on how hard it is to two-putt for a win. Instead, Kenny just took his audience along on an honest wave of emotion. While Kenny loved that a career journeyman was about to notch a rare win, the shot of little Brooke eagerly "reading" her dad's face sent him over the top. It particularly resonated because, for decades, one of Venturi's favorite charities was Guiding Eyes for the Blind; over the years he's helped raise millions for that cause. One month after the International, a Guiding Eyes dog saved a blind man from the debris on the seventy-first floor of the World Trade Center on 9/11. The grateful survivor, Omar Rivera, later told the audience at a Guiding Eyes benefit dinner, "That dog came from Ken Venturi."

Yet another powerful reason why Brooke Pernice so captured Kenny's heart was that Venturi himself had had a handicap to overcome—he was a stammerer. His condition was so serious that he couldn't pronounce his own name out loud until he was thirteen. That's why he felt so comfortable with golf, because he could stand on the driving range in solitude, talking to himself *internally* in perfectly constructed sentences, without the pressure of trying to communicate with teammates.

As with Billy Packer, I had grown up listening to and admiring Ken Venturi. He, too, was old enough to be my father, and in certain ways he has fulfilled that role, especially since we began to work together at a critical juncture in both of our lives. In 1994, Pat Summerall left CBS for Fox, and two years later, Ben Wright and Frank Chirkinian were retired. Kenny and I loved these dear friends and colleagues, and their departures left a void in our CBS golf family that seemed magnified because we were both struggling with intensely painful personal issues at home. My dad had suffered his stroke in 1995, and over the next five years his situation progressively deteriorated. Meantime, Kenny's wife, Beau, was battling terminal brain cancer. In short, we were more than broadcast partners—we were a two-man therapeutic support group.

One of the keys to surviving an on-the-road lifestyle is to

have a supportive family. For example, it means so much to a golfer to see his wife in the gallery, knowing that she'll still give him a consoling hug if he misses a putt or shoots 80— even though such mistakes might cost a couple of hundred thousand dollars. I've often thought that many of the same dynamics apply to sports television. In this regard, Beau Venturi was exemplary. She did wonders for Kenny's confidence and morale.

By the spring of 1997, Beau's condition was grave, and she wanted to experience the magic of the Masters one last time. Kenny removed the seats from the back of his van and installed a mattress for Beau to lie on as they made the eleven-hour drive up from their Marco Island home to Augusta. There, while the rest of the planet was transfixed by twenty-one-year-old Tiger Woods and his record-shattering performance, a devoted and loving couple shared a sweet and tender moment, a romantic lunch on the back lawn near the giant oak tree, and watched the golf world go by.

Two months later, Ben Crenshaw was in the tower with us as we prepared to sign off from the Westchester Classic. As usual, Lance had choreographed the back-timing of the broadcast perfectly, leaving just enough time for a final on-camera. Intuitively, we had all sensed that this would be the last time Beau would ever see "her Kenny" on TV. With a lump in my throat, I signed off the air saying, "We hope you enjoyed the show today, Beau."

Following Beau's death, just a week later, in July of 1997, Kenny wanted to retire. I knew, however, that the worst possible thing would be for him to sit alone grieving on Marco Island. Fortunately, we were able to coax him into coming back to work for five more years—between his CBS schedule and his charitable endeavors, Kenny was able to bounce back from his painful loss.

. . .

Venturi was in the prime of his playing days when he suffered a back injury in 1961 in a car accident. He could not play golf, which was his livelihood, until he had fully recovered, which would at best take some time. At one point in his recuperation, Kenny recalled, "I told God, 'You put the clubs back in my hands, and I promise I'll give back.'"

He has kept that promise. In addition to Guiding Eyes, Kenny has raised money for numerous charities, including the Stuttering Foundation of America, the Beau Venturi Home for Abused Women and Children, and the Loma Linda University Medical Center, which planned to create the first hospital-based proton-therapy cancer-treatment center.

A significant influence on Kenny's life in many ways, including his philanthropy, was Frank Sinatra, who was his best friend, and roommate, when both were bachelors in Palm Springs. In fact, it was "Ol' Blue Eyes" who paid for Venturi's wedding and walked Beau down the aisle in church. "Frank would scan the daily newspapers," Kenny told me. "If he saw that some family was in desperate need, he would donate money to them anonymously. He just loved helping people."

At about the time that I began partnering with Kenny regularly, Charlie Epps, the golf pro at the Houston Country Club, suggested that Fred, Blaine, and I launch a charitable organization in Houston—and the Three Amigos was born. Each of us, in his own way, had felt the call to return to the city where we had all first met and do something special for the community.

Fred had just lost his mother, Violet, and so he chose to

memorialize her through a cancer research foundation. Blaine's wife, Claudia, suffers from a rare eye disease known as PXE (pseudoxanthoma elasticum), so that's where he earmarked his donations. I chose to support Alzheimer's research, and I selected this in honor of our influential coach, Dave Williams, who was afflicted with it.

Coach Dave, the "father of college golf," couldn't make all of his players into champions, but from the first day of our freshman orientation, he championed each of us. Sometimes, he believed in our dreams even before we ourselves did. So it was only appropriate that he was our first honoree that year, and I don't know who was beaming more that night, Coach Dave or my dad.

No one in the audience was bothered when Coach's remarks periodically veered into incoherence; it was disconcerting to those of us who knew him and loved him, but everyone knew it came with the territory of this awful affliction. Little did I know when I had designated Alzheimer's research as my charity that a cruel twist of fate awaited me half a year later, when my own father began his long, painful descent into that same neurological netherworld.

My dad had been ecstatic about the whole concept of the Three Amigos, from the continuation of our friendships to the important philanthropic contributions. Years later, when he could barely hold a coherent thought in his head, I would sit at his bedside and play name games with him, as part of my ongoing attempts to help him "exercise" his mind. Almost as though I were a contestant on *Password,* I would feed him clues. "*Ken-ny . . . Ven . . .* C'mon, Dad, I worked with him on golf. . . . Kenny *Ven . . .* ?" Finally, he'd mumble, "Kenny Venturi," and I felt as if we had scored a victory. Then we'd try another one. The last clue that he ever responded to in our name game was "Hey, Dad, me and my buddies ... the *Three ...*"

"*Amigos,*" he responded, staring blankly ahead.

. . .

For Ken Venturi, his all-too-brief playing career climaxed with his legendary winning performance at the 1964 U.S. Open, when he survived severe dehydration and heat exhaustion in a 36-hole finale at the Congressional Country Club outside of Washington, D.C., an epic feat of courage and perseverance that earned him *Sports Illustrated*'s Sportsman of the Year honors. Venturi came close to winning a number of other majors, and all of these near-misses came at Augusta National. In 1956, he came closer than anyone else to fulfilling Bobby Jones' dream that an amateur would one day win his tournament. But Kenny three-putted six times en route to a final round 80 and lost to Jackie Burke by a stroke. In 1958 and again in 1960, Venturi was beaten out on the second nine by Arnold Palmer. The 1958 defeat was especially painful for Venturi because he perceived that Palmer had got a favorable ruling on the 12th hole. The controversial call turned a 5 into a 3 and helped Arnie capture his first major title, and the first of his four Green Jackets.

Unfortunately, the ensuing "he said/he said" dispute spawned a frosty private relationship. What saddened me about this situation, which stems back to an event before I was born, is that, knowing both men and admiring them as I do, it's clear that they shared so much in common that they really *could have* and *should have* been very good friends.

. . .

Back in 1998, I took the liberty of writing a long and detailed letter to PGA Tour commissioner Tim Finchem. In it, I laid out the case for why he should appoint Venturi as captain of the 2000 U.S. Presidents Cup team. Among the reasons why I felt that Kenny was so deserving was that nobody knew the players better—he'd been out observing them for twenty weeks a year—and that the event was going to be held near Washington, D.C., which was where Kenny had enjoyed his greatest moment as a golfer, winning the 1964 U.S. Open. The captaincy, I wrote, was an honor that would surely stand as the crowning achievement of Venturi's distinguished career.

Several months later, much to my delight, not only did Commissioner Finchem act upon my suggestion, but Kenny himself was thrilled beyond belief. The good news was delivered the week of the 1999 NCAA basketball Final Four in St. Petersburg. Taking advantage of the timing and proximity, I went down early to spend a day celebrating with Kenny on Marco Island. Over lunch at Pelican Bend, where grouper is the fish of the day *every* day, Kenny solicited my advice on whom to name as his assistant captain. We tossed out any number of names of veteran Tour players, then realized that, for one reason or another, they wouldn't work out. I suggested Paul Marchand, and Kenny replied, "He's *perfect!* That's it!"

Kenny had met Paul on numerous occasions—at the Three Amigos charity events that Paul helped run with Charlie Epps, and from Paul's many visits to our booth. Moreover, Kenny knew that as a respected instructor of Tour players and as the head golf professional at the prestigious Shadow Hawk in Houston, Paul was organized and understood the game at the highest level. Together, Kenny and I concocted a plan to surprise Paul with the news at Augusta two weeks later. I called Paul back in Houston, and I asked him to join me on my annual Wednesday-afternoon walk around the course. Casually, I mentioned that Ken Venturi said that he might also join us that day to talk about some Masters' memories.

Paul's personal history with Augusta predated his helping Fred win the Green Jacket in 1992. Paul's dad, Walter, was a Baptist minister in Franklin, Indiana, twenty miles south of Indianapolis. One day, after the Reverend Marchand had officiated at a wedding, the father of the bride handed him an envelope in appreciation for the beautiful ceremony; inside, much to the minister's surprise, was a pair of tickets to the 1971 Masters. And so began what became an annual father-son pilgrimage to Augusta.

In 1997, Paul and his dad were walking the course to follow Fred. Suddenly, Paul (but not his father) noticed a message posted on the bottom of the 9th-hole leaderboard: "Paul Marchand call home."

Paul's mother had been seriously ill, and he feared the worst. Carefully shielding his father from seeing the alarming message, Paul told his dad that he had to attend to some business and that he would rejoin him later along the second nine. When he returned the call, Paul's suspicions were confirmed— his mom had passed. Knowing this would likely be the last time they would ever experience Augusta together, Paul waited to break the devastating news to his father until the end of their walk.

Almost two years to the day after Mrs. Marchand died, Paul was making the walk with Kenny and me when we reached the famous twelfth.

"Paul, why don't you give me your video camera," I suggested. "You haven't been in any of these shots so far."

"By the way, there's one other thing that I wanted to tell you, Paul," Kenny said, picking up on my cue. "I got a call from

Commissioner Finchem a couple of weeks ago. He told me some news that he would like me to keep private for another month."

"What's that, Mr. Venturi?" Paul inquired.

"He asked me to captain the United States Presidents Cup team in 2000."

"That's *fantastic!*" Paul reacted. "What an unbelievable honor! Nobody deserves it more. I'm so happy for you."

"Well, there's more," Kenny continued, when Paul had settled down from his excitement.

"More?"

"You know, Jimmy has told me about your special memories here at Augusta with your dad, and I know they go back a long way," Kenny said, as I trained Paul's camera on my old college buddy. "So I think this would be the perfect place to create another special memory for you. Paul, there isn't anybody in the world that I'd rather have to serve as my assistant captain . . . than *you*." Paul was thunderstruck, and he doubled over in astonishment. It wasn't quite Sarazen's "shot heard 'round the world," but it may just as well have been judging from the stunned disbelief. Unlike the Squire's immortal double eagle, this magical moment *was* captured on video. And just as I would suggest on the air five years later when voicing over a replay of Phil Mickelson's winning 18-foot birdie putt, you could see Paul's life change right there in front of the lens.

·   ·   ·

In August of 2000, we were wrapping up our golf season at Akron and Kenny was a month away from captaining the U.S. team in the Presidents Cup when he dropped a surprise of his own on me.

"Jimmy," he said during a quiet moment after our final-round broadcast, "I'm going to tell you something that no one else, other than my oldest son, Matt, knows, and I'm going to trust you that this will stay that way." I assured him that he had my word. "Good, Son," he replied. "Because I've been diagnosed with prostate cancer."

He saw the concern and amazement in my face, and before I could say anything, he beat me to the punch. "Don't worry about me," he said, looking me in the eye. "I'll get through this one, too."

Here was a man who had already overcome, among other traumas, childhood stammering, a major car accident, carpal tunnel syndrome in both hands that prematurely curtailed his professional playing career, and the loss of his beloved wife, Beau.

When I caught my breath, Kenny told me that his doctors had calculated that the best treatment option for him was proton therapy. There was only one operational proton-radiation therapy machine in the country—the very one at Loma Linda that Venturi had been raising money for years to purchase and install. Kenny was determined not to let this setback get in the way of his mission to regain the Presidents Cup for the United States; he begged me to honor this confidence so that his health would not be a motivating factor or an excuse in the ultimate outcome.

Frank Chirkinian and I flew to Washington to watch Captain Venturi and former president George H. W. Bush lead the opening ceremony at the Robert Trent Jones Golf Club in nearby Virginia. For me, it was a rare reunion of three of the most influential men in my life since the onset of my dad's dementia. As it turned out, Venturi's team won by a landslide.

Now Kenny faced another, more personal challenge, and as usual, he attacked this one head-on. He flew to California and moved in with a friend in Palm Springs, where for thirty-nine straight days he drove an hour each way to Loma Linda for radiation treatment. By day three of this regimen, Kenny was feeling tired and fatigued. What's more, it was January 17—Beau's birthday. Nonetheless, a friend prevailed upon him to go out for dinner at a local Palm Springs restaurant where a gentle blonde lady with a beautiful smile caught Kenny's eye. They chatted, and she volunteered to keep him company during those lonely two hours of daily desert driving.

The proton therapy worked. What's more, during their shared commute, Kathleen and Kenny fell in love; ultimately, they married. His cancer was cured—and so, too, was his broken heart.

CHAPTER FIFTEEN

The 2007 Masters was the coldest on record. Normally, the azaleas enjoy a head start, bursting into colorful bloom about two weeks before the tournament begins. This time, though, Mother Nature never got the memo. On top of the cold snap, which had everyone bundled up, Georgia was also in the throes of a major drought. The long dry spell made the greens run quick. The weather, I knew, would clearly play a role in elevating scores—and leveling the field—at Augusta National. Earlier in my journey, the Indianapolis Colts and the Florida Gators had won their respective 2007 championships as widely expected. Here at Augusta, Tiger Woods and Phil Mickelson were atop everyone's pretournament list of favorites, but if ever there was a setup that could play into the hands of an underdog, this was it. Surprises, I suspected, lurked around almost every turn.

. . .

"Excuse me, sir," the man said politely as the elevator in our downtown Pittsburgh hotel made its way up from the lobby on a frigid Saturday in late January of 2002. "But aren't you Jim Nantz?" I nodded in acknowledgment, weary from the freezing weather and a long day rehearsing at Heinz Field in preparation for the Patriots-Steelers AFC championship game.

"Well, I just wanted to tell you that my wife and I enjoyed watching clips of you hosting *The Early Show* in Las Vegas," he said to my astonishment. "Of course, I knew you from watching golf and the NFL for so many years, but my wife had never heard of you before; but she liked you and rated you highly." I wondered, "what was this guy talking about—rated me highly"? Something strange seemed to be going on. I had filled in for the vacationing Bryant Gumbel on a few occasions the previous year, just for kicks. But since then, I'd been totally absorbed with football and *The NFL Today*.

"Would you mind if I got off the elevator with you?" I asked him. "I would really like to hear more about this." When we alighted on his floor, he told me that he and his wife had received coupons "to see some new shows" at CBS's Television City at the MGM Grand Hotel—which is really a state-of-the-art market-research facility, where they take advantage of the demographic cross-section of America that visits Vegas to test-market different programming ideas. Unbeknownst to me, someone at CBS had spliced together some of my appearances to gauge the public's reaction through a variety of research techniques, including response meters and focus groups. So much for "What happens in Vegas, stays in Vegas."

To make a long (and politically sensitive) story short, I was ultimately extended a generous offer to co-host *The Early*

Show. In the absence of my father, who was always my principal sounding board for these kinds of career matters, former president George Bush was kind enough to pinch-hit and help me think through the complex pros and cons of a midcareer jump to news. In keeping with how my dad would've handled this, 41 never told me what I should or shouldn't do. Instead, he brilliantly formulated the right questions with which I was able to frame the decision-making. Ultimately, after agonizing deliberation, I declined.

Ironically, my father was the one person who always envisioned me working in news. "You're going to be the next Walter Cronkite," he would say. I suspect, however, that it was a reflection of his own worldly curiosity, and that it was his way of trying to encourage me to broaden my interests beyond the narrow scope of the sports pages.

Years earlier, Roone Arledge had invested his considerable resources and personal charm in trying to recruit me for *Good Morning America.* At Roone's behest, I even secretly taped an audition with Elizabeth Vargas and George Stephanopoulos. Arledge was, after all, the Zeus of sports and news television, and he was accustomed to getting what he wanted. One time, when our schedules were not compatible for a lunch in New York, Arledge shocked me the next day by showing up in the seat next to mine on a cross-country flight to California, thus ensuring a captive audience for five and a half hours during which he could make his sales pitch.

I was flattered and tempted by the *GMA* offer, but back then, I also concluded that I was already blessed with the job of my dreams. Even without the certainty that CBS would regain part of the NFL package, I was still working the right mix of events that I loved—therefore, "if it ain't broke, don't fix it!" Or as my dad used to counsel me, "Don't do it for the money,

Son." In the end, saying no to Roone Arledge proved to be one of the toughest things I've ever had to do in my career.

By the time I showed up in Augusta for the 2002 Masters, I was confident that this latest flirtation with a job in early-morning news was finally behind me. But I had underestimated the power of the grapevine. And, of all people, who should approach me to raise the topic of my career path but none other than Arnold Palmer!

It wasn't as if we were enjoying a private dinner conversation: he was about to tee off for what at the time appeared to be his farewell round at the Masters. As he walked out of the clubhouse, with thousands of people jostling to see him on this historic occasion, he pointed at me, walked over, and gave me a big handshake and a hug. "I need to talk to you, Jim," he said.

"Sure, I'll find you after your round," I replied.

"No, we need to talk right now. Come with me to the putting green."

I followed Arnie and his caddie (and son-in-law) Roy Saunders through the ropes and onto the practice green. "I want to ask you something," Arnie said, while rotating three golf balls in his huge hand. "Somebody told me that you're thinking about leaving CBS Sports and all of this to go to work for CBS News. I said, 'I *know* Jimmy Nantz, and there's no way he's giving this up.' So what's the story?"

"Arnold, the bottom line is that you're right," I said. "But I already made my decision a couple of weeks ago, and I'm not going." I reassured him that I was staying right where I was.

"Well, I'm really glad to hear that," he replied. "I'm sure it was a very good offer."

"Yes, it was. But, believe it or not, the most difficult part for me was that for the first time I felt an overwhelming sense of loss in that I couldn't ask my dad what he thought I should do."

Arnold gently tapped me on the heart and said softly, "Jimmy, he's *right there*! What you must understand is that he prepared you your whole life to make this decision. You heard his voice, you just didn't realize it."

While this chat was taking place, Arnie had yet to even hit a single practice putt on this morning when the air was so thick with emotion for him. "Believe me," Palmer continued, "right now, I'm thinking about my own dad. You see, my dream was his dream—to come here to Augusta to play in the Masters. This was something we shared together, and I never thought about my life being at a point where one day I wouldn't be playing in this tournament. All through this round, I'll be thinking about my father."

.   .   .

I had met Arnold Palmer on numerous occasions, but our close friendship really developed in 1994. We were seated at the same table, as we are each year for Rolex's U.S. Open dinner. This time, Arnold was bidding farewell to the U.S. Open, which was being played at Oakmont, just outside Pittsburgh. Also at our table was my tennis broadcast partner, Vitas Gerulaitis, a legendary gentleman and total golf fanatic, and Arnie invited us to come out early the next morning to see his family home in Latrobe, only forty miles to the east.

The King didn't have to issue his royal invitation twice. The mere thought of seeing the iconic tractor that Arnie rode in those Pennzoil commercials made Vitas and me giddy with anticipation. We arrived at seven-thirty, thinking that we were

probably too early. But Palmer and his wife, Winnie, were already out walking their dog on the famous, but modest, course
that his father, Deke, had owned and operated—the Latrobe
Country Club. Arnie gave us the full tour. He took us through
the pro shop, his dad's workshop, and even the spot where his
parents are buried. All the while, he reminisced about his father, their times together, and his glorious career.

With his telegenic charisma and bold, risk-taking approach
to the game, Palmer was instrumental in making golf a main-
stream sport. In his own way, Gerulaitis helped facilitate tennis's
transition from the Stone Age to the rock era.

On the way back to the airport, Vitas claimed that he had
just enjoyed one of the greatest days of his life. It was fascinating to see how a New York City kid, who thrived in the international jet-setting clubbing crowd, could be so inspired by a
rustic shrine from an era right out of *Happy Days*. Perhaps it
was the relaxed sense of order at Latrobe and the personal
peace that the Palmers exuded that had the biggest impact on
the normally frenetic Gerulaitis.

Sadly, three months later, and just one week after we
worked the 1994 U.S. Open Tennis Championships together,
Vitas died in a tragic accident. Of all things, he had been watching our coverage of the first Presidents Cup golf competition
when he fell asleep in a guest cottage on a private estate on
Long Island. Alas, there was a carbon monoxide leak from a
faulty pool heater, and Gerulaitis never woke up.

This was not supposed to happen to a happy-go-lucky
forty-year-old champion who had the world on a string—and
had a heart that was as golden as his hair. He had conquered a
drug problem and was just making his mark in television—and
playing as much golf as humanly possible. In a final tribute to

Vitas's obsession with golf, his younger sister, Ruta, slipped his five-iron into her brother's coffin. You could make the case that Vitas was cheated out of so many days of his life, but no one ever crammed more life into every day that he lived.

. . .

If Arnold Palmer was the Johnny Unitas of golf—the popular, clean-cut man-of-the-people hero—who ushered his sport into the television era, then Tiger Woods was the game's Michael Jordan, the transcendent player/personality with global appeal. I first met Tiger in 1992, when he played in the L.A. Open and missed the cut. What struck me was that most sixteen-year-old high school golfers would have been thrilled just to experience playing with the top pros in a Tour event. But watching Tiger, it didn't appear that he was thinking that way; he had it in his mind that very week that he could *beat them*— right there and then.

After turning pro and winning a pair of tournaments at the end of the 1996 season, Tiger came to the 1997 Masters surrounded by plenty of buzz. At twenty-one years of age, Woods attacked Augusta National with a combination of power and finesse unlike any ever seen at the Masters. By the end of Saturday's third round, Tiger's nine-stroke lead made victory a foregone conclusion.

Saturday night, as always, was a heavy work night for Tommy Spencer, my one-man golf think tank, and me. We pored through every note that we'd ever cataloged about Tiger. Then we began choreographing potential themes, ideally built around stories that had never before been told. We found all kinds of things: Tommy, as only he could do, unearthed a copy of a beautifully crafted letter that Woods had written to Augusta National in 1995, thanking the club for the opportunity to play in the Masters as an amateur. We knew that we'd want to read excerpts from it on the air the next day.

We also looked at the sociological importance of the first player of African-American or Asian descent to win the Masters, noting that Tiger's presumed win coincided with the national commemoration of the fiftieth anniversary of Jackie Robinson's breaking baseball's color barrier. Then there was Tiger's link to Jack Nicklaus. While growing up in Cypress, California, Tiger had taped a list of all of Nicklaus's records just above his bedpost, so that he could dream about them at night and wake up motivated to challenge them.

It's impossible to know, on the night before the last round, just how the final sequence will unfold. But we did know that however Tiger closed out the tournament, the clip of his final putt had the potential to be the defining sports moment of our lifetimes, a highlight that might be played twenty, fifty, perhaps even a hundred years from now. And we knew it was imperative to have the appropriate narration to accompany that clip.

As we pondered the nature of Woods's imminent achievement, I was flooded with memories from my youth, when I would painstakingly tape-record every major golf telecast. I could almost hear immortality being conferred upon the great champions Arnold Palmer and Jack Nicklaus by the legendary voices of McKay, Schenkel, Whitaker, and Summerall. This time, *they* would be the ones watching and listening as I took my turn chronicling a new chapter in golf history.

I felt them looking over my shoulder as we brainstormed and tossed out options. The many aspects to Tiger's impending triumph made it somewhat akin to writing a haiku. A barrage of statistics would only trivialize the moment. The pictures would do most of the talking; what we needed was a short, evocative, and memorable summation. Finally, we hit upon "a win for the ages."

Meantime, Lance Barrow, producing his first Masters after working with Frank Chirkinian for twenty-three years, was formulating his own final-round game plan, and for this one time only, it represented a radical departure from the traditional CBS Chirkinian system of quickly cutting from action to action that Barrow still follows to this day. Instead, we were going to follow Tiger on camera as much as possible. As a practical matter, Lance reasoned, Tiger wouldn't really be competing with any of the other golfers on the course. Woods was challenging all of Augusta National's glorious history.

Woods himself also spent that Saturday night preparing, trying to script out in his mind every shot that he wanted to make the next afternoon. Sometimes, a golfer with Woods's unique skills and mental discipline can pretty much follow the script, and Sunday, April 13, 1997, was one of those times. Everyone had goose bumps when Tiger knocked in his final four-foot putt for par and a record 270 for the tournament. Lance also executed his plan. Richard Sandomir of *The New York Times* reported that Tiger was on the air for 55 percent of the actual golf coverage that day. The result was one of the highest-rated rounds of golf in Nielsen history—culminating with a video clip . . . for the ages.

. . .

By the summer of 1999, two years after his landmark Masters win, Tiger went on a tear of sustained brilliance that brought him eight victories that year, including his second major. That triumph came at the PGA Championship, which was staged that August at Medinah Country Club, just west of Chicago. There, he created my favorite Tiger memory.

Following his second round on Friday, I caught up with Tiger as he was signing his card outside the scorer's tent. I asked him if he would mind coming up to our studio behind 18 to tape an interview for our late-night highlights show. He graciously consented. "Oh, by the way," I said, as he followed me up the steps. "My little girl, Caroline, is in there. She's five years old, and she's really excited to meet you."

When I opened the door, as expected, everyone was in place and ready—CBS was not going to make Tiger wait around. Neal McCaffrey was manning the camera; Kevin McHale, the audio expert, had the microphones in his hands all ready to go. My wife, Lorrie, and her friend, Sarah Blumenstein, were seated in the far corner. I scanned the room, but couldn't see my daughter, so I motioned for Tiger to sit down; I, too, did not want to take too much of his time. "Just give me one second here," Tiger said. "I need to say hello to someone first."

"Where's Caroline?" I whispered to Lorrie. She pointed across the room, where Caroline was all curled up hiding beneath a chair. She was timid, as all children are at that age, about meeting someone for the first time. "Oh, Caroline, where are you?" Tiger called out, adopting the pitch and cadence that kids use when they play hide-and-seek. "Caroline, come on out so we can play."

He walked around the set theatrically. "My goodness, is she . . . *over here*? . . . *No!* . . . Let me check *over here*. . . . Still no Caroline over here." Then Tiger got down on all fours and crawled over to look under the chair where, as he had known all along, she was hiding.

"*There* you are! Peekaboo, I see you! My name is Tiger.

Why don't you come out, Caroline, and say hello?" This gentle moment revealed a wonderfully human side of Tiger that rarely breaks through his tournament game face or his carefully crafted corporate persona.

. . .

Woods continued his dominance into 2000, winning the AT&T at Pebble Beach in February, then returning four months later to win the U.S. Open there by a remarkable fifteen shots. Now all eyes pointed to the British Open, where Tiger had a chance to become only the fifth golfer to win a career grand slam, joining Gene Sarazen, Ben Hogan, Gary Player, and Jack Nicklaus.

The 2000 British Open was being staged at the Old Course at St. Andrews, Scotland, where golf was born six hundred years ago. Even though it was ABC's tournament to broadcast, and not CBS's, I had already planned to attend once I learned that it would mark Jim McKay's final appearance on a golf telecast. But now, there was even more significance.

On Saturday night in St. Andrews, I caught up with Tommy Spencer and some golf writers at a local pub. On a whim, we decided to make a midnight excursion to the old cemetery on the north side of town. There, we located the grave sites of Old Tom Morris and his son, Young Tom Morris, two of the founding fathers of golf in nineteenth-century Scotland. As lovers of golf history, we paid our respects by the light of the moon in the wee hours.

The next morning, I arrived at the venerable Rusack's Hotel on the right side of the 18th fairway, and called up to McKay's room. As I walked down the narrow hallway, I felt as if I were about to be granted an audience with Pavarotti backstage before his final concert. I was taken aback by how dark and small McKay's room was, certainly not much more than ten by twelve feet. He had a little twin bed in the corner with a tiny nightstand and a reading lamp. On the windowsill was a bottle of red wine that was uncorked but looked hardly touched. A small desk was loaded with reading material. In the euphemism of today's sports marketing, we'd call it a "throwback" room.

Seeing the patron saint of sports commentators sitting on the corner of the bed, all dressed for work and looking over his notes, I thought to myself that this must have been typical of the kind of spartan conditions he'd faced early in his career, when he traveled extensively behind the Iron Curtain or to third-world countries to bring his wide world of sports into the comfortable New Jersey den of my youth. My dad, who was always curious about other countries and cultures, used to sit next to me riveted by McKay's descriptions of these exotic locales.

Now just two months shy of his seventy-ninth birthday, McKay's mind was brilliantly sharp about every last detail as we chatted about his career, about golf, and about Tiger's place in history. He was bursting with pride as he spoke about the accomplishments of his children, Mary and Sean, and his grandchildren at the time, James and Maggie. What made the biggest impression on me, though, was how totally focused he was on simply getting home to be back with his wife, Margaret. He missed her so much, it was just palpable.

Here was my professional idol and role model all suited up, but he no longer had any appetite for the life of the lonely road warrior. While I still get excited about traveling and the opportunity to visit favorite restaurants, look up old friends, and see new sights, it struck me that the man whose adventurous life I dreamed of emulating was providing me with my first glimpse of a future that I had never envisioned before. This was a look at what may happen *after* I live out my dream.

We walked outside and I rode with him on a golf cart over to the ABC Sports compound. I wished him well and safe travels, then McKay headed into the trailer for a production meeting. I was left to speculate about how he would regale the audience back in the States one last time.

Now I had the chance to play spectator on a busman's holiday. I wasted little time hustling over to the links. I longed to walk the entire eighteen holes and immerse myself in their history and magic. Ultimately, I located Fred Couples, whom I followed around until Tiger took the stage at 18 with an eight-stroke lead. I stood at the elbow of the 17th fairway looking all the way down the final hole at the huge throng as Woods claimed the Open championship trophy, the Claret Jug, and his first career grand slam.

. . .

I've known of Mark O'Meara since our college days, when he was an All-America at Long Beach State. O'Meara is one of Tiger's best friends. But even he isn't 100 percent exempt from the Game Face, as I witnessed first-hand one year at Jack Nicklaus's tournament, the Memorial. Mark was in the locker room after warming up for Saturday's round, and we got to chatting about a course that he had designed out in Utah, when Tiger walked up to us. "Hey, Mark, how're you doing?" Woods said, completely oblivious of me. "It must be hot out there—look at your shirt! What did you shoot?" It was an especially muggy day, and O'Meara had come in to change clothes after his warm-up. "Well actually, Tiger, I was just out there getting loose," he replied. "You know, I'm one behind you, so I haven't teed off yet."

"Oh, okay," Tiger said, waltzing off. "Way to go, Mark." Although he'd made the effort to make small talk with his buddy, Tiger oddly, seemed to have no idea that his closest pal on the Tour was in contention with him for the tournament lead.

"That was kind of weird," Mark said to me. "Plus, Tiger didn't even say hello to you. Have you guys got some issues?"

"No, not at all," I said. "I'm six foot three, but I guess I've become a little invisible these days."

A few minutes later, as I related this peculiar incident to Lance Barrow and Jack Nicklaus over lunch in the clubhouse, Jack roared with laughter. He, too, had experienced Tiger blowing right past him, so deep in concentration that Woods didn't even acknowledge the tournament host—and the man who holds all the records that he's chasing. "So what are you going to do about this, Jimmy?" Nicklaus challenged me in between hysterics.

"I'll tell you what I'm going to do," I thundered with all the mock indignation I could muster. (In my peripheral vision, I could see Lance rolling his eyes, as if to say, "Oh, Lord, please don't let Nantz start World War III with Tiger on our air!") "If he won't recognize me, then I won't recognize him. I will not mention his name once today, that's all."

Jack was incredulous. "That's *impossible*! We've got him for eighteen holes, and he'll probably be near the top of the leaderboard all day. How can you *not* mention his name?"

"Just watch me!" was my final word on the subject, as Jack continued shaking his head in disbelief. My first order of business was to race back to the compound and re-record the opening tease. Although it was the same video montage about Woods, this time I took pains never to say *Tiger* or *Woods* in my narration. Instead, it was all generic: "He comes here to Muir-field Village ranked number one in the world.... He's the three-time champion here at the Memorial."

Then for four hours I continued my private protest, all in jest, although with each passing hole, it became increasingly difficult to work around the two self-forbidden words. During commercial breaks, the guys in the truck and my colleagues around the course would be laughing and egging me on. Finally, Lance had his associate directors, Jim Rikhoff and Sellers Shy, put together a one-minute package of close-ups and slow-motion replays of Tiger's day at the Memorial with which we would go off the air. In short, they tried everything to trip me up, but I was resolute in my determination to take the "I" out of the Tiger.

After the show, I mentioned this to Fred Couples at dinner. He got such a kick out of it that he said that he nearly wet his pants. Of course, what I didn't expect was that the next day Fred would run off and tell Tiger about this on the practice tee. Happily, Tiger seems to have understood that this was done in the spirit of good fun, and he has never brought it up with me once. But then again, most of the time when I see him, I can never tell what's going on behind his famous game face.

. . .

Tiger's continued success demonstrates that supreme focus and mental discipline are extremely beneficial when it comes to winning majors. But in an unscientific survey, I've found another, much easier, method that will enhance a player's chances of earning that coveted Green Jacket: just serve as my runner at the NCAA Final Four.

This admittedly offbeat strategy worked for Fred Couples

in 1992. When I mentioned it during an interview on *Charlie Rose*, the host, a graduate of Duke and its law school, immediately put me on the spot and asked if he could be a runner at the '93 Final Four in New Orleans.

During a commercial break in the first national semifinal game, between North Carolina and Kansas, producer Bob Dekas told me something bizarre in my headset: "Jim, we're getting word from security that Nick Faldo and two others are at the press entrance demanding to know where their tickets are that you were supposed to have left for them?"

"*Nick Faldo? . . .* This sounds like a scam." I replied, incredulous. "Why would I leave tickets for him? Hey, just in case, do me a favor. Can somebody go out there and see if it's really him—and if so, let's try to get him in." I knew Faldo, but only as an acquaintance, not really as a friend or dinner companion. Suddenly, the three-time British Open and two-time Masters champion materialized at midcourt just as we threw it to Pat O'Brien for the halftime show.

"I've been watching this big event since I've been over here in the States playing for a few weeks; it's quite fascinating, you know," he explained sheepishly. "You're the only person I knew who had anything to do with this event. I was hoping that you could get me in." I told him that it would have been helpful if he had given me a little advance notice, explaining that outside of the Masters, the Final Four may be the toughest ticket in American sports. Duly chastised, Faldo asked if there was anything he could do now that he was here.

"Nick, say hello to my partner, Billy Packer," I said. "By the way, are you as hungry as I am, Billy?"

Packer, who loves this kind of stuff, jumped right in. "I can't believe you read my mind, Jimmy. I really could use something to snack on. Nick, you wouldn't mind fetching us a couple of ice cream bars, frozen fruit bars, or something, would you?"

I reached into my pocket to hand Faldo a couple of bucks. "No, no, no!" he protested. "It's on me, and I'll do it with great delight—anything you want." I replied that what I wanted was for him to hurry back because we were going on the air again in just a couple of minutes. I don't know how many people were in the line that he cut in front of, but I saw him scurry down the steps and jump back over the railing to press row— all the while delicately balancing two ice cream cones, which Billy and I rather enjoyed.

"By the way, Nick," I said, as we sat down at our positions, "don't be surprised one day, when you're on the sixteenth hole of the final round at the British Open, and the marshal stops you just before you hit your tee shot and says, 'Some guy named Jim Nantz is over by the front entrance, and he insists that you were supposed to leave him a couple of passes.' Am I correct in assuming that I won't have any problem getting in?" Faldo chortled and headed for the stands. As he left, Charlie Rose wandered up to inquire whether Billy or I needed any- thing else. Yes, I thought silently to myself, we need to stop hiring celebrity gofers.

. . .

I had been dreading the day for years, but on June 2, 2002, Ken Venturi stepped down after thirty-five years at CBS Sports, first with Jack Whitaker, Vin Scully, and Pat Summerall, then with me, ending the longest tenure of any lead analyst in tele- vision sports history. We chose the Kemper Open for the fare- well broadcast, because the TPC at Avenel was, as Kenny put it, "a par-5 away" from the Congressional Country Club, where he had won the 1964 U.S. Open. It was also close to Robert Trent Jones Golf Club in Virginia, where he'd captained the U.S. Presidents Cup team to victory.

"I don't care if you have to call Nancy, Frankie, Tina, or Barbara Sinatra," I told Chris Svendsen, one of our golf producers at CBS. "But we've got to get the rights to use 'My Way,' and if you tell them it's for Ken Venturi, they'll make it happen." Chris was putting together the special tribute to Kenny that we would go off the air with and to my mind, only one song, by only one singer—his former best friend—would do the piece justice.

On this moving afternoon, one by one, each golfer finished the final hole, then looked up to the tower. They waved, saluted, tipped their caps—or in the case of Greg Norman, tossed the ball right out of the cup to Kenny. Here was the man whom they, like me, grew up listening to as a friend from afar. And for those privileged to play on the Tour or work at CBS Sports, Kenny became so much more than that.

As I led into the "My Way" tribute and reflected on our seventeen-year partnership, I told Kenny that I would think of him every time I sat in the 18th tower. With that, we rolled the video, which Kenny was seeing for the first time. And when the song ended, he looked into the camera for one last good-bye.

"The greatest reward in life is to be remembered," he said, choking back the tears. "Thank you for remembering me. May God bless you, and may God bless America." Kenny turned, put his arms around me, and wept on my shoulder as I hugged him back. They stayed on that shot for a couple of seconds, then dipped to black, ending a television run that began with the Palmer-Nicklaus rivalry and carried over to the current Woods-Mickelson generation.

.   .   .

Lanny Wadkins, the 1977 PGA Championship winner, was named to succeed Kenny, and to his credit he read the situation well. He knew that he was replacing a legend for whom there was considerable affection. He never tried to "compete" with Venturi; instead, he went out of his way to praise him. "I loved the way Kenny would say thus-and-such," he would tell the audience.

Professional golfers are "independent contractors" who engage in a solitary pursuit. Other than for the Ryder Cup matches, where he played brilliantly, this was the first time in his professional career that Lanny really got to enjoy being part of a team—and he was a wonderful teammate. But, truth be told, at one period during his playing days I would never have envisioned Wadkins fitting in so well with us at CBS.

Back in the early 1990s, we were at the Greater Greensboro Open, and I was in the tower on the 15th hole. All of a sudden, I felt the whole rickety structure rocking violently back and forth as if we were having an earthquake. I looked over my shoulder and saw Lanny climbing into our booth. He was steaming mad as he motioned for me to take off my headset. Apparently, one of our cameramen had mistakenly moved during Wadkins's backswing, and the disruption caused him to mis-hit the shot.

"You tell Frank Chirkinian," he ranted, "that the next time his camera guy doesn't get behind me in time, he's going to find a sand wedge up his [expletive]." Lanny might not have been the most polished orator at that moment, but even then, you could tell that he could communicate forthrightly.

.   .   .

Beginning in 2006, I produced a one-hour retrospective that would air immediately preceding our Sunday coverage of the Masters on CBS. The first topic was a natural, as this was the twentieth anniversary of Jack Nicklaus's sixth Green Jacket—and my Masters debut.

I went down to Florida to interview Jack for the program. After going through the 1986 highlights and talking about his other five Masters titles, we talked at length about his farewell round at Augusta, which had taken place only a year earlier in 2005.

"What did you say to your son, Jackie, when you walked off the last green?" I asked Nicklaus. Jack got all choked up and shook his head to signify that we couldn't go there. Then he composed himself. "I'm all right, Jimmy. Go ahead and ask me again," he urged me, and I did.

Once again he tried to get through the answer, but couldn't. Meanwhile, I was taken aback by his rare display of emotion and by his determination to reveal a very private moment that he had never shared with his public before. "I really want to say this," he told me. "I've never told this story before, but it's important. So let's do it again."

On the third attempt, he managed to tell the story of how his father, Charlie, a Columbus, Ohio, pharmacist who introduced Jack to golf, was being wheeled into the operating room for emergency surgery. Charlie Nicklaus looked up at Jack from the gurney and said, "Don't think it ain't been charming."

"So is that what *you* said to Jackie—your *father's* final words—as you walked off Augusta National for the last time?" I asked.

Jack nodded. "Don't think it ain't been charming."

From that moment on, whenever I see Jack, or one of his

and Barbara's children, I always think of that farewell line that links three generations of one great family.

. . .

After the Nicklaus retrospective aired on Masters Sunday 2006, Phil Mickelson went out and won for the second time at Augusta. Phil and Tiger were now exchanging Green Jackets just like Nicklaus and Palmer used to do back in the 1960s. And I was reminded of Jack's comment that rivals bring out the best in one another. Mickelson has often said that there isn't a golfer on the Tour who doesn't appreciate what Tiger has done for the game, especially when it comes to television ratings and prize money.

Without Arnold Palmer to pave the way, Tiger Woods would not have reached the popularity that he enjoys today. Yet, none of today's players had ever seen the King in his heyday. So the day after the 2006 Masters, I called Chris Svendsen, whom I consider the Tiger Woods of special video projects. "I've got an idea," I said, bubbling with enthusiasm and already wanting to get started planning the following year's special. "Great!" he said (which I knew was his polite way of saying "Uh-oh!")

"Remember how we talked about doing something with Arnie for 2007? Well, what if we took the 1960 Masters telecast—and *colorized* it?"

Chris immediately threw himself into researching the feasibility of such a project. Back in 1960, there were no videotape machines, so the only way to capture a live broadcast was to make a kinescope by locking down a film camera in front of a television screen and *filming* the TV show as it aired. Svendsen went into the CBS storage vault in New Jersey and somehow located the decaying old kinescope of the 1960 Masters. He found it in barely salvageable condition, with the film almost deteriorated beyond repair, and what a pity it would have been to have lost such a precious historical record. Then, Sven located a West Coast–based company called Legend Films, which had just colorized *It's a Wonderful Life* and the entire *I Love Lucy* series.

Now it was up to me to convince the Augusta National that we would not turn the Masters footage into a hokey cartoon, which was a legitimate concern given the results of earlier generations of colorization technology. But this was cutting-edge, computerized, frame-by-frame image enhancement that employed teams in San Diego and India around the clock. The process took more than *ten thousand man-hours* of labor to complete—and I know, because the invoices were addressed to my office!

When Arnie found out what we were doing, he was ecstatic that he would get to "play" again on Masters Sunday. He had never seen the CBS broadcast; in fact, no one had, not even Frank Chirkinian, who produced it. That's because, back in 1960, there was no mechanism to record or to play back the programs, other than these cumbersome kinescopes.

When you watched the start of the 1960 broadcast, you saw Kenny Venturi tap in from a foot out to par the last hole, and you could see him freeze for a moment as if to tell himself, "I just won the Masters." But then, Arnold Palmer came along and birdied 17 and 18 to clip Kenny by a stroke. It was especially poignant watching the footage of Bobby Jones conducting the interviews, first with Kenny and then with Arnold. Palmer accepted congratulations from the Augusta National founder, but added that he was only sorry that by winning he had to take the tournament away from Kenny. This truly genuine moment may have been lost on both men, since they had never seen the CBS broadcast. This interchange between Palmer and Venturi was particularly moving as it came just two years after the 1958 contretemps on the twelfth hole at Augusta.

· · ·

"Mr. McKay, *happy Easter!*" I said cheerfully into the phone on Masters Sunday 2007.

"Jim, you're so great to call," came the warm reply in the familiar, if somewhat weaker, voice.

"You're about to go on the air here on CBS in forty-five minutes, sir. You remember that show I told you about several months ago, the colorized rebroadcast of the original 1960 Masters? Well, Mr. McKay, the nation is once again waiting to hear your voice, since you were the anchor back then. As you know, it's been almost a half-century!"

It meant the world to me to be able to "put Jim McKay on the air" again. Just as I hoped that the current generation of golfers and fans would finally see what Arnie and Kenny were all about in their prime, I also hoped hearing Jim McKay once more in all his glory might touch others, just as his words and delivery had once inspired me.

The taped program aired on the network as we finished our production meeting in Lance's office. Nick Faldo, who was my new broadcast partner, and I headed over to Butler Cabin to rehearse and open the day's live Masters coverage show. Many observers have suggested that in recent years Faldo has worked as hard on revamping his personality as he once did on his swing. Be that as it may, the once dour Englishman has become the life of the party. I personally don't believe that Nick has undergone such a radical transition, because on each of the three occasions that I saw him in Butler Cabin to claim his Green Jacket, I detected a fire and passion in his eyes. He was emotional about winning at Augusta.

As we went on the air, a handful of players, including Tiger Woods, remained in serious contention, and Nick opined that this might be that rare day when Tiger slipped up and allowed someone else to sneak through and capture the tournament. After the opening, we went up to the tower at 18, but after a few minutes in the biting cold and wind, I said, "This is nuts, Nick. I'm going back in. Do you want to come with me?" But Nick wanted to stick it out in "the commentary box," as the British say, so I called the action from a monitor in Butler Cabin, and we handled it the way Chet Huntley and David Brinkley used to do, always ending our comments with the other man's name as a cue.

Normally, the Tiger factor would intimidate the rest of the contenders. But although he briefly grabbed the lead, Woods could not hang on to it. Meantime, from out of nowhere, Zach Johnson, a salt-of-the-earth kid from Cedar Rapids, Iowa, slipped into the lead by playing solid, methodical golf. Not only was Zach resolute in sticking to his strategy of hitting fairways and greens, but he played without an ounce of anxiety. Normally, you can tell if a player is nervous by his hands; but Johnson feathered some of the softest chip shots you'd ever want to see, particularly at the 72nd hole, where his deft touch from off the green saved par.

At the end of his round, we saw Zach go over to kiss his wife, Kim, and their fourteen-week-old son, Will. At that moment I understood why Johnson was unfazed by having Tiger behind him. Next to the blessed experience of becoming a new father, everything else pales by comparison—even the chance to win a Green Jacket.

Zach Johnson wasn't the marquee star, the Peyton Manning of the Masters. He was the Dan Klecko. They're the guys you never really get a chance to root for, but when their turn comes around and they do win, they radiate a glow that emanates from within rather than from the preprogrammed reactions of those accustomed to being in the spotlight. It's such an honest joy that you can't help but feel happy for them. Good people with good stories—my dad would have loved it. To him, *that* was what sports, and sportsmanship, were all about.

Walking back from Butler Cabin through the nippy chill as dusk descended upon Augusta, I felt richly fulfilled by the events of the day. In a sense, my television special had given new life to McKay, Palmer, and Venturi, while assuring that future generations, including Will Johnson's, would be able to witness them in their greatness. And no matter what else Will's dad, Zach, achieves in his golf career, he will always be able to say that he has a Green Jacket, just like Arnie and Tiger.

. . .

Where *did* the sixty-three days go? It seems now as if they have all vanished into a blur. Wasn't it just yesterday when I was in Miami with Devin Hester set to receive the opening kickoff of the Super Bowl? That night, the 2007 Masters seemed far beyond the horizon. The "journey," as we called it, turned out to be as intriguing as advertised. But the best moments along the way didn't always involve the players we expected to star, nor did the most touching events happen in the three major championship destinations.

One of the truly special occasions during this unique nine-week stretch was February 13, 2007—only nine days after the Colts defeated the Bears—when *Jim Nantz Remembers Augusta: The 1960 Masters* held its premiere before an overflow crowd at the Bel-Air Country Club in Los Angeles. Arnold Palmer flew in for the occasion, and much to my delight Ken Venturi accepted my invitation to come over from Palm Springs, as well. Kenny had suffered a serious heart attack two months earlier and this was his first public appearance since recuperating from quintuple bypass surgery.

Almost immediately as the restored video jumped to life on the giant screens, the room fell into a deep hush. For the entire hour, you could feel the audience riveted: No one talked, no one moved, no one sneezed. When the show ended and the lights came back on, I stepped to the microphone and said, "And now, here is your 1960 Masters champion, Arnold Palmer." The Bel-Air room erupted into a huge ovation, as if they had just seen the King win his Green Jacket *live*.

Then I introduced Kenny, who had no idea how prominent a role he had played in that CBS broadcast. And like Arnold, he could not get over how he was magically young, vibrant, and truly at the top of his game—in living color. Frankly, I was holding my breath, not only about Kenny's physical stamina, but also about how he would react given his reluctance to let go of the 1958 ruling incident with Palmer. Kenny came up and gave me a big hug. He turned to Arnold and clenched his fists for a moment—the way Muhammad Ali used to playfully tease Howard Cosell—then, with a big smile on his face, he reached out both arms, inviting Arnie to embrace him—which he did.

"Jimmy," Kenny said. "I just can't believe that I'm here and that I just watched the 1960 Masters. You have no idea how special this night is for all of us. But there's one thing that I'd like to say above all: Those kids who are out there today, the Tigers and the Phils—and I'm their biggest fan—but I hope they know that they owe everything to *one man*." With that, Kenny pointed to Palmer and walked over to hug him yet again, as the crowd leapt to its feet in applause.

We'll never know whether Kenny's brush with mortality changed his perspective. Maybe the surgeons magically mended his heart figuratively as well as literally. Or perhaps, he just woke up in his hospital room and realized that life is too short to carry around grudges. In any event, the next morning at a special screening for the press, Arnie confided to me, "You have no idea how much it meant hearing what Kenny said last night."

When I witnessed this long-overdue reconciliation of these two great men who have meant so much to me in my life, I knew that this project had been worth all the hard work, expense, and aggravation that went into it. What I had undertaken as a labor of love for the game itself ended up taking on a far deeper and infinitely more satisfying meaning.

While my dad would have loved seeing me call the Super Bowl, the Final Four, and the Masters, he would not have hesitated to trade them all in for this one night in Los Angeles. Above all, my father was a peacemaker: He would compromise, he would cajole, he would do anything within his power to heal relationships. Throughout the process, and all evening long, I felt Dad's presence. In his eyes, this would have been his son's greatest accomplishment in a year unlike any other.

EPILOGUE

Saturday, October 27, 2007

We had just finished our meetings with the Carolina Panthers, who would be hosting Peyton Manning and the defending Super Bowl champion Indianapolis Colts the next day in Charlotte. I got into my rental car and headed west to "the country." At this time of year autumn begins to take hold in the Piedmont. The last vestiges of the previous night's heavy rainstorm were moving out, and peeks of the famous Carolina blue skies were starting to pop through the remaining overcast. The stiff breezes that were moving the storm clouds were also shaking the multicolored leaves from their treetop summer homes.

Within half an hour, I was in Mt. Holly, where I made my way to the small town cemetery. I walked over to the prominent granite headstone bearing the family name: NANTZ. Beneath it are buried my great-grandfather Mark, and his wife, Maude Nantz. To the right of them lies my great-uncle, who was a boy of but eleven when he died back in 1913. Over on the far side of this multigenerational family burial plot, a towering fifty-foot juniper tree appears to stand as an honor guard above my grandparents' resting spot. Right beside James Sr. and Velma is the lone remaining vacant grave. *This* was the real estate that I came to inspect.

Between the conclusion of the 2007 Masters and the start of another NFL season, my father had suffered a number of medical setbacks, including a bout with pneumonia that necessitated a brief hospitalization. Fortunately, years back, we found an angel from heaven in the person of Laverne Moran, who cares for Dad with enormous compassion. Already this October, I've flown to Houston four times to see him. I would sit in his room for a few hours, and since conversation was futile, I would squeeze his hand, cradle his head, and periodically kiss him on the forehead. Regardless of what I tried, he did not respond. Only thirteen years ago, he was widely sought out for his wit and wisdom, and I was at the head of that line. Today, words literally fail him.

What truly breaks my heart is that Caroline never had the joy of knowing my father when he was physically robust, mentally sharp, and the life of the party. She sees him only on periodic family visits to Houston. Nonetheless, she walks right into his room and says, "Hey, Granddaddy! How are you doing today?" She slows down her words and raises the pitch of her voice, as if she were talking tenderly to an infant. Lorrie and I burst with pride at how Caroline showers Dad with the same unconditional love that he lavished upon his own children. Yet he cannot reply to his granddaughter's kindness. His once-powerful arms and torso that so easily dispensed hugs must now be raised by special mechanical power lifts. The once-twinkling eyes that radiated affection are more often shut than open.

No, I realized after painful sessions alone by his side, this was *not* my beloved father. This was a tortured shell of a human, a nearly emptied vessel. Defying all logic and whatever little that modern neuroscience really knew about this horrible disease, I found myself hoping against hope that perhaps a few viable neurons still remained with which to fire up a final synapse or two—any kind of mental flash that might indicate to him on some level that his family is okay and loves him through it all. At other moments, the hopelessness becomes so overwhelming that I just want to blurt out words I never thought I could ever bring myself to say: "It's okay, Dad.... You don't have to worry about us any longer; we'll be fine.... You put up an incredible fight.... *But now, if it's time to go, Dad ... it's okay.*"

The doctors had suggested that we should be prepared to activate some contingency plans. That spurred another round of discussions among my mother, my sister Nancy, and me about what Dad would really want. Knowing how patriotic he was, and the pride that he took in his army service, we had plans for interring him in the nearby National Cemetery. Yet Nancy had insisted for years that, as much as Dad loved Houston, he always longed to return to his native North Carolina.

. . .

Following a morning-long scrimmage with the clouds, the sun finally claimed victory, but the wind continued to rustle the leaves. Across the street, I saw the building where my father and his twenty-seven classmates attended high school back in 1944. Just beyond it was their grammar school, with the flagpole out front, just like the one that my dad and my uncles Mark and Kenny, and their cousin Henry Kale, used to climb. Seeing it conjured up many memories of my own youth and all the old stories my father and his siblings would regale us with at the Sunday family get-togethers after church.

Leaning against the juniper tree, I tried to take it all in— and to focus on my fundamental question: Did this *feel* like the right final resting place for Dad?

The cemetery and the school are perched upon a gently sloping hill. At the base, some five hundred yards off in the distance, is the football field where my father once played. A game was in progress, and when the wind abated, I could hear the muffled sounds of the PA announcer, the music, and the cheers wafting up the hillside, luring me down there. As often as I've visited Mt. Holly, I never had occasion to walk that football field before. Working my way toward the main entrance, I felt the energy pulsing through the crisp fall air. It was a perfect football Saturday. The whole setting was idyllic, as though it had been lifted right out of a movie.

I bought a $3 ticket and began to walk a lap around the field, just as I try to do in my pregame routine on Sundays during the NFL season when I seek out those extra details that may help express a larger story. In this case, it might be the legend above the scoreboard that proclaims MT. HOLLY—THE LITTLE CITY WITH THE BIG HEART. Continuing around the perimeter, from the far side of the field I could look up and see the cemetery on top of the plateau, with the regal juniper tree jutting out above the field of tombstones. My dad used to say that before you consider a solution, try to visualize it from every possible angle. Looking around, I saw the players and cheerleaders with MT. HOLLY emblazoned across their jackets. Which of these kids, I wondered, would use sports as a springboard to a college education, a career, and a chance to explore the mysteries and riches of the wider world? That's what my father did, and his journey got its modest start right here on this timeworn but hardy patch of grass and dirt.

Returning to the cemetery, I sat at the base of the juniper and called Houston. "Mom," I said softly into the cell phone. "I just wanted you to know that Nancy was right, this is *exactly* where Dad would want to be. When it's time, we're going to bring him home to Mt. Holly." I could hear the relief in her voice. She herself had grown up down the road in Charlotte, and she understood as well as anyone the magical allure that the Tar Heel State could exert on her sons and daughters. What's more, we now had a plan in place. That fact, alone, removed a huge weight from her shoulders. I could tell just sitting here that she was at peace; as a result, so was I.

In one panoramic sweep, I could take in most of the formative sites of my father's youth. I could hear the sounds that made him happy, from the cheering of the fans to the spirited football fight songs. All was in perfect readiness to welcome back a long-lost favorite son. It all felt *so right.* And we all knew that it wouldn't be long before Dad would be coming home.

Afterword

As the clock approached midnight on Saturday night, June 28, 2008, Dad passed away in Houston, and finally "came home" to Mount Holly four days later. Wednesday, July 2, was as perfect a Carolina summer day as you could imagine. It was warm, but not oppressive, with bright blue skies as far as the eye could see. As the funeral procession turned off of I-85 South, we saw the locals pulled over to the dirt shoulder on the side of the road to pay their last respects; some got out of their cars and pickup trucks and were saluting. The windows of the Main Street shops glistened in the morning sun. The playing fields of the local parks were green and inviting. This was still Small Town America, and we were returning one of its own back to his roots.

With a military bugler's fanfare, two soldiers folded the American flag on Dad's casket and presented it to Mom with the "thanks of a grateful nation." Each member of the immediate family had a single long-stem rose to place upon the gleaming coffin of a man whose brilliant full bloom was prematurely withered by the early frost of Alzheimer's disease. Dr. William Jeffries, the senior associate pastor of the Providence United Methodist Church in Charlotte, officiated at the graveside funeral beneath an open-air tent that shielded family and close friends from the midday sun. Dr. Jeffries read passages from the Old Testament and the New Testament. Then he called upon me to read aloud passages from the epilogue, just a few pages earlier. Standing beneath that same large juniper tree, I recalled my vision from eight months earlier. And as I described the field of my father's boyhood dreams, the mourners craned their heads to the left in unison, and there it was at the base of the promontory. This was truly a case of life imitating art. The moment was at once magnificently perfect, breathtakingly beautiful, and oddly surreal.

From there, it was back to Charlotte, where an even larger crowd awaited us in the very church where I had been baptized some forty-nine years earlier. I was stunned and deeply touched by how many CBS Sports colleagues, business acquaintances, and friends of the family made the effort to be with us on the visitations Monday night in Houston, Tuesday night in Charlotte, and here at the memorial service. It was a solemn occasion, but much as had been the case only three weeks earlier at Jim McKay's funeral in Baltimore, I wanted this to be a *celebration* of a man we loved and of a life well lived.

At McKay's memorial service, I was honored to have been asked by his son, Sean McManus, to serve as a pallbearer and to deliver one of the tributes. It was one of the very few times in my life that I found myself unable to trust my ability to stand up and tell a story extemporaneously. Once again, I was intimidated by the sweetest, kindest, most gentle—and least intimidating—of men. Instead, I read about my last visit with him at St. Andrew's from the manuscript of Chapter 15. While it came off fine, it felt very unnatural to me. I made a mental note that I would not read from a written script if and when the time came for my father's funeral. Rather, I would trust my instincts, speak from the heart, and just "let it rip."

Dr. Jeffries began with some readings and remarks. Then, Dad's two grandchildren, my Caroline and Nancy's Holton, jointly read the 23rd Psalm. On behalf of the family, my father's brother, Uncle Mark Nantz, and my first cousin Brad Wells (whose father, my uncle Bob, was married to my mom's sister Barbara), delivered heart-felt eulogies. Lance Barrow and Billy Packer, representing my CBS family, also offered moving tributes. Finally, I tried to share with the congregation a sense of Dad's last days. As noted previously, some of my fondest memories are of those times that we had spent together as father and son on the golf course. I had really thought that we'd lose Dad on that Friday night before, which was June 27. So as I sat in his room at the hospice in Houston, I clutched his once powerful hand in mine and we "played" one more round at Pebble Beach. We played every hole of that scenic layout, and I described each shot from every replay angle that we had at CBS. It may have been my all-time-best running golf commentary—and it was commercial-free. With his favorite jokes and good-natured gamesmanship between each of our shots—along with a few periodic pauses to admire the natural splendor of the setting—it took us four hours to virtually walk the entire Pebble Beach course. Dad enjoyed the best round of his life. I had him down on the scorecard for eighteen pars. *He shot 72 at Pebble!* Somehow I felt that if I could prolong our round together, then maybe I could sustain him until daylight on Saturday morning; if I couldn't, then at the very least he'd die with images of Pebble surrounding him—and what could be better than that?

Somehow, Dad lasted until just shortly before the stroke of midnight on Saturday night. When the moment that we'd all been anticipating with dread finally arrived, it caught me by surprise. With one final loud gasp, Dad's eyes, which had been essentially sealed shut for days, abruptly popped wide open.

Out of nowhere, his gaze was intense and clear. It appeared that, if only for those few remarkable seconds, his mind was clear and whole once more. Although doctors dismiss this phenomenon, I could swear that he was communicating that, at long last, he could *see* me and tell me that he "knew" the herculean effort of caregiving that my mom and my sister, Nancy, had put forth on his behalf—and that he loved us so very much. For the rest of my life, I will always be thankful that I was able to be there with him for that startling good-bye. Then I noticed that all the color seemed to drain out of his body from his forehead on down. Just like that, it was over. Thirteen years and one month after he had suffered a mini-stroke at the base of my broadcast tower in Fort Worth, Dad's long nightmare had ended. In that sudden instant of death, as in his modest, yet noble life, Dad's love felt unconditional and unceasing.

The memorial service concluded with a hymn, "Sing with all the Saints in Glory," set to the melody of Beethoven's "Ode to Joy," which elicited so many happy memories of watching the Olympics with my father on ABC, and which was also the processional hymn at Jim McKay's farewell. Ironically, the backdrop for this book was my assignment to broadcast three high-profile events—Super Bowl XLI, the NCAA Final Four, and the Masters—in one sixty-three-day stretch. In another of those peculiar quirks of fate, my uncle Bob would die of a sudden heart attack on Saturday night, August 9. Once again, I would have to speak at a funeral service. So in the exact same time frame, I had sustained the loss of one of my broadcasting fathers, my real father, and my godfather. Sixty-three days, three eulogies. To borrow McKay's most famous comment: "They're all gone."

. . .

Tuesday, April 10, 2007, would prove to be an unexpected turning point in my life. Scarcely forty-eight hours after completing our coverage of the Masters, I met with Gotham

Books' publisher Bill Shinker and his team about this book project. Rather than feeling the routine physical exhaustion and emotional letdown following this nine-week, three-major-championships sprint, I found myself strangely elated and energized. It was as though I had a new mission to fulfill; moreover, I felt that Dad somehow had a new lease on life. I must admit that there were a few scary patches during the writing and editing process when we were afraid that Dad might pass away at any moment. But he kept holding on. Then, as I embarked upon a nonstop promotional whirlwind, I was seized by the irrational, yet almost palpably tangible, notion that as long as I was out on the stump talking about the book I was somehow keeping Dad alive. In part, I suspect that such illogical "magical thinking" was a very human response to feelings of utter vulnerability and helplessness; in such times, we desperately search for an idea, an object, a person, or a place, something—anything—that might give us the comforting perception, no matter how illusory, of *control* over events and offer hope.

I also found myself drawing strength from the overwhelming reaction to the book. Nowhere was this more apparent than at the 2008 U.S. Open at Torrey Pines. I had flown to San Diego to sign books immediately following Jim McKay's memorial service. It was the run-up to Father's Day weekend, and the hardcover edition had jumped to number three on the *New York Times* Bestseller List. All day long—Thursday, Friday, and Saturday—people waited patiently in lines for an hour to reach my signing table. Almost everyone had a personal story to relate, and I could see how important it was and how cleansing it felt for them to share it with me. Many told me that they had been moved when they heard me talking about Dad with the likes of Rush Limbaugh, Matt Lauer, Larry King, Don Imus, and David Letterman—or they had read excerpts in that month's *Golf Digest*. Some of the stories I heard there—and everywhere that I go to speak—involve wonderful father-son or father-daughter relationships, usually with sports as a common bond. Other folks often say that the book has served as a "wake-up call" about the transitory nature of life. From now on, they insist, they are consciously making the effort to spend more and better time with their own children. Still another group are those whose families have been touched in one way or another by Alzheimer's disease, dementia, or other terminal illnesses. Although I must have signed roughly 1,500 books at Torrey Pines, I'm sure I could have easily tripled that figure if I was more ruthlessly efficient. But I wanted to give everyone a moment, a smile, an acknowledgment of his or her own story. That's certainly the way my father would have done it—and that's how he taught me to treat everyone. Eventually, that Saturday afternoon, they had to shut down the line. By the time I got to the last person, I was so emotionally spent that I just completely melted down. I had tears in my eyes, and my hand was shaking so hard that I could hardly sign my name. I've always felt that when I was signing my name I was also signing my dad's name—and technically, I was— but now that the book tour was over, I had the awful premonition that I was signing off on his life.

It has been—and continues to be—incredibly rewarding to witness how Dad's life meant something special to so many people. He rose up from his humble mill-town roots to build a career, raise a family, and see the world. But he always believed that the true measure of a man's life was never in terms of success, but rather whether that individual had lived a life of *significance*. My father's story is one that encompasses such universal themes as hope, comfort, faith, and love—as well as an innate appreciation for how very precious life is, even in its most limited state. And in the course of sharing his old-fashioned Mount Holly values with the public at large, he leaves behind a legacy far greater than he could have ever imagined. So we had come full circle, returning my father, as planned, to that "little city with the big heart."

Rest in peace, Dad. Now and forever.

ACKNOWLEDGMENTS

Writing this book has been quite an odyssey—wrenching, uplifting, painful, cathartic, and joyful. Right away I realized that this project was tantamount to writing my father's eulogy in advance—and maybe this was Dad's final blessing, inspiring me to tell this story and enabling me to feel a deeper appreciation for life and for love. Now, after a prolonged absence, I can actually hear music again in my life.

There is only one place to start, and that is to give thanks to my remarkable co-author, Eli Spielman. We spent thousands of hours talking and writing over the past year. A close friendship that was spawned nearly a quarter-century ago when I first walked into the CBS studios has now turned into a brotherhood—and I am so grateful.

Book publishing is the ultimate *team sport*—and I'm deeply appreciative for all the wise coaching and solid in-the-trenches support that have enabled this project to become a reality. As always, my exceptional agents on this project, Barry Frank and

Sandy Montag and my entire team at IMG, were quick to spot the potential but careful to make sure that it was fulfilled with utmost professionalism; literary agent par excellence Scott Waxman helped refine the concept and found a perfect match in Bill Shinker, the visionary founder and publisher of Gotham Books. Bill's outstanding cadre of creative and editorial talent—especially Lisa Johnson, Brett Valley, Patrick Mulligan, Ray Lundgren, and Beth Parker—have been a joy to work with from day one.

My invaluable right arm, Melissa Miller, pushed her marketing and organizational skills to the max—calling time-out only to deliver her baby, Jake. Where would I be without her? Another indispensable part of the team is my man for all seasons, Kevin McHale. Tommy Spencer, who is my second set of eyes above the 50-yard line and in the tower at 18, proved to be a rich resource for story ideas and background information. The incomparable John Kollmansperger applied his legendary zeal for accuracy in fact-checking every detail. Drs. Susan Bressman, Robert Goodman, and Joseph Zeitlin provided valuable medical background. Jean Becker and Jim McGrath of President George H. W. Bush's staff shared their reminiscences of the Bush-Clinton summits and other stories involving 41 and his family.

My CBS "family" has been wonderfully supportive of this endeavor; without them, in fact, the sixty-three-day, three-championship "journey" that served as the genesis of this project would not have been possible. While I wish that I could name everyone at the network whom I had the privilege of working with through the years, regretfully that is not practical. I would, however, like to especially thank CEO Les Moonves; CBS News and Sports president Sean McManus; CBS Sports executive vice president Tony Petitti; CBS Sports senior vice president of communications LeslieAnne Wade; CBS Sports executive director of communications Robin Brendle, and her associates, Jerry Caraccioli and Jen Sabatelle; and CBS photo editor Paula Breck. In addition, I am indebted to all of my producers, directors, on-air colleagues—and a heartfelt thank-you to the greatest technical crew in sports television.

Again, I am so happy to have made this trip with Eli. May I add how thankful I am to all the Spielman boys—David, Avi, and Josh—for "sharing" their dad; and their mom, Yael, who offered keen editorial insights while helping care for her own Alzheimer's-stricken father. The late Rabbi Leon Spielman, Eli's dad, and Harman Avery Grossman graciously volunteered to read through the final manuscript.

As for my family, I hope that through their active participation, every one of them had occasion to relive their memories of happier days. I trust that when Caroline grows up she will be able to appreciate all that my dad stood for, and why his life meant so much to all of us. Dad was a great man—and as a popular song describes it so sweetly, he will always be my "whisper in the wind."